LOVES OF YULIAN

MOTHER AND ME, PART III

# LOVES of YULIAN

## JULIAN PADOWICZ

ACADEMY CHICAGO PUBLISHERS

Published in 2011 by
Academy Chicago Publishers
363 West Erie Street
Chicago, Illinois 60654

© 2011 by Julian Padowicz

First edition.

Printed and bound in the U.S.A.

Library of Congress Cataloging-in-Publication Data

Padowicz, Julian.
Loves of Yulian / by Julian Padowicz.
p. cm. — (Mother and me; pt. III)
Continues: A ship in the harbor. Chicago, Ill. : Academy Chicago
Publishers, 2009.
ISBN 978-0-89733-616-1 (pbk. : alk. paper)
1. Padowicz, Julian. 2. Padowicz, Julian—Relations with women.
3. Padowicz, Julian—Childhood and youth. 4. Jews, Polish—Brazil—
Rio de Janeiro—Biography. 5. Immigrants—Brazil—Rio de Janeiro—
Biography. 6. Holocaust, Jewish (1939–1945)—Biography. 7. Mothers
and sons—Brazil—Rio de Janeiro. 8. Rio de Janeiro (Brazil)—
Biography. I. Padowicz, Julian. Ship in the harbor. II. Title.
F2646.9.J4P33 2010
940.53'18092—dc22
[B]
2010053282

This book is dedicated to my two handsome sons Tom and Joe
and the people they love.

# PREFACE

ON A SUNNY DAY in the spring of 1986, I took the lady, who would soon become my wife, to visit the sadly abandoned campus of the boarding school, in northern Connecticut, where I had spent five poignant years from 1941 to 1946. You can imagine my surprise and embarrassment when we discovered that the distance from the Main Building to the Schoolhouse, between which, I had told her, we used to have impromptu, but important to us, foot races, was only about fifteen yards, and the great lawn to the side of the Main Building, on which we had played monumental games of "kick the can" or touch football, was like the postage stamp-size front lawn of the typical suburban development. What this told me was that things remembered from one's childhood are not necessarily the way we remember them fifty years later.

Undaunted by this reality, I have plunged ahead to tell the story, experienced just prior to that time—1940–1941 to be exact—when my Mother and I were in Brazil, still waiting for our chance to enter the United States. I have not gone back to Brazil to check out the *pension*, the hotel, the café, or other places where the story was set. I don't think I would be able to find them, or even recognize them if I did. I do, however, hold a powerful image of them in my mind—with a full understanding, now, that that image may be badly distorted.

What I do not have much of a memory of is the time interval between some of the events. The events themselves and the feelings they generated, are unforgettable. But the unmemorable time in between, has proven exactly that, unremembered. So there I've had to, simply, create intervals. There are also some intentional distortions where I have changed the names and some of the characteristics of several individuals, so as to render them unrecognizable. Mother had a propensity for getting involved with people who were prominent, or who would eventually become prominent in their environment. While most of those individuals can be presumed to have passed on, I did not want my very subjective recounting to impinge on their memory. The one exception is the great Polish poet, Julian Tuwim, whom I have presented as accurately as I remember him.

And, as for the dialog, we both know that I could not, possibly, remember it all word for word. But what would a story be without dialog? So in the interest of providing a coherent and comprehensible narrative, I have taken the liberty of reconstructing much of that dialogue to produce the remembered effects.

What *is* totally true in this story, or as true as I can recall them, is the feelings. And this is a book, not so much about events, as about feelings.

In the first book of this series, *Mother and Me: Escape from Warsaw 1939*, which takes place almost entirely in Poland, I began the convention of transliterating certain proper names to give the English-speaking reader a better sense of the sound of the Polish language. Thus, my name *Julian*, for example, which happens to be spelled the same way in Polish, but pronounced differently, became *Yulian*. But because most of the names in this book are Latino and more familiar to American readers, I have suspended that practice, except for names like *Yulian* that carry over from the two previous books.

As a guide to Polish words in general, let me say that the combination of *cz* is pronounced like *ch* is in English, as in *church*, and *sz* like *sh*, as in *shush*. The Polish letter *w* is pronounced like *v* in *vodka*, and *u* becomes *oo*, as in *tool*. The name of the great Polish poet, Tuwim, mentioned in the book, should be pronounced *Tooveem*.

And now, good reading.

# CHAPTER I

WHENEVER MOTHER ADDRESSED ME in French, I knew it was for someone else's benefit. I was eight and a half, and I understood these things. We were Polish, and what we normally spoke to each other was Polish. But Mother's new friend, M. Gordet, with the pomaded-down black hair and the mustache, who had bought the bottle of red wine at dinner last night, was sitting on Mother's other side now, and she was telling him about the book she was going to write about the two of us, once we got to America.

The three of us were dangling our legs in the pool that the sailors had erected on deck that morning. They had assembled a large wooden frame, draped a tarpaulin inside it, and pumped in seawater. Because it was July and we were getting closer to the Equator every day, the makeshift pool was a very welcome relief, but the problem for me was that there was no shallow end.

"It is so hot *Julien*," Mother had just said to me in French. "Why don't you get into the water and swim?"

"B... but there is no sh... sh... shallow e... end," I answered. "I don't k... k... know how t... t... to swim." I was stuttering badly again. I had just acquired the stutter in the last two or three months, and sometimes it was worse than at other times. But I had been, in a way, sick.

This was nineteen forty, the war had been going on for almost a year, and I had gotten sick in Hungary three months ago. Before that, Mother and I had escaped from the Bolsheviks who had invaded the eastern part of Poland where we had gone when the Germans had attacked from the west. And, in Hungary, I had done something very bad. Except that I couldn't remember what it was that I had done.

I knew about the man down on the floor of his shop where, Mother had explained to me, I had tripped him on purpose. Mother wasn't supposed to explain that to me, the doctor had said, because it was best for me to remember it on my own. The reason that I could not remember it yet, he said, was that it was so upsetting to me that my mind didn't want me to remember it. There had been several weeks following that happening when, apparently, I had lain in bed and people had had to feed me, but I could remember just bits of that. And when I was well enough to get out of bed, I had begun stuttering.

The doctor had said that, eventually, I would probably remember everything, but it would take time. And when I did, the stuttering might well go away. But my stuttering really embarrassed Mother in front of other people. Many times she had told me to think of what I was going to say before I opened my mouth and then just to say it. But that's not the way it worked. I knew very well what I wanted to say, but, for some crazy reason, I just couldn't say it. Once she had even started really yelling at me to stop doing that, as though I was doing it on purpose, but I knew that she was just trying to help me, so that didn't work either.

Then, when we were in Lisbon, just before getting on the ship, she had taken me up to our hotel room after lunch and said, "You can't go on the ship talking like that," and, in spite of what the doctor had said, she had gone on to tell me what I had done in Hungary, in the hope, I expect, that, once I knew, I would stop stuttering. She told me that, while we were staying with Count Baresky, I had become great friends with his chauffeur Carlos, who had taught me to use tools and even to shoot a gun. That part I remembered. But then she told me that Carlos, who turned out to be a crook like his employer, the count, had had an argument with a shopkeeper over some merchandise that had been stolen, and I, in order to show off to Carlos, had stuck out my foot and tripped the shopkeeper on purpose. Then she had sat there looking at me, and I knew that she was waiting to see if I would still stutter. And when it turned out that I still did, I heard her say, "*merde*," under her breath, which I wasn't supposed to hear. So now I knew what it was that I had done, but only from Mother's telling me and not from remembering it, and I still stuttered.

Mother and I were Jewish, but, because the Nazis were hunting and killing Jews, we pretended to be Catholic—which delighted me. Kiki, my governess before the war, had been Catholic, and she had said that, if I wanted to go to Heaven some day, which was where she was going when she died, I would have to become Catholic like her. Kiki had been my entire world, ever since I could remember, because Mother and my stepfather Lolek were very busy with travel and cocktail parties, and, on the rare occasions that she took a day off, I was inconsolable. So the idea of spending a whole eternity away from Kiki was something too horrible to even contemplate at the time.

Exactly where Jews went after they died, was a question to which Kiki did not have a ready answer. Bad Jews, she said, went to Hell just like bad Catholics, but where good Jews, like my late father, went, was part of the Great Mystery.

The question had not stayed long unanswered in my own mind. When Kiki and I had to go someplace far, such as to visit my cousin Fredek, we took a trolley, and on warm summer days, Warsaw trolleys had an odor that wasn't altogether pleasant. One of the fixtures on these trolleys was the black-coated, black-hatted, bearded Hassids, to whom Kiki referred simply as *Jews*. I came to associate these long-coated, long-nosed men with the trolleys, and, in my five or six-year-old mind, I had come to see good, dead Jews, like my father, riding these sweaty trolleys into eternity.

In order to avoid such a fate for myself, I had taken to learning the Catholic prayers that Kiki taught me so that God would have mercy on my soul and so that, some day, I could get baptized and join her in Heaven. Kiki had also explained that the reason that Jews were barred from Heaven, was that we had cruelly nailed God's son, Jesus, to a cross many years ago, which, I realized, meant that He couldn't get food or anything to drink and must have starved to death—to say nothing of the embarrassment of soiling his loincloth.

My mother and my stepfather, Lolek, did not dress like the Jews on the trolleys, and spoke and ate like everyone else. We had lived in a beautiful apartment in Warsaw where Kiki and I slept in the same room. But, when the war began, last September Kiki had gone back to her own family in Lodz. Losing Kiki had been very hard for me, at first, but now it was almost a year since I had seen her, and I had gotten used to it.

"Of course he can swim," Mother was saying now to the man with the mustache, M. Gordet. "He and his governess spent every summer before the war in Yurata, the most expensive summer resort in Poland, where they had the bay on one side and the Baltic on the other, both within walking distance of their beautiful hotel, and swimming instructors and everything."

This was all true, except for the fact that I had never had any swimming lessons. Kiki and I had these inflated floatation pillows that we strapped to our waists and mimed people we had seen doing the breaststroke, but in only half a meter of water. But I had become accustomed to Mother telling stories that weren't always true. When we were living with the Bolshevik Russians, and there were shortages of everything, including food and firewood, she had often gotten them to help us by making up a story—usually about me being sickly or even sick.

Mother was very beautiful. Her name was Barbara, and before the war all her Warsaw friends had called her, *Beautiful Basia*. She had a round face, darkly blond hair, which I now knew wasn't really blond, but brown like mine, and large, round, brown eyes. She had even had a "screen test" a few years before, in Warsaw to see if she could be a movie star, but nothing seemed to have come of it.

Now she turned back to me. "You see how the others are swimming, don't you? See how they move their arms and their legs?"

The people she was pointing out were doing what Kiki and I had done, wearing our floatation cushions. We had called it, "doing the frog."

"Just do the same thing they're doing, and you'll swim," Mother said. "If they can do it, so can you. And if you have any trouble, M. Gordet, here, is an excellent swimmer, and he'll, of course, pull you out, won't you George?"

Then, turning again to M. Gordet, she said, "The first thing I'm doing when we get to Rio will be to hire a good governess for him, to give him some routine and some discipline again. He was brought up so well in Poland. He had such beautiful manners, but with the war, he's become very undisciplined. Just a few weeks ago, he even yelled at me."

The incident she was talking about in Lisbon was after she had yelled at me first for breaking a porcelain figurine that one of her men friends had given her, when it wasn't I who had broken it. But I had learned that Mother would often talk about how bad I had been to her in order to gain people's sympathy. And since my protest would just cause her to say, "You see what I mean?" I didn't say anything and hoped she would forget about my going in to swim.

Then she turned to me again. "Go ahead, get in," she said. "M. Gordet and I are right here."

I wasn't at all sure that M. Gordet could even swim—I hadn't seen him in the water yet. He had a nice tan and fair muscles, but I wondered how he would feel about getting his hair wet.

"Go ahead," Mother said.

I lowered myself into the water, took a deep breath, released the board I had been sitting on, and began to "do the frog."

And I swam. I did, indeed, swim. And, as I slowly breast-stroked my way the length of the little pool, keeping within reach of the side, I was suddenly very excited and aware of several things at the same time. One was that, in finally learning to swim, I had passed onto a new level of maturity. Another was that I had made that passage by myself, without the elaborate swimming lessons that I had seen older children receiving from swimming instructors on the bay side of the Yurata resort. A third was that my poor Kiki, who had been my constant companion until the war began and then had to go back to her own family in Lodz, most certainly had not had the opportunity to learn to swim under the current occupation of our country by the Germans. This meant that I had undoubtedly passed her in that area of development.

A fourth realization did not occur to me till a few minutes later, when M. Gordet suggested that the three of us had had enough sun for one session and should go inside. And that was that, with fresh ocean water being constantly pumped in and out of our makeshift pool, I and my fellow swimmers were, in a sense, swimming our way across the Atlantic.

Our ship was taking us not to America, which *was* our final destination, but Rio de Janeiro, Brazil. We had left Lisbon, Portugal a few days earlier and would have to wait in Brazil until we could get a visa to the United States under the Polish immigration quota. But, at least, we were putting an ocean between ourselves and the war in Europe. And when we finally did get to America, which was a very big and very rich country, Mother would get to write her book, and we would become American and rich again.

We had been rich before the war. My stepfather, Lolek had owned a shirt factory, and we had had a big apartment in the best section of Warsaw. But when the Germans had started bombing Warsaw, on September first, Lolek had gone into the army, Kiki had gone back to her family, and Mother and I had gone to a farm in southeastern Poland to get away from the bombing. Then the Bolsheviks had suddenly invaded from the east, while our soldiers were busy fighting the Germans in the west, and we had spent six months living with the Russians. The moment they arrived, there was almost no food in the stores and no firewood, and people would be detained for questioning and then disappear without a trace. So Mother and I had escaped over the Carpathian Mountains into Hungary, walking eleven hours in the snow, after our hired guide had abandoned us, and everyone called it incredibly courageous on Mother's part, and a miracle that we had survived.

Of course, before our escape, everyone had told Mother that she was crazy. Yes, people had escaped that way, but they had been strong men, not women with children, and it had been before the mountains were covered with snow. But Mother had just laughed at them, as though they were saying silly things.

That escape was what Mother's book was going to be about, along with stories about how brutally the Germans treated people in the part of Poland that they occupied. We couldn't talk about the book while we were still in Europe because the Germans who had spies everywhere, didn't want Mother getting to America, which wasn't in the war, and writing her book. But right now, we were very poor.

Not because she expected to need them, but because of the falling bombs, Mother had wrapped up all of her jewelry in a blue pillowcase, when we left Warsaw, and packed them in one of the suitcases we brought with us. We had not expected to be gone long, since Poland had a mutual defense treaty with Britain and France, and the two of them would surely push the Germans back into Germany in a matter of weeks. But that hadn't happened, and Mother had had to start selling off her jewelry for us to live on and to get from one place to another. The guide who had been supposed to lead us across the Carpathians had been paid from the proceeds of the sale of some of that jewelry, and Mother had sewn the rest into the lining and buttons of our clothes before our mountain adventure.

But travel through Europe on a Polish passport was both hazardous and expensive in nineteen forty, and our, often urgent, financial needs made it a definite buyer's market in diamonds. Our supply of precious stones was being quickly depleted. Our challenge at this point was to reach America, where Mother could sell our story to a publisher, before the supply of jewels ran out altogether.

Not only did I understand all this very well, but I must have actually understood it somewhat better than Mother, because in Lisbon she had gone out and bought a new bathing suit and three new outfits, including a long evening gown, that she said were just for the ship, which would only be a two week trip. All I had gotten for the trip, and all I needed, was a bathing suit, and I could have even done without that, and just worn my brown shorts. She had said that it was important for her to look nice, but she didn't really need new clothes to look nice. Nor did she need to go to a hairdresser in order to have her hair washed, since you could buy shampoo at a pharmacy. I understood that women were more concerned about their looks than men, but we were running very short on finances, and who knew how long we would have to wait for our turn in the Polish quota for immigrating to America.

Of course, I also understood about temptation. I knew what it was to see something in a store window that you wanted to have. I, of course, had never had the opportunity to just walk into the store and buy what I wanted, but for somebody who did, I could well see how that might be hard to resist. And my mother just didn't seem very good at resisting that kind of temptation. Mother could only speak a few words of Portuguese, which was what they spoke in Brazil, and she couldn't type or cook or drive a car or even sew—I could sew buttons on better than she could—so I didn't see any way for more money to be coming in until we got to America and she got to write her book. So it might well be up to me to make sure that our funds lasted for as long as it took to get to America.

"He's very sickly," I heard Mother saying to M. Gordet, as he helped her to climb down from the swimming pool on the ladder that was nailed to the side. Mother had on open-backed shoes on very high, wedge heels and I could tell she was going to have trouble. Of course, I also knew she was talking about me again, and I dearly hoped she wasn't going to tell him about the problem with my memory and what I had done in Hungary. I was relieved to hear her say, "He's just gotten over scarlet fever. He caught it in Barcelona, where there wasn't any medicine, and I didn't know if he was going to live."

The part about scarlet fever in Barcelona was true. I had had to stay in bed in our hotel room for several weeks and been allowed to eat nothing but boiled, unsalted potatoes and boiled, unsalted fish, both of which were disgusting. Mother was out most of the time, trying to sell her jewels or get a visa to Portugal or, maybe, Brazil, and the boredom had been terrible too. The reason why there was no medicine was that, in nineteen forty, Spain had just gotten over a civil war, and they were out of almost everything. On the other hand, the part about my being *sickly* wasn't true at all. But Mother had told that lie so often, that, I supposed, she had just come to believe it.

Soon after leaving Lisbon, Mother had explained to me that our ship, which had a huge Brazilian flag painted on each side so that German submarines would not torpedo us, was a "mixed freighter" and not a "liner," which meant that it carried both freight and passengers, and was smaller and not as luxurious as a liner, which carried mostly just passengers. On the other hand, it was also less expensive, which I had been happy to hear. The ship would make several stops along the way to pick up and drop off both cargo and passengers, so the trip would take longer than it would have on a liner.

But we weren't in any hurry, since we would have to wait months, maybe years, once we got there because America only allowed in so many people from any one country each year. Because the war had begun in Poland, there were a lot of Poles on the waiting list. But she assured me that we would get to America eventually and become Americans. America, she said, was the safest country in the world because it had a huge ocean on each side, and it was the strongest and the richest. Before the war, a friend of Mother's, who worked in the Polish embassy in America, had brought me back a watch that he had bought for just one dollar in a pharmacy. Anywhere else in the world, you had to go to a jewelry store to buy a watch and pay a lot of money. America was also where they made movies, where they had cowboys, and the buildings were hundreds of stories tall.

Mr. Gordet, whom Mother had met the second day of our voyage, was, Mother had told me, a vice president of the shipping line, and made the trip to South America quite often. He knew a lot of people in Rio, and would introduce Mother to people who were likely to buy some of her jewels. He also got Mother and me transferred to the captain's table in the dining room, where he ate his meals. To be at the captain's table, which seated ten people, like each of the other three tables, was considered a great honor, though the captain only ate with us two evenings. His chair, an armchair with a blue cushion on the seat, stood empty the rest of the time. One of the ship's officers sat at each of the other tables, and I found my eyes constantly attracted to their blue and braid uniforms. In Poland, all the schools, except the one I went to, had navy blue uniforms with brass buttons. Since their meeting, Mother and M. Gordet had spent a lot of time together.

The talk in the dining room went on in several languages, of which I understood the French and very little of the Portuguese and Spanish. On the second day out, we had a "lifeboat drill." At supper the previous evening, one of the officers had explained to us, in several languages, that we would hear a siren over the public address system, which meant that we should put on the life jackets that were under our beds and report immediately to the spot on deck that we were assigned to by the chart on our cabin door.

Coming out of our cabin, we saw a steward, already in his bulky life jacket, who then helped us to tie our own jackets properly and hurried us onto the deck. Once there, we stood in little groups beside each lifeboat that the sailors were doing something to. One of the officers explained to our group that in a real emergency we would be instructed to climb into the boats and be lowered into the ocean. Also, that there would be a crewmember in charge of each boat, and we were to obey his every command since he was trained in these matters. Then, he went on to reassure us that the Brazilian flag painted on either side of our hull would keep German submarines from torpedoing us.

It seems that there were two other children on board, besides me. They were two brothers from Holland, who looked exactly alike, except that one had his hair parted on the right side and the other on the left. Mother asked me why I didn't go play with them, and I explained that I didn't speak Dutch, and it wasn't likely that they spoke Polish. Mother answered that they probably spoke some French, as I did, and, if they didn't, it would be fun communicating through hand gestures and mime, which certainly didn't sound like fun to me.

Even if they had spoken Polish, I would not have been anxious to make their acquaintance. I had not had a good experience playing with other boys. They always wanted to pretend we were soldiers, and that I was their prisoner being tortured or that they were cowboys, and I was a robber about to be hanged.

At the hotel in Barcelona, there had been a girl, almost a year younger than me, who was also Polish, and we made believe that we were riding in a car, with me driving, up and down the halls, or climbing the Carpathian Mountains the way Mother and I had done, to get away from Soviet border guards. But it turned out afterwards that it was she who had given me my scarlet fever, since she was just getting over it when we began playing together.

But, with M. Gordet translating, Mother discussed the issue with the Dutch brothers' parents, while sitting in deck chairs, and reached the agreement that the three of us boys would all benefit from playing together, while the four of them had cocktails. Then, the three of us proceeded to sit cross-legged on the deck, while I stared at them, and they stared at me.

The four grownups seemed to fare a lot better, with no shortage of conversation. After a while, following some whispered conversation between the two brothers, one of them stood up and motioned for me to follow. While I would have preferred not to, I could imagine Mother telling me that I wasn't playing nicely, so I got up and followed.

The brother who had first signaled me to follow, led the way around to the other side of the ship, and the other walked along behind me. When we reached the section where the lifeboats stood, the leader indicated that I and his brother should stand together in front of one of the boats so that he could take a picture of us with the imaginary camera he now held in his hands. This, at least, was something to do, and it was something I had seen a lot of the grownups do with real cameras, so I took my place willingly, planning to propose a picture of the two of them, once each had been photographed with me. Watching him "photograph" us, I realized that I could mime the procedure much better with things like fiddling with the lens and turning the little knob that wound the film.

But, suddenly, they had each grabbed one of my arms and were pushing me backwards, between two boats, towards where there was no railing between the deck and the ocean. Now I realized that they were trying to push me overboard. I couldn't imagine that that was, really, what they were doing, since my absence would be quickly discovered and traced to them. This had to be a game—some kind of Dutch game. Looking down, I could see in my peripheral vision the wavy ocean rushing by and getting closer. But, on the other hand, they could just lie and say they didn't know where I had gone. Or even that I had been showing off by standing near the edge on one foot and fallen off.

Then I found that I could wrap one hand around one of the lines by which the boats would be lowered. Holding tight to this line, I kicked out blindly with my foot. I felt it hit some target and heard a cry from one of the brothers. His hands released me immediately, as he grabbed for his eye. His brother let me go as well, as the first boy burst into loud sobs. In a moment they were both running back the way we had come, the sobs warning me that I would not be greeted with cordiality on my return.

I took my time on the way back, and, true to my fears, found the one brother sitting in his mother's lap, a napkin full of ice against his eye, the other in his father's lap. Seeing me arrive, Mother and M. Gordet both stood up. M. Gordet gripped me firmly by the elbow, and I was marched down to our cabin and told not to come out.


There were two other Polish-speaking people on board, a Mr. Kosiewicz and his wife, Mrs. Irena. The woman looked a little younger than Mother, and they were both very good looking. Mr. Kosiewicz was tall and thin, with wavy blond hair and blue eyes, and Mrs. Irena had long, chestnut hair that fell in thick waves onto her shoulders, soft looking cheeks, and large, green eyes. She was taller than Mother and even more beautiful, which Mother as much as admitted.

"That woman is so beautiful," I heard her say to M. Gordet, as we saw the couple dance to a phonograph record in the lounge, before dinner. This was the day after my affair with the Dutch brothers, and I had not been allowed to leave Mother's side all day.

"They're Polish, you know, Basia," M. Gordet said and Mother said, "Oh, I didn't know that. They look like professional dancers, don't they?"

The two were pressed very close together, and they moved like one person.

Then M. Gordet whispered something in Mother's ear, and I saw her eyebrows go up a little. "Well, it's wartime, you know," she said.

I understood what she was saying. It wasn't as though M. Gordet didn't know that the Germans had occupied Poland and France and were, right then, bombing England. It was just that saying, *It's wartime*, meant that certain things were all right, which wouldn't have been all right in peacetime. But what all that had to do with the current situation, was a total mystery.

"And they look very much in love," she added, with a little laugh. I tried to guess what it was that M. Gordet had whispered in Mother's ear about the two, but came up empty.

When the record stopped playing, Mother said, "Why don't we invite them over for a drink with us, George," and M. Gordet got up and crossed the dance floor to where the two were stand-ing. They spoke for a moment, then the three of them walked back to our table.

"Mme. Padowicz, may I present Mr. and Mrs. Kosiewicz," M. Gordet said, though he had a lot of difficulty pronouncing both names, "and this is Madame's son *Julien*."

I stood up, as I had been taught, and shook hands firmly, with both of the guests, trying to look each directly in the eye. As I had discovered with many other grownup men around Mother, Mr. Kosiewicz did not shake my hand firmly or look me in the eye. His attention, I could see, was on Mother. But his wife gave me a warm handshake and looked at me from under her eyelashes with what, to me, was clearly an expression of shyness. I didn't know that grownups could be shy as well.

"I understand you and your wife are Polish," Mother was saying, in French, to Mr. Kosiewicz. "My son and I are from Warsaw, but M. Gordet doesn't speak Polish."

Now I could see exactly what it was that held Mr. Kosiewicz's attention. It was Mother's diamond ring. It was, I knew, the ring that Lolek had given her as an engagement present, and it had two large diamonds set side by side. The two were exactly alike and each one was as big as just about any diamond I had ever seen. I had seen the ring attract the attention of numerous people in the last few months, when Mother wore it. A lot of the time it actually spent in the lining of Mother's dress, just below the waistband, where there were some tucks and a bulge wouldn't show. A woman mother had met in Yugoslavia had fashioned a little pocket for her there, so she could get it in and out without resorting to needle and thread each time, which Mother wasn't very good at. Actually, there were several pockets like that in the dress, but they were all empty now except for one that held the round, diamond broach, which Grandmother had given Mother just before the war began, and which Mother said she would die before selling because, some day, my wife would wear it. This sentiment was one that, at my age of eight and a half, I did not appreciate the way she did, and hoped that, if the need to sell it arose, as I could well see it happening, Mother would change her mind.

But, while the broach almost never came out of its secret pocket, there were many times when Mother would display her double-diamond ring. As she had explained to me, she and my stepfather had been planning to divorce before the war, so the engagement ring had only monetary value for her. And in restaurants and hotels, I had seen many eyes attracted to the stones, which, I understood, was Mother's intention. But as for Mr. Kosiewicz, there was something in his expression that seemed to say something more than mere admiration. Right then and there I decided that I didn't like the man, and it occurred to me that, as a result, in my thoughts and when talking to my friend, Meesh, who was in our cabin at the moment, I would refer to Mr. Kosiewicz not by his name, but, simply as Mr. K.

Meesh was a small, white teddy bear, though he was turning a little gray now. I had acquired him just before our escape from the Bolsheviks, when I was still seven and a half. At that time, I had considered him my son, and I would carry him everywhere, in the crook of my elbow. When we were escaping over the mountains, he had been in my backpack. But we were both older now, and Meesh spent most of the time in our room. When we traveled, he now rode inside my suitcase, rather than in the crook of my arm, because he really didn't like meeting new people. But we could still talk to each other, even across a large room, though not through walls, in our silent language. We spoke to each other in words and sentences, just the way other people talk to each other, except that we did not need to say them out loud. And, when I got back to our cabin this evening, I would tell Meesh about meeting the greedy-looking Mr. K and his shy, pretty wife, whose first name I didn't yet know, but didn't want to call by Mr. K's name.

Now, as Mother and M. Gordet conversed in French with Mr. K., I noticed that Mrs. Kosiewicz, sitting on my left, sat quietly in her chair looking down at her hands. When the waiter came to take a drink order, Mr. K ordered something for her without even asking what she wanted. It occurred to me then that maybe she did not speak French. If this were so, then my duty as a gentleman, I knew, was to engage her in a conversation in Polish. The duties of a gentleman, such as pulling chairs out for ladies, picking their napkins up when they dropped them, opening doors, entertaining them at the table, and keeping your own nails clean and your hair combed, were things that Mother had been lecturing me on ever since we had arrived in Hungary. But exactly how one went about beginning a conversation with a lady one doesn't know, was something I had not learned yet.

On the other hand, I did have one weapon that had served me well a number of times in difficult social situations. That was the copper washer that I kept well polished and in my pocket at all times. A man to whom we had given a ride in our truck, when we were escaping from Warsaw and the bombs, had taught me how to palm a coin, making it disappear and appear again out of people's ears and places like that. The coin that he had given me to practice with, Mother had taken away from me, because I wasn't allowed to accept money from strangers, but, long ago, I had found the washer lying on the ground, polished it, and had been practicing with it ever since. So now I slowly reached into my pants pocket and, hoping that Mrs. Kosiewicz did not see me doing it, maneuvered the washer out of the handkerchief that it was entangled in and into my palm. Then just as slowly, I proceeded to withdraw my hand and place it in my lap. For maybe a minute, I sat there looking around at the room, and finally turned to Mrs. Kosiewicz, on my left. "Oh, p... please Missus," I said, in the awkward way the Polish language does these things, "did M... Missus know that th... there is s... something in M... Missus's ear?"

I saw Mrs. Kosiewicz blink in surprise. "My ear?" she said in a quiet, but genuinely surprised voice.

"Yes," I said. Then I reached over and produced the washer, as though out of her ear.

"Oh," she said. "You did a magic trick." As a child, *you*, was all the form of address that I was entitled to.

"A m… magic t… rick?" I said, as though that was the furthest from the truth.

"Why, you pretended to pull that thing out of my ear," she said.

She was smiling as she said it, and I was suddenly emboldened by an idea. I noticed that her surprised voice had made the others turn to look at us. "W… what th… thing?" I said, making the washer disappear again. "W… what th… thing is M… issus t… talking about?"

To my very great delight, Mrs. Kosiewicz laughed.

Then I saw Mr. K give his wife a quick, annoyed look, then turn back to Mother with a smile. "She doesn't speak French," he said, confirming my suspicion.

"That was very clever," Mrs. Kosiewicz said. "Can you do any other tricks?"

I shook my head. I knew that shaking my head wasn't polite, but, with her asking for more tricks, my self-confidence had left me. I had hoped she would show me a trick, herself, or tell me a joke or something. But she was looking at me and smiling, as I was at her, but didn't seem to know what to say either.

This was a very new experience for me. In the past, all of Mother's grownup friends had had lots of questions to ask me about where I had been, what I liked to do, what I liked to eat, what grade I was in, where I had spent the summer, and so forth. But not Mrs. Kosiewicz. I put it down to the fact that she hadn't been grown up long enough.

On the other hand, since I knew some of those conversation-starting questions, why shouldn't I ask her them? Mrs. Kosiewicz certainly seemed friendly enough not to feel insulted.

"S... so tell me, please M... Missus," I began. "Where has M... Missus been spending the s... summer?"

"Well—I'm sorry, I don't know your name."

I realized that M. Gordot's introductions had been in French. "It's Y... Yulian," I said.

"That's a beautiful name."

Everyone said that.

"My name is Irena. You can call me Irena, if you want, instead of the Mrs. Kosiewicz. In fact I'd like that better."

I had never had a grownup lady tell me to call her by her first name before. Except, of course for Kiki, but I had been calling her that as long as I could remember, and it had probably started before I was old enough to call her Miss Jane. "All r... right... " I had intended to add the *Irena* to the end of that statement, but, somehow, it wouldn't come out.

Then I remembered that now that we were out of Europe, I could talk about our escape. I hadn't been supposed to tell anyone about it before, in case the story got back to the Nazi-sympathizers who were looking for us to stop Mother from writing her book in America. That's not to say that it hadn't slipped out a few times, when we were in the company of people who I was sure weren't Nazi-sympathizers, particularly when I had to correct distortions that my mother made, like when she said that I had fallen into the stream and she had to pull me out, which was totally untrue, or left out the little fact that, if I hadn't found a strong stick and moved that tree branch off her leg, she would still be sitting there in the woods. And Mrs. Irena—I had no trouble calling her *Mrs. Irena*—who only spoke Polish, certainly wasn't a Nazi-sympathizer.

"My m... mother and I e... scaped from the R... Russians, who were oc... c... cupying Lwow, where we were s... staying, by w... walking across the C... Carpathian M... Mountains into Hungary for e... eleven hours, last F... February," I said.

"Oh my, that's quite an adventure," she said.

"T... the g... g... guide that we h... had h... h... hired d... didn't g... g... get out of the s... sleigh, when w... we d... did, but just d... drove off, and my m... m... mother and I w... wandered in the w... woods a... a... alone, until we f... found a v... v... village by a... accident."

"You must have been very scared."

"Well, yes, p... please M... Missus, we were." It was funny that now it didn't bother me at all to say that I had been scared. Before the war started, when I was only seven, I would have been ashamed to admit to being scared of anything. "How did M... Missus and Mr. K... Kosiewicz get out?"

"Well, we drove out just before the war started. Tadek, that is, my husband, had a car and we drove out because we knew there was going to be a war."

"W... were you s... cared?" This was a question people had frequently asked me.

"Well, I certainly was, but not Tadek. He's not afraid of anything."

Suddenly I could see Mr. Kosiewicz looking at his wife and me. His eyes were darting back and forth between us and Mother and M. Gordet, as though he was trying to pay attention to both conversations. Mrs. Irena must have seen it too, because she stopped talking suddenly and lowered her eyes. "My husband is a very brave man," she said after a moment, and I had the impression that she wanted him to hear it.

At supper, the Kosiewiczes did not sit at the same table with us, and I heard M. Gordet say to Mother, "He certainly showed a considerable interest in your ring."

"Do you think he's interested in buying it for his wife?" she asked.

"I don't know, but I'd lock my cabin door securely."

"Oh, I don't think so. He has such beautiful manners. He doesn't speak French so well, but did you see how manicured his fingers are?"

Mother's mention of manicured fingers set off a sour note in my head.


On Sunday, one of the passengers, who was a Catholic priest, said mass in the passenger's lounge. As she had done in Hungary, pretending to the count that we were Catholic, Mother decided that we were going to attend this mass as well. Now that I knew that you didn't have to be Catholic to go to Heaven, I had cooled considerably from the religious fervor that had gripped me less than a year earlier. And, since we were rapidly putting miles of ocean between ourselves and Europe, where the Nazis and Nazi-sympathizers hated Jews, I could not see why Mother was so concerned with maintaining the charade. But, fortunately, this time, unlike the experience in Hungary, where she had insisted on taking Holy Communion and then chewed the Host, instead of letting it melt into her soul, Mother did not try to take Communion, and I was much relieved.

Soon after my scarlet fever in Barcelona, Mother had informed me that two Polish priests would come and instruct us in Catholicism, following which we would be baptized. A year earlier, this would have been the best news I could possibly have heard. To receive my visa to Heaven, where Kiki would, some day, reside, and, at the same time shed my detested Jewishness, would have been the fulfillment of all my dreams. But in the course of that year, Kiki's prestige had been diluted somewhat by the several new women who had passed in and out of my life, and when Mother had explained, prior to our escape from the Bolsheviks, that good Jews did go to Heaven along with good Catholics, that concept did conform more closely to my idea of an all-loving God. And, while the idea of Mother and myself being instructed in a subject in which I was better versed than she, had a definite appeal, like the fantasy of one of the fathers posing a question and me having the answer, while Mother didn't, I certainly didn't receive the news with the same enthusiasm that I might have at an earlier time.

The two young Polish priests in their long, black cassocks with their multitude of buttons, did pay two visits to our hotel room and talked about God and Jesus, original sin and the sacrament of baptism, but, somehow, the plan never did get off the ground. We were still Jewish, though Mother continued wearing the little gold cross, which she had obtained before our escape from the Bolsheviks and telling people that we were Catholic. And when, the two times that he did dine with us, the captain asked for the Lord's blessing, Mother crossed herself along with most of the company. Except that she touched her right shoulder before her left one, which was, of course, the wrong way around.

It was a couple of days after we went to Mass, that the whole ship went crazy. We were crossing the Equator and, in keeping with tradition, a gang of sailors, dressed garishly as make-believe undersea beings, searched the ship from stem to stern for all passengers and crew who could not produce a certificate of Equator-crossing baptism. Those of us who could not, were marched to the afterdeck at the urging of wooden tridents in our backs, to cheers and jeers from those already initiated. Once there, we were painted from head to toe with some slimy green substance and made to kneel individually before a bearded, seaweed-draped, crowned, and enthroned King Neptune who ordered each of us to be thrown into the sea. It was fortunate that we had a pool full of seawater right there on the deck, so that no one had to be thrown overboard.

One of the officers had forewarned us about this at dinner, the evening before, telling people to wear their bathing suits or old clothes, and Mother had explained to me that this would be all in fun. So I knew the shouts, the grunts, and the tridents in our backs to be all an act, though I could not help the feeling that some crewmembers were taking more pleasure in the charade than they were supposed to. As I sailed, covered in green slime, into the pool and then proudly swam away from the sailor stationed there to rescue non-swimmers, I saw my beautiful mother, in her bathing suit and an orange scarf covering her hair, being permitted to lower her own self carefully into the pool to rinse off the small globs of green slime that had been applied symbolically to her shoulders and upper arms, without getting her hair wet.

A small group of passengers and crew stood around King Neptune on his throne, up on a specially-constructed platform on the deck beside the wood-framed pool. Some were in bathing suits, some in regular clothes, and many showed evidence of having been in the pool. They cheered as new neophytes were led into the king's presence to receive their sentence and then forced up the ladder and into the pool.

I joined this group and cheered with the others as a stout, gray-haired man whom we had all seen promenading the deck in a spotless white suit, a Panama hat, and a walking stick, was being coated with the green slime before being led into the king's presence. He was without his jacket, hat, stick, or tie, and stood barefoot as the "sea creatures" applied their goo with large paintbrushes, making his shirt and trousers cling to his body. The crowd seemed to take particular enjoyment in seeing the proud man humbled.

He didn't struggle, and, when the sailors led him into the king's presence, he bowed respectfully before kneeling to receive his sentence. Then, directed with more grunts and gestures, he climbed the pool ladder, and I could hear a loud splash, accompanied by an even louder cheer from us spectators. In a moment, he had climbed down again with his wet clothes, nearly transparent, clinging to his skin. His wife handed him a towel, and suddenly there was spontaneous applause for the good sportsmanship he had shown in playing along with the game.

A moment later there were more grunts from the sea creatures, and I saw Mr. K. being led into view by two of them. But, unlike the man of the white suit who had walked willingly between his two captors, Mr. K walked, jerking his elbows trying to free his arms from their grasp. He was yelling something at them that I couldn't hear, and his face was distorted with anger. Like the man before him, he was dressed in a shirt and trousers, except that he still had his shoes on.

Cheers went up as extra measures of green slime were applied to his body and even rubbed into his blond hair. It took three men to force him to kneel before King Neptune.

And then, I suddenly saw Mrs. Irena standing beside me. She was in her bathing suit, her wet hair indicating that she had already undergone her baptism. Her bare shoulders were hunched and she had the tip of one thumb in her mouth in her excitement. "Oh, Yulian, they want to kill him," she said. She put her arm around my shoulders and hugged me close to her side. I knew that she wasn't really afraid for his life, and then I heard her give a little giggle and realized that she was actually enjoying this scene. "He was hiding under our bed. He said he wasn't going to let anyone treat him that way again."

Mr. K was permitted to remove his shoes before climbing the ladder to the pool. Then, as he climbed, yelling something over his shoulder that was drowned out by the jeering of the crowd, I wondered what sort of treatment in the past it was that he had referred to. I remembered Mrs. Irena telling me that they had driven out of Poland before the war had started, so I didn't suppose they had been exposed to any of the Nazi brutality that we had heard about. But I didn't consider this an appropriate time to ask such questions. I decided, instead, to enjoy the touch of Mrs. Irena's soft skin against mine. Unfortunately, I didn't have much time to enjoy it, because her husband came over, took her other hand, and immediately led her inside. Mrs. Irena managed to turn her head and blow me a kiss before disappearing through the doorway.

Dinner was very noisy that evening with much laughter, stewards bringing bottles of wine that people had ordered, and talk of the day's happenings. More than once I heard the name Kosiewicz mentioned, though usually the context was in a language I couldn't understand and generally followed by more laughter. Concerned over how this was affecting Mrs. Irena, I discovered their places to be empty. Then I heard Mother comment on their absence.

"He did make quite a spectacle of himself," M. Gordet said.

"Well," Mother said, "he's probably a gentleman of the older school and just isn't accustomed to being treated this way by common sailors. I know that if they had tried to do that to my father, he would have given them such a look that they wouldn't have dared touch him."

"I don't know just how much of a gentleman he is. He does have very formal manners, but I couldn't find out anything about him."

"You mean you check on the passengers, like the secret police, George?" Mother laughed as she said this.

"We do have to be very careful these days, Basia."

"So what have you found out about me?"

"That would be giving away my secrets, wouldn't it?"

"But it's *my* secrets we're talking about."

There was a tone in their voices now that grownups sometimes get when they don't really mean what they say, and the other person knows that they don't mean it, but they say it anyway, and it's all some kind of grownup game. I could understand how Mr. K could be too embarrassed by his own behavior to show his face in the dining room, but I sincerely hoped that Mrs. Irena didn't have to go without supper because of him. Then, as we were having dessert, the captain came in, made a little speech about how glad King Neptune was to have made the acquaintance of all of us, and began calling out names of people who had been initiated that day. As I waited, anxiously, for my name to be called, I tried to remember what King Neptune had looked like to see if it may have been the captain behind the beard, but decided that it wasn't.

My certificate had the name of the ship and of the shipping company printed in beautiful gold letters, my own name written by hand, and a lot of words in a language I did not recognize. But I knew that when we re-crossed the Equator on our way to America at some future time, I would be one of the initiated, the people who got to cheer and to jeer and to stay dry.

# CHAPTER II

I DIDN'T SEE ANYTHING more of the Kosiewiczes until we arrived in Rio, except for our second lifeboat drill. It turned out that their lifeboat was right next to ours, and, after the public address had dismissed us, I saw Mother exchange a few words with them. I was glad to see that Mrs. Irena looked quite well and decided that they must have been eating their meals in their cabin.

Then, when our ship finally docked in Rio de Janeiro, Mother spoke to the Kosiewiczes again, and she and Mr. K. both wrote things down, which I presumed to be each other's Rio address. I was very sure that that was what they were doing and felt quite proud to be able to make such assumptions. I wondered who of my peers back in Poland had seen as much of the world or understood grownups as well as I.

M. Gordet had a car and a chauffeur meet him at the dock, and he gave Mother and me a ride to the *pension* that he had recommended for us to stay at. On the way to the *pension*, we drove along a long, curved beach with waves and bright sand and people with skin several shades darker than I was used to seeing. I understood that, in a warm place like this, people would be heavily tanned, but I felt a thrill as I saw that some of the people had the very black and curly hair or the flattened noses that I recognized from a book I had had before the war, as "Negro" features. I had never seen *Negros* before.

While on one side of our car was the ocean, the beach, and a sidewalk inlaid with "S" shaped, black and white stripes, on the other side was a city, which I knew to be the capital of Brazil, with tall buildings, offices, stores, and traffic. And the idea of such a city being equipped with its own beach was another concept that had to work itself into my mind slowly. Back in our own capital, Warsaw, if one wanted to go to the beach, he would have to pack a suitcase, go to the train station, buy a ticket, wait for a train, ride that train for a long time, and finally get off at a resort on the Baltic sea and rent a hotel room. Here, all one had to do was cross the street. And on top of all that, as Mother had told me, here it got hotter during the winter and colder in the summer. When I had asked why that was, Mother had said that it was because the earth was round so that it rotated around the sun.

Our *pension* was a ways away from the downtown part of the city, and was surrounded by a big, fenced-in yard with grass and trees, and M. Gordet came inside with us and introduced us to the woman who owned it. She was a small and thin woman, like Mother, only older. She had black hair with a considerable amount of gray and very dark skin that looked almost like leather. She had a thin face, a bit of a mustache above her lip, and a gold tooth right at the front of her mouth. Her name was Sra. De la Vega, and M. Gordet said she would take good care of us. This made the senhora smile, lighting up her face with two rows of perfectly even white teeth, except for that one gold one. She spoke French to Mother and M. Gordet, though I could tell that she had difficulty with it.

I had not been paying much attention to their talk until I heard her mention the word *beach*. "I go to the beach every afternoon," she was saying, "and your son can come with me. It's just short walking, you know." And it was arranged right then that directly after lunch today, I would accompany her to the beach.

Our room was a corner room, with windows on two sides, which Mother opened immediately, letting a fresh breeze into the warm room. The furniture was wicker, something I had never seen indoors before, and there was only one bed. This meant that I would have to sleep with Mother, something I had done before in some of the hotels and *pensions* across Europe, but preferred not to. Whenever I rolled over or even scratched my leg, Mother would complain. "Don't do that, Yulian," she would say, even though I thought she was sound asleep. If I got out of bed, however slowly and carefully, Mother would wake up. And since Mother went to bed considerably later than I did, and since my bladder tended to get very full during the night, mornings were particularly difficult for me, when I didn't have my own bed.

But I noticed that the bed had sheets with green vines and blue flowers printed on them. I had never seen sheets with anything printed on them before, but these might give me something to look at as I lay in bed with nothing to do, while waiting for Mother to wake up. And these vines and flowers certainly went well with the wicker furniture.

When we went downstairs for lunch in the *pension's* dining room, Mother and I were both surprised to see M. Gordet waiting for us. Whether he had been waiting all that time or gone out and come back, I had no idea, but Mother kissed his cheek as though she had not seen him for a week. He would have lunch with us, he said, and Mother told him how pleased that made her.

M. Gordet translated the lunch menu into French for us, after which Mother asked, "What do you want to order, Julien?"

I looked at Mother in surprise. Nobody had ever asked me what I wanted to eat before. If I had heard Mother correctly, her question marked for me a transition into a higher state of being...

which, on reflection, made perfect sense since this was our first meal on a new continent. Mother gave no indication of there being any sort of significance attached to her question. In fact, there was a definite possibility that she had asked the question quite absently, since M. Gordet had just lit her cigarette, from a pack with a label I had never seen before, and Mother seemed to be in the act of savoring its essence.

"They're American," M. Gordet said about the cigarettes.

Whatever meaning lay behind Mother's question to me, I decided that I should assume my original impression to be correct and respond in kind. One of the items that M. Gordet had read off was an omelet with ham and some other ingredients, whose French names I did not recognize. I loved eggs in any form—scrambled with chopped spinach, they even made that dismal vegetable palatable—and I was sure that this is what Mother expected me to order. But, as I now knew from experience, an omelet of some sort was likely to be on the *pension's* lunch menu on most days, and I would get a chance at it tomorrow. On the other hand, the acknowledgement of my maturity that I assumed to have just been handed to me, deserved an equally mature selection. There was a fish item on the menu. On numerous occasions Mother had tried to make me eat fish, and it had never been a pleasant experience for either of us. When I had scarlet fever in Barcelona and had had to eat that boiled, unsalted fish, that had been really awful. But the fish on the menu here was described as fried in butter, which even made cauliflower taste good, and also some kind of almond things.

"I... I... I would like the f... f... fish," I said. I seemed to have more trouble getting the words out than I usually did, which tended to happen when I was excited about something.

"Don't do that," Mother said in Polish, and I knew it was the stuttering she was referring to, and not the fish. Then she turned to M. Gordet. "When he gets excited about something, he does that," she explained. "The doctor said it's just temporary. It's from the stress of what we've been through and having to move all the time. It'll stop once he's settled and in school." This wasn't the first time that she had tried to explain my stuttering to M. Gordet.

I certainly had not heard the doctor say anything about school, but I knew how much my stuttering embarrassed Mother.

"The fish," M. Gordet repeated. He had a little piece of paper on which he was supposed to write our order for the waitress.

"Y… yes M… monsieur," I said.

Then the waitress, who seemed to know M. Gordet, brought two Martinis on a little tray and took the order slips from him.

"George, how nice," Mother said, but I could tell that she wasn't really at all pleased. Anything stronger than one glass of wine, tended to make Mother sick. But they clinked glasses and M. Gordet leaned his head toward Mother's, as he had not done in the ship's dining room, and talked in a low voice.

Unlike some of the men that Mother had met during our travels, he did not seem like a bad sort. I had definitely not liked the photographer in Lisbon, who had shot photographs of her in his studio, which she wouldn't let me see afterwards, or the fat man in Rome who had taken us to his old mother's house for dinner, tried to make me eat octopus, and then laughed at my revulsion. I didn't even hold it against M. Gordet that he had marched me to our cabin that way when the two Dutch brothers had tried to push me off the ship. They must have told him some story regarding that kick in the eye, and he had no reason not to believe them. No, while M. Gordet rarely spoke to me and did have a habit of running his comb through his hair quite frequently, I did not have any negative feelings toward him.

I counted eight other tables in the dining room. The furniture here was wicker, just like in our room, but painted a light green, and the tablecloths had floral designs on them, just like our bed sheets, though not the same design. I saw no other children in the room, which was a relief to me, though some of the tables were empty. When our food arrived, I was further relieved to discover that, as I had hoped, the fish was quite good. This was particularly welcome since, so far, Mother had taken no notice of what I had, voluntarily, ordered.

I had finished my canned pears and was staring out of the dining room window, when I sensed somebody standing behind me. Turning, I saw that it was Sra. De la Vega in a beach jacket and a scarf tied around her hair. A pair of very large sunglasses covered her eyes and made her small face look even smaller. "Time to go to the beach, my little one," she said.

"Ah, Sra. De la Vega," Mother exclaimed, noticing her for the first time.

"Gabriella," the senhora corrected.

"Gabriella, you're on your way to the beach," Mother said. "I'm so grateful to you for taking my son."

"He can help carry my things," she said. Then, to me, "Go upstairs and put on your bathing suit. Do you like lemonade?"

I said that I did.

"Go upstairs, shoo! I will wait for you on the front porch."

I went upstairs and exchanged my pants for my bathing suit. In Poland everyone had always brought a second bathing suit to the beach, so you could change into a dry one when you came out of the water, but I only had the one.

Sra. De la Vega had a folded beach chair, a beach blanket and two thermoses, besides her large, flowered cloth purse. I had expected to be handed the two thermoses and/or, possibly, the folded beach blanket, but the senhora surprised me by handing me the folded, wood-frame-and-canvass beach chair, plus the blanket. The beach chair wasn't heavy, but, because of its size, awkward for me to carry. The senhora had held it with ease, because she was taller than I was, but I had a great deal of difficulty keeping it off the ground. I tried to manage it with as little struggle as possible, so that she would not take it away from me, but, much to my delight, I saw that the senhora took little interest in my problem and set right out down the street. Several times I had to stop and shift the load to my other hand, but my companion didn't embarrass me by stopping to wait for me. A few running steps brought me even with her each time, before having to set it down and switch it to the other hand.

The beach was only one block away, and the senhora set a brisk pace. And she didn't make me hold her hand to cross the wide avenue or even tell me to look both ways. She crossed the street by herself, and I, some paces behind, decided to wait for some cars to pass before plunging ahead. Making this decision was also a first for me, and I couldn't help a little pride.

Sra. De la Vega was a considerable distance ahead of me by the time I reached the sidewalk with the "S" shaped mosaic lines that I had seen from the car. As I crossed this sidewalk, I tried to determine whether it was white with black "S"s or the other way around. There were a lot of people on the beach already, some in the water, some on blankets, and two men and a lady smacking what looked like a beanbag with feathers, back and forth with their hands. The bathing suit that this lady was wearing was not the one-piece kind that I had always seen on women before, but what looked like the panties and brassier that my mother wore under her dress.

Sra. De la Vega did not seem to stop and look for a good spot, as Kiki and I always did when arriving at the beach, but walked directly to a spot as though it had been reserved for her. As she passed other people, they seemed to know her and exchange greetings with her.

Once she had reached her spot, the senhora stopped and waited for me to catch up. With both my arms sore now from the load, I had had to stop for a short rest, and was embarrassed now to keep her waiting. I hurried as fast as I could, my feet sinking into the soft sand at each step.

When she had taken the blanket from me and spread it out, and then set up her chair, the senhora removed her beach jacket, revealing a bathing suit similar to the one worn by the lady playing with the feathered beanbag, though a different color. Except that, while the top half of the other lady's suit had covered the lower half of her breasts, the senhora's top was so much smaller and her breasts so much longer, that a good three quarters or more of each leathery breast was open to the air.

I looked away quickly. Back in Poland, people coming out of the water, would frequently change from a wet bathing suit to a dry one right in plain sight, and you were supposed to, automatically, turn your head away and not look. That had been fine with me, and when, on occasion, someone did catch me inadvertently looking at them, I would be very embarrassed. But now, the smooth swellings above the suit top of the lady playing the beanbag game had a fascination I had not experienced before. Suddenly I found myself watching in the hope that in stretching for the feathery projectile she would, somehow, stress the mechanism holding up that top to the point where it could no longer perform its function and I would be treated to a glimpse of one or both of the hemispherical treasures.

There were some things to this whole business that I didn't understand. I knew that men had, what Kiki called, *birdies*, and women didn't. I had one, but Mother did not. In place of a *birdie*, Mother had hair, and she would, sometimes, come out of the bathroom with nothing on, but holding one hand over her hair, while covering her breasts with the other forearm. It always embarrassed me for her to see me looking at her. Had she not been able to see me, I would have looked more closely to find out exactly what was there.

But Kiki had also told me that, if I touched my *birdie* when I didn't need to, such as when I had to negotiate it out through the leg opening of my shorts to go to the bathroom, I would go crazy. I could not understand how simply touching a part of your own body could make you go crazy, but, as with God and Jesus, I had taken it on faith. On the other hand, since I understood it to require a certain accumulation of touches to achieve that dreaded result, I had developed an inexplicable craving to tempt fate by sneaking my hand under my nightshirt, at night, and make split-second contact between the tip of my finger and the purple tip of the hazardous organ. But, once I knew Kiki to be wrong on the subject of Jews and Heaven, and particularly since I believed myself considerably more grownup than my peers, rather than going crazy, I had accepted her as being wrong on the subject of *birdies* as well and the entire adventure lost its appeal.

"Be very careful in the water," Sra. De la Vega was saying now, "because there is a very strong current."

I had been taught to face anyone addressing me, and I automatically turned back toward the senhora. But the senhora had seated herself on the reclining beach chair, and I saw that the bottom half of her suit was as limited in its coverage as the top, ending a good distance below her brown bellybutton. Had these same body areas belonged to the beanbag lady, and had they been similarly displayed, I would have feasted my eyes for as long as I could manage. But, things being as they were, I only turned away in embarrassment.

"I... I... I am not s... s... supposed to go in the w... w... water so soon after ea... eating, S... s... senhora," I said, looking toward the water.

"So sit down next to me," she said, patting the blanket. I sat down, still examining the ocean.

Sitting beside the senhora and facing the huge expanse of ocean, I realized that what I was hoping for from that other lady's bathing suit top had scant chance of happening. She had, undoubtedly, played this beach game many times before and was well familiar with the limits of her equipment. On the other hand, I reasoned that, on this beach, there must be other ladies, more youthful than the senhora, but similarly reclining and similarly exposed. And if I were to equip myself with a pair of sunglasses, like the senhora wore, I could wander this beach, harvesting all those sights, without fear of embarrassment.

But the moment I thought that, I realized that sunglasses would be an unessential drain on our precarious budget. I could tell Mother that the sun hurt my eyes very badly, and then she would certainly buy me a pair. But, in my self-appointed role as sentinel against unnecessary spending, I could not justify such a subterfuge to my own conscience.

"You are so quiet, Julien," the senhora said, breaking into my reverie. Suddenly I was embarrassed. I knew that there were certain people who could read minds, and what if the senhora was one of them?

"Are you missing your home and your little friends in Poland?" she asked.

"Y... Y... Y... Yes, S... S... S... Senhora," I said. I tried to think about Warsaw and Kiki to cover my shameful thoughts from her sight. And I was stuttering terribly. The senhora would certainly tell me to stop and think of what I wanted to say, and then to just to say it, as everyone else did.

"Give me your hands, Julien," the senhora said suddenly.

"M... M... My h... h... hands?" With both my hands in hers, she would be able to read my thoughts even more thoroughly. Or was it so that I wouldn't be able to get away?

"Just turn to me and give me your hands," she said.

I turned to face the senhora in her beach chair and saw that she had sat up and turned her shoulders and those long breasts squarely towards me. A cigarette was dangling from her lips. She held her palms up, and I carefully laid my fingers on hers.

I felt her fingers draw my hands until they had a solid grip on them. She was looking into my eyes, and I didn't dare turn away. Her eyes were very dark brown, and she had thick, black eyebrows.

She was looking inside my head now. I tried to picture myself and Kiki walking to the park in an effort to give a benign image to my thoughts.

The softness of Sra. De la Vega's hands surprised me. I had expected the feel of leather.

There was a black disk in the center of each of the senhora's eyes, but now they seemed to be receding so that I felt that, maybe, I was looking inside *her* head too, even though there was nothing to see. But I didn't have the power to read minds. I wonder if, in my eyes, she could see me and Kiki, walking along the street to the park, as I was visualizing us.

"I want you to say after me, *My name is Julien, and I don't have to stutter*. And say it without stuttering." I felt the Senhora's tight grip on my hands.

"My n... name is J... julien, a... and I d... don't have to st... tutter," I said, trying hard not to stutter, but it not working.

"Pay attention," the senhora said severely, and she shook my two hands for emphasis.

"Say, *I used to live in Warsaw, but now I am in Rio de Janeiro*."

I stuttered my way through her sentence.

"Look deep, deep into my eyes," she said.

I tried to look more intently into her eyes. I opened my own eyes as wide as I could, and now her black ones were beginning to rotate in little, tight circles. "*I used to live in Warsaw*," she repeated, her voice seeming to come from further away now, as though our arms had stretched several meters. "*I used to live in Warsaw*," she said again. "Say that!"

I had made her impatient with me. I wanted desperately to say
it correctly for her. I watched her eyes describing their circles. "I...
used to l... ive in W... arsaw," I said, dragging out the first sound
of each word, but not stuttering.

"Say it again, quicker."

"I used to live in Warsaw." I said it without stuttering.

"But now I am in Rio," the senhora prompted.

"But now I am in Rio," I said.

"Rio is a magic place."

"Rio is a magic place."

"That's good. That's very good. Now go play. You won't need
to stutter anymore." I felt her release my hands, and her eyes
stopped circling. The senhora had picked up her book and was
reading again, her head tilted to avoid the cigarette smoke.

I was in no mood to go play. Sra. De la Vega had cured my
accursed stutter. I wouldn't have to stutter anymore. Of course,
if she had the power to cure my stutter simply by looking into
my eyes, it was very likely that she had also read my mind, which
must, surely, be easier than curing a stutter, just as *looking* at a picture is much easier than drawing one, and so she must have seen
my embarrassing thoughts. But she hadn't said anything about
them or looked upset about it, so it was best to just leave it alone.

I didn't want to disobey the senhora, after all she had done
for me. If she didn't see me playing, as she had told me to do, she
might think that I wasn't grateful or something, so I began digging a hole in the sand with my hands.

The feeling came gradually, but I was, now, aware of being
filled with the thrill at being able to speak, again, like normal people. I wanted to savor the thrill more intensely, so, with my back
turned to the senhora, I began to, silently, mouth the first thing
that came to mind, which happened to be *The Lord's Prayer*. I had
no difficulty with it.

At the same time, I was also aware of the appropriateness of this particular text—that the first normal words out of my mouth were a prayer. Contrary to my zeal of a few months earlier, I was no longer totally sure, anymore, that there even was a God who listened to prayers, but, if there was, then I had scored some points with Him.

How surprised Mother would be when she heard me speak!

Ordinarily, I would have grown quickly bored with an activity like digging a hole in sand that kept pouring back in to fill the hole. But my mind was playing a film in which I come back to our room, Mother asks how the beach was, and I, casually, begin telling her about the people playing with the feathered beanbag, and I don't stutter anymore. And then I run into Mrs. Kosiewicz on the street, and I say, "Good morning, Please Missus," and she says, "Oh Yulian, you don't stutter anymore. How wonderful!"

Then there was a scene in which I'm walking along the street with Mother, and I see Mrs. Kosiewicz about to cross the street, but she doesn't see a bus that's about to hit her, and I shout, "Irena, watch out for the bus!" I address her as *Irena,* because it's a faster way to get her attention, and then she says, "Oh Yulian, you saved my life." At one point, I even found myself mouthing the dialogue.


After quite a while, the senhora looked down at her wristwatch and said that I had had enough sun for my first day, and should go back to the pension. Since I didn't see her make any move to get up, I realized that she meant for me to walk back by myself. I had never been allowed out on the street by myself—to say nothing of crossing the thoroughfare, but I did not say this to the senhora. And, suddenly, I was quite nervous about surprising Mother with my new speech.

I thanked the senhora, ostensibly for bringing me to the beach, but implying her curing of my speech impediment. Careful, lest I stutter again and shatter the new reality, I spoke very slowly and deliberately, dragging out the first sound of each word.

The senhora patted my cheek, and sent me on my way.

When I got back to the pension, M. Gordet was finally gone, and Mother was sitting cross-legged on our bed, playing solitaire. By the expression on her face and the way she laid the cards down—almost throwing them down—I could tell that something more than the solitaire had gone badly.

"Did you have a good time at the beach?" she asked. Her tone made it almost an accusation.

I took a breath in preparation for my stutter-less performance. But, with a stack of un-played cards still in her hand, Mother suddenly swept all the cards together, spilling some onto the floor. "Well, it turns out," she said, "that M. Gordet is no gentleman."

Each time Mother brought the word, *gentleman*, into play, I would find myself cringing inwardly a little. Over the past months, Mother had found a number of men—as well as myself, with my dirty fingernails—to fall short of that designation. And, except in the case of my nails, the reason for this demotion was always rather unclear, but charged with angry emotion.

"The only man that I can trust is you," Mother said. "You are my knight in shining armor, aren't you?"

She had called me her knight before, and, while I had, at first, felt complimented, I had soon come to identify it as an appeal for either my support or my collaboration in some impending crisis. And, in the end, it had never turned out well.

"This is something you want to remember, Yulian," she said, but sounding as though it was I who was being accused.

"Remember it for when you grow up. A woman will give anything to a true gentleman."

"D… d… did h… he t… take y… y… your r… ring?" I stammered.

Mother didn't seem to have heard me. But I could see the ring still on her finger, and breathed a sigh of relief. On the other hand, I had had no idea how insecure our possession of that ring actually was. Apparently, had M. Gordet been a true gentleman, she might well have given it to him.

On the one hand, I couldn't imagine Mother giving away her ring—really *our* ring, now that it represented our joint security—to someone just because he was a gentleman. On the other hand, I well knew how many incongruities and contradictions to my vision of the world were presented by life all the time. And, perhaps, what Mother was really telling me was to be on my guard against the eventuality that she might meet a true gentleman and be inclined to give those twin diamonds away.

"Tomorrow we're moving out of this *pension*," Mother went on. She had gotten down from the bed and was packing our suitcases again.

"M… M… M… Moving?… " And I stopped before finishing, because I was, again, aware that whatever it was that the senhora had done for my stutter, had just come undone.

"Yes," Mother went on. "It seems that this *pension* is where M. Gordet likes to bring his lady friends."

It was clear that this was not a time for us to be moving, since I, evidently, needed another session with the senhora. "W… W… Why is that a r… reason to m… m… move?" I asked.

Mother put her fingers to her forehead, "Will you please stop that stuttering!" she said.

I knew that she knew that I could not do that. What she was saying now was out of exasperation. She was upset by whatever it was that M. Gordet had done, and, when she was upset by some-thing, my stuttering disturbed her more... just the way that my stuttering got worse when I was upset.

Mother must have realized something of the sort as well, because she sucked in her lips and raised her hand in a gesture that seemed to imply an apology.

With a great effort, the kind of effort that I hadn't needed when speaking to the senhora, I repeated my question, "S... o w... hy is th... at a r... eason to m... ove?"

"It just is," Mother said.

I knew that Mother didn't want to talk about it any more. "W... here w... ill w... e m... ove t... o?" I asked. There was more than just curiosity to that question. It just might, I hoped, make Mother realize that we didn't know any other places. "We d... on't kn... ow anyone else i... in R... io."

"I'll find us another *pension*."

That remained to be seen.

# CHAPTER III

I HAD FORGOTTEN ABOUT Mr. and Mrs. K. I had seen Mother
exchange addresses with Mr. K. before disembarking, so now it
was him that she called the next morning, and, that same afternoon, we were unpacking again, this time at the Kosiewiczes'
hotel, in a suite right above theirs.

The hotel was closer to the center of town than the *pension*
had been. It was a totally urban setting, and there were stores and
apartment buildings across the street. We were on the fourth floor
and had a bedroom and a living room with a cot, meaning that
I would have my own bed. We also had a telephone on a little
table next to my cot.

On the bad side, however, was the fact that we were in the
same hotel with Mr. K, whom I didn't trust to begin with, and
had even more concern about now, in view of Mother's confession
of the previous day. My concern increased when he telephoned
Mother that same afternoon and then came up from their suite on
the floor below to talk with her.

I had hoped that Mrs. Irena would come with him, but she
didn't. He did, however, bring a briefcase from which he produced
a diamond necklace and some earrings to show to Mother. They
sat together on my cot, and he let Mother hold them. She turned
them one way then another in the light, as I had seen people do
with jewelry. I could tell from her expression that she liked them.

spoke quietly, so that I wouldn't hear, but, if he was hop-
sell them to her, he was barking up the wrong tree because
ad no money. Of course, it could have been a trick. I had
rd of pickpockets, people who would distract you in some way
that you wouldn't notice them robbing you. Kiki and I had
even seen a stage performer who could take the watch off your
wrist or the wallet out of your pocket, without your knowing it.
And so Mr. K. could have been trying to get Mother so interested
in his necklace and earrings that she would not notice him sliding
the diamond ring off her finger.

It was, as I thought about it, a rather clever trick. You put
somebody off their guard by giving them something valuable
of *yours* to hold so that they don't suspect that you are actually
*robbing* them. But I wouldn't let it work here. Sitting in a little
armchair by the window, I had my eyes on Mother's ring every
second, and, if he tried anything, I would see it.

On the other hand, what if he simply asked for the ring and
Mother gave it to him because she considered him a gentleman?
No, that couldn't happen. There was no way that Mother could
just give her ring to Mr. K. I must have misunderstood Mother's
statement yesterday. Or, what was most likely, there were certain
conditions under which this was true, conditions which Mother
had been too distraught to specify.

I was relieved to see Mother finally hand the necklace back
to Mr. K. and him pack it back in the briefcase—with the ring
still on Mother's finger. I thought he might go home now, but he
didn't. Instead, he pulled a large broach out of his bag, and they
went on talking quietly.

Then Mother looked at me. "Yulian," she said, "Mr. Kosiewicz
says that his wife hasn't been to the beach yet. Why don't you
take her."

Nobody had ever put it that way to me before. It was always
someone who was taking *me* somewhere. If Mother's suggestion

had been just that, a suggestion, it would have presented a temptation that was hard to resist. But I knew that I had no choice in the matter anyway. And, as far as the ring was concerned, if, in my absence, Mother's ring were to disappear somehow, we would all know who had taken it, and all we'd have to do is call the police and tell them. And, because Mr. K. knew this as well as I did, he would not try anything.

Mr. K. was already on the telephone, telling his wife that she was going to the beach with me. I went into the bedroom to put on my bathing suit, then waited a long time out in the living room for Mrs. Irena to arrive. This time, I determined, I would call her *Irena*, as she had asked me to on the ship, when I hadn't been able to.

When she finally knocked on the door and I let her in, she had what must have been one of her husband's shirts over her bathing suit. The shirt was unbuttoned, and I automatically checked to see if she had on one of the skimpy, two-piece suits I had seen on the beach the day before, but she didn't, and I was disappointed. It was the same white bathing suit she had worn on the ship. Her beautiful brown hair seemed even fuller and more luscious than I remembered it. A green headband crossed over the top of her head, over which she had a pair of large sunglasses, which I immediately envied.

She shook hands with Mother, then with me. "How are you today, Yulian?" she asked.

"I'm f... ine, Mrs. I... rena. How are y... ou?" I was speaking very slowly so as not to stutter.

"*Mrs. Kosiewicz*," Mother corrected.

"Oh no, please Missus," Mrs. Irena said. "I asked Yulian to call me Irena. I hope that's all right."

"Well, as long as he's respectful."

"It'll be fine," Mrs. Irena said.

"Go get a towel from the bathroom," Mother said to me, "and you'd better get a blanket out of the closet."

I saw that Mrs. Irena had brought neither blanket nor towel, so I brought an extra towel from the bathroom. "Let me carry the blanket, and you can take the towels," she said. I handed her the blanket.

"So, are we ready to go?" Mrs. Irena asked me.

"Y... es M... rs. I... rena," I said.

I had expected her to lead the way into the hallway, but she didn't. Then I realized that I should open the door. "P... lease, M... rs. I... rena," I said, holding the door open.

"Thank you," she said, stepping through. Then, when the door had closed behind us on the landing, she said, "When we're alone, *Yulek*," using the familiar form of my name, "just call me *Irenka*. The *Missus* makes me feel like an old woman. And I don't look like an old woman to you, do I? Your mother and Tadek probably won't like it, so you can call me *Missus* in front of them, but when we're alone, we'll just be two friends. It'll be our secret."

I knew that this was going to be hard for me to get used to. But without the *Missus* in front of her name, I would be free of that third-person form of address. Not only was the third-person awkward to use, but I felt that it put a barrier between people. It was as though I had to wear a glove to touch her hand. As we rode down the hotel's one elevator, I searched for some equally-intimate response I could give.

"I have a b... ear n... amed M... eesh," I said, as we reached the lobby. "W... hat I m... ean is that h... e is a t... eddy b... ear." As we walked through the little lobby, I realized that I had a problem. I wanted to hold Mrs. Irena's—or Irenka's—hand once we reached the street, but I didn't want her to think that it was because I was a little boy who wasn't allowed to walk in the street without holding someone's hand. I still remembered how soft it was, from the two or three times we had shaken hands, and the idea of walking the three blocks to the beach, nestled in that pillowy hand, seemed suddenly like a short sojourn in Heaven.

If she were to ask to hold my hand, as she well might, I decided, I would comply, because that would not indicate that that was my normal practice, but just her *supposition* of my normal practice. But for me to take *her* hand, could well be interpreted as though, on the street, I was always held by the hand. .

"Which way do we want to go?" she asked as we stepped out into the sunlight, and she lowered the sunglasses down over her eyes.

"T... he b... each is j... ust th... ree bl... ocks str... aight ah... ead," I said. "so w... e can g... o either l... eft or r....ight

"All right. So which way do you want to go?"

I realized, suddenly, that it was I who was supposed to be taking Irenka to the beach, so it was up to me to make those decisions.

"To the r... ight," I said, and began walking in that direction. Irenka caught up to me, but that put her on the street side of the sidewalk, the side on which, I knew, the gentleman was supposed to walk. I crossed behind her to place myself on the proper side. As I did, I passed the two towels to what would now be my outside hand.

"Oh, you are such a gentleman, Yulek," she said. To the best of my memory, that was the first time that anyone had actually credited me with that elevated status.

But the blanket stayed in Irenka's left hand, dashing any of my dreams for the softness of her palm. Then I remembered that I had begun confessing to her about my relationship with Meesh.

"I g... ot M... eesh w... hen we w... ere in L... voof and I w... as a lot y... ounger," I said. I explained that, at first, I had pretended that he was my son and carried him everywhere, but, later, when we got to Hungary, and I was older, he didn't like being carried around anymore, but we would still talk together in our secret language.

It had not been an easy confession to make, as I felt myself laying my soul bare in front of my new friend.

"I hope I can meet your bear some day," she said, and, as I fantasized introducing Meesh to her, the feeling I had was of a sacred bond being sealed between us.

And suddenly, to my horror, I found that, inadvertently, I had slipped my hand between Mrs. Irena's palm and the blanket.

At what point in my confession I had done that, and how long it had been there, I had no idea. And now I wasn't even sure that she was aware of what I had done. Possibly, I reasoned, it had happened as we crossed the street.

We had turned the corner, and I could see heads of people as they moved about the beach, some three blocks in front of us. I walked very carefully now so that my hand wouldn't jiggle against hers and alert her to its presence. If the issue came up, I would pretend that I was as unaware of the situation as Mrs. Irena seemed to be—that it had happened inadvertently, as it had, and that, for all I knew, it was she who had initiated the action.

As we walked now, I tasted again the deliciousness of the words she had spoken on the hotel landing, when she had told me to call her *Irenka*, and hoped that she had another luscious intimacy to share with me. But then I chided myself for my greed.

"It's good to have a friend you can talk to, isn't it?" she responded, at long last. And then I realized that what my frantic thoughts had construed to be a passage of time, had only been a few seconds.

"Y... es," I said.

"I'm sure that your Meesh is very discreet, isn't he?"

I had heard the word *discreet* before, but wasn't exactly sure of what it meant. "Y... es," I said, hoping that she would clarify it.

"Things that you say to him he doesn't repeat to anyone, does he?"

I assured her that he didn't and suddenly got an inkling of where this might be going.

"And do you keep the secrets that he tells you, too?"

There really weren't any secrets that Meesh ever told *me*, but I assured her of this as well, because I would have if there had been any.

"You know that, when somebody tells you a secret, you can't repeat it to *anyone*."

"Y… y… yes," I said, my stutter getting the best of me this time.

"Well then, maybe you could become *my* Meesh."

Suddenly I could feel my heart thumping. Of all the things that an eight-and-a-half-year-old boy could become, I could think of none I would rather be than Irenka's Meesh.

Now Irenka was saying something else, and I had missed it. I didn't even know if it had been a statement or a question. "Y… es," I said. For the first time, I was glad for my slow speech, since it enabled my response to be taken for either an answer or an acknowledgement. And my *yes* was an unequivocal agreement to anything she might have proposed.

Now I felt Irenka give my hand a little squeeze. "You and I are going to be very good friends, aren't we," she said. Overwhelmed, I responded by giving her hand a firm squeeze in return.

"We'll have a nice talk when we sit down," she said, smiling. And the smile stayed on her face, as we completed our walk to the beach in silence.

The next thing I heard from Irenka was her exclaiming what a beautiful beach it was, as though she had not seen it before. "And look how long it is," she said.

"I w... as ... here ... yesterday," I said, though I was sure she already knew it. "N... ot ex... actly h... ere, but f... urther up. N... ear where our p... ension w... as."

"Where shall we spread our blanket?" Irenka asked.

There were a lot of empty spaces in front of us, but I didn't know if she liked to sit near the water or far from it. "H... ow ab... out there?" I said, pointing to a space half way down, though I wasn't sure she could tell which one I was pointing to.

"Fine."

Then I realized that she was waiting for me to lead the way, so I stepped down from the sidewalk, onto the sand.

When we had spread our blanket, and Irenka kneeled down and began to twist her shoulders in order to remove her shirt, I could see a lot of people watching her, and I was suddenly glad that she was not wearing one of the skimpy, two-piece bathing suits. In fact, I would have preferred that, in front of all these people, she even not remove the shirt. I looked her directly in the eyes and even raised my chin so that she would know that that was where I was looking. "The s... un is ... very h... ot on th... is beach," I said, "m... aybe M... issus, I m... ean y... ou sh... ould k... eep *your* sh... irt on."

"You're right, Yulian. I'll put it back on in a few minutes," she said, "but the sun feels so good on my shoulders." Then she put her hands down on the blanket and lowered herself to her stomach. She removed her sunglasses, and then I watched Irenka's hands reach back and unbutton the two shoulder straps from where they attached at waist level behind her back. "Would you lay the straps down on the blanket for me?" she asked, crossing her forearms as a pillow under her cheek.

I reached carefully for the strap nearest to me and laid it, with equal care, across her upper arm. Irenka now raised her arm to make the strap drop to the blanket. As she did so, she raised her shoulder exposing, for an instant, the entire side of her round, white breast, with its pink nipple.

I instinctively turned to see if anyone had seen it. To my great relief, nobody who might have seen past me seemed to be looking in our direction.

This still left the strap on the other side, where her breast would be exposed to viewing by anyone looking in this direction. I gathered up the strap and laid it carefully on the blanket, through the space between Irenka's upper arm and the back of her head so that she wouldn't have to move her arm.

"Thank you, Yulian," she said. "Now, why don't you lie down beside me where I can tell you something."

I did as asked.

"We were talking about secrets," she reminded me, "remember?"

I assured her that I did.

"So now if I tell you a secret, will you promise that you won't tell it to *anybody*?"

"Y… es."

"You're sure?"

"Y… es."

"All right. Well, you see, Yulian, Tadek, and I did something really bad."

"Y… y… you d… d… did s… something b… bad?"

"I feel terrible about it, Yulian, and I've wanted to tell it to someone for the longest time. You won't tell anyone, will you?"

I assured her that I wouldn't.

"You see, back in Poland, we were servants in somebody's home. Tadek was a chauffeur with the Romanskis, and Mrs. Romanski was teaching me to be a maid and to do hair. Then, when the war began and the Romanskis were in Italy, Tadek took an axe from the tool shed and broke through the wall, where they kept their valuables in one of those safes, and he put all the jewelry into a little crocodile leather bag, and we drove away in the Romanskis' Packard car."

"B... b..but it w... was w... w... wartime," I broke in, anxious to relieve her guilt with the explanation that the Germans or the Bolsheviks would have gotten it anyway..

But Irenka continued talking. "I wanted Tadek to take Alicia, the cook, too," she said, "but Tadek wouldn't take her. He said that he had a plan. Because he and I knew manners and could speak properly, we could pass for gentry as a newly married couple on their honeymoon, but Alicia, who spoke like a peasant, would give us away."

It was the *pass-for-a-newly-married-couple* part that hit me the hardest. "Y..you m... mean y... you and y... your h... husband aren't m... m... married?" I stammered, incredulously.

"No, we're not, but, remember, you can't tell that to anyone. You promised."

"No, i... t's a s... ecret," I said, but my mind was racing to grasp the fact that what she had just shared with me was much more grownup than I had expected. There was a major transformation taking place at this moment—Mrs. Irena was changing from just a lady who permitted me to call her by her first name to somebody who really wanted or needed something from me.

I felt myself overwhelmed by the confidences being revealed to me. She was telling me not only her own secrets, but Mr. K's, meaning that she was becoming friendlier to me than she was to him.

"I told Tadek that we should take her with us because the Germans were coming, and it was dangerous, but he wouldn't. We just drove off without telling her."

Now my Irenka was lying there with her eyes closed, and I had the fantasy that she was waiting for me to say something comforting to her. But I had absolutely no idea what to say. I tried hard to think of something. Irenka—my Irenka—was feeling guilty and sad because they had left Alicia, the cook, behind, and I had no idea how to make her happy. I knew that pulling a brass washer out of her ear wouldn't do it. Besides which, I didn't have the washer with me.

I realized that I had started tracing and re-tracing a small circle in the sand with my finger. I had made a little hollow, but, as my finger continued going around, the sand kept sifting in from the sides and prevented the hollow from getting bigger.

It was interesting the way that worked. Just turning my finger around in a tight circle had created the hollow. If I lifted my finger out of the sand, the hollow stayed there until, I supposed, something came along to disturb it, like someone stepping on it. But when I put my finger back in and continued turning, it wouldn't make the hollow any bigger. The faster I turned it, the faster the sand sifted back into the hollow.

I cupped my hand and scooped out a handful of sand. It made a bigger hollow, and sand, again, sifted in from the sides, filling in part of the hollow, but not all of it.

"You won't tell anyone, will you?" Irenka was saying.

I shook my head, without turning to look at her. And I hoped she wouldn't tell me anything more.

Then I thought of going into the cool water. Ordinarily, I would have asked for permission, but I had the sense that my relationship with Irenka was such that it wasn't required. On the other hand, my simply announcing my intention to her seemed unfeeling. And to just stand up and go, would have been rude. I pondered my course of action.

To ask permission, as had been my custom with Kiki, certainly would not have been in any way rude, but it would also mean the surrender of a certain prerogative that I felt in this unique relationship. The term, *prerogative,* of course, was not a part of my vocabulary at the time, but I had an unmistakable sense of its presence there on the blue hotel blanket with Irenka and myself. Now that I knew her to not be married to the nasty Mr. K, I saw Irenka, lying there with the straps of her bathing suit unbuttoned and, possibly, asleep, as someone needing my protection. While I, kneeling at the edge of the blanket, was someone desperately in need of protecting her.

And then the solution to my dilemma presented itself in all its obvious logic, while I chided myself for not thinking of it sooner.

"I... renka?" I asked, not sure that she was awake enough to hear me. I saw her open her eyes. "W... ould y... ou l... ike to g... o into the w... ater wi... th me n... ow? Just don't f... orget to do up y... our sh... oulder st... raps."

To my relief, I watched Irenka's hands feel for the straps on the blanket without her raising either shoulder. In a moment she was kneeling, safely secured within her bathing suit. "I saw how well you swim, on the ship," she said. "Would you teach me?"

I lowered myself from my kneeling position to sit on the blanket, as Irenka was doing. There was a definite purpose in this. I wanted to compare my height to hers and to see if, by some phenomenon, a length of time had elapsed without my realizing it, and I was now a grownup. The things that my companion had said to me since leaving our hotel would, certainly, support such a conclusion.

But, as I had to tilt my face up in order to watch Irenka tuck her long hair into a rubber bathing cap, I realized that the suspected phenomenon had not, after all taken place.

Now I turned my mind to recalling exactly how I had gone about learning to swim. I could remember standing on a dock, two or three years earlier, with Kiki and looking down at people doing the breaststroke in the water. Then, at some point, we had acquired the orange, inflatable floatation cushions with the straps to tie around our waists. In water that came up to my chest, we had let the cushions support us as we did our best to imitate the swimming motions that we had seen, and found ourselves actually moving forward a little. It was, of course, the incident with Mother and Mr. Gordet on the ship that had taught me that I did not need a floatation device to stay afloat.

"Y… ou h… ave to go l… ike th… is," I said now, demonstrating the arm motion, sitting there on the hotel blanket.

Irenka seemed to imitate my example without any difficulty. "Th… at's r… ight," I said. "And w… ith your l… egs y… ou… " I paused to lie down on my stomach, "go l… ike th… is."

"I see," Irenka said.

"No," I said, "Y… ou tr..y it n… ow."

Irenka copied my arm movements.

Then I told her to lie down and do the leg kick. "Th..at's all there is to sw… imming," I said. "J… ust do th… at in the w… ater and you'l sw… im."

"I want to try it now," Irenka said, getting up. "You'll make sure I don't sink, won't you?"

I nodded my head. Irenka started running down towards the water, and I followed.

But the moment we were knee-deep in water, I realized that it would be unlikely that either of us would be able to do any swimming, as waves, much bigger than the ones I had seen in Yurata, came crashing, one after the other, onto the sand. Quite a ways further out, I could see people's heads bobbing on the bumpy water, but those near the shore only dove into the oncoming waves and let them redeposit them close to shore.

"I don't think we can do any swimming here," Irenka said, and I agreed. Then I watched her plunge headfirst into an oncoming wave.

Diving headfirst was not an action I had yet attempted, but I knew that I had little choice, but to follow her example. In fact it was I who should have set the example. I straightened my arms in front of me, closed my eyes and lunged into the next wave as it bore down on me. Instantly, I felt myself whirled around by the force of the water, turned upside down with salt water going up my nose. Then, as I thrashed to reach the surface, my head hit something very unyielding, which I realized must have been the bottom. I had been going in the wrong direction. Now panic grabbed me as I felt the lack of oxygen in my lungs. I tried to turn so as to put my feet against the sandy bottom and thrust myself toward the surface, but the force of the wave had not finished with me, and I felt myself lifted again and suddenly crashing against the beach, face and shoulder first.

"That was wonderful!" I heard Irenka shout and realized she was sitting on the wet sand right next to where I had landed. "Let's do it again!" She stood up and reached for my hand.

My shoulder hurt, my face hurt, and my head ached from my impact against the sand. But I let my companion pull me to my feet. Hand-in-hand we charged the next incoming wall of water.

# CHAPTER IV

OUR HOTEL OCCUPIED HALF the space between two larger buildings. This would have provided an alley between the side of the hotel and the building to its left, except that the hotel lobby took up one story of that empty space. So that what you saw from the street, was an entrance to a small, single-story, flat-roofed structure sandwiched between a large building on one side and the five stories of the hotel on the other. Except that, inside, the lobby had a big opening into the dining room and the elevator that were the bottom of the hotel.

Our bedroom window, on the fourth floor, looked out onto that space above the hotel lobby, and the two windows of our living room, where my day-bed was, faced the street. One creaky elevator served the hotel grudgingly, and the stairs, which I preferred to use, also had windows that opened on the alley space above the lobby roof.

As Mother and I had our supper the first evening, I could not keep my eyes from wandering to Irenka and the man pretending to be her husband, at a table across the room. I noticed that they didn't talk to each other, which made me glad. There was so much that she and I had had to talk about that afternoon. And then there was that glimpse I had had of her bare breast, with its pink nipple, like a plump little mushroom.

As a matter of fact, Mother and I weren't talking to each other either. Mother ate only a salad, which she just picked at, and she smoked all through the meal. This concerned me. My Uncle Martin had died from smoking cigarettes. And Kiki had not approved of people smoking. She never actually said that people who smoked or drank alcohol or wore makeup weren't nice, I suppose because my mother did all those things, but it was easy to tell that she didn't approve.

And once, a few months ago, when Mother and I were in Yugoslavia and Mother was very tired from trying hard to get us a visa to go somewhere further away from the Germans and the Russians, I picked up a cigarette that she had left burning in an ashtray and put it in my mouth. I had done it to show my support and appreciation of Mother and all her efforts to get us out of danger. The cigarette tasted terrible, but I had thought that my doing such a grownup thing would please Mother and demonstrate that I did not disapprove of her anymore, the way that Kiki had.

But Mother's reaction had expressed the very opposite. She had torn the cigarette from my surprised fingers and crushed it out with quick, angry gestures. Then, a few moments later, in a calmer tone, she told me that I was never, ever to touch a cigarette again. She said that cigarettes made people sick. She told me again about Uncle Martin dying from cigarettes, which I had already known about from Kiki, and said that she only smoked them because they calmed her nerves, but would stop when she didn't have to worry about our safety anymore. She even told me that some day she would buy me a gold lighter so that I would be able to light cigarettes for ladies, as was expected of a gentleman, but I was never to smoke, myself.

Well, what would happen if my mother were to get sick and die? There I would be, all by myself in a hotel suite in Rio with no idea how to go about selling Mother's diamonds or what to do once that money ran out.

"You sh… shouldn't be s… moking so m… uch," I said avoiding my stutter almost totally with my new technique of dragging the words out instead of repeating the same sound.

"Yes, I know. I will stop as soon as we get to America," she answered.

"Are you u… pset because M. G….ordet isn't a g… entleman?" I had the sense that there was something to his failure in the *gentleman* department that went beyond the dirty-fingernails and failure-to-light-cigarettes issues. In fact, for some time now, I had had the feeling that what I knew of life was, like the lobby of our hotel, just an antechamber to some great mystery which, once I was introduced to it, would explain a whole lot of things. And I had to confess to myself that my question regarding M. Gordet had been motivated only partly out of concern for Mother's feelings and partly as a probe into that mysterious realm.

"We will never speak of M. Gordet again," Mother said, instantly slamming the door on my probe.

"Tomorrow I will have to telephone Sr. O'Brien, to make an appointment to see him," she announced, as though she had just made a difficult decision. "He's a very rich man, and his wife is Russian. He should be sympathetic to us. I have his telephone number and a letter of introduction from Sr. Santos. Do you remember Sr. Santos, the photographer in Lisbon?"

I remembered Sr. Santos very well. He was the one who made me go to the waiting room after I had watched him shoot some pictures of Mother with her hair blowing from a big fan, because he was going to take some more pictures that I wasn't supposed to see. As for Sra. O'Brien being Russian, Mother had had considerable luck with Russian people, due to her command of the Russian language. Her own mother, my grandmother, was Russian, and Mother had grown up speaking both Russian and Polish. Before our escape, Mother had been able to gain special consideration from several Soviet officers, due to some degree to her fluency in that language. Russian people always seemed to be particularly pleased when they heard somebody, outside Russia, speaking good Russian.

Now I watched Mother light a fresh cigarette from the end of the old one and hoped we would be going to America real soon.

"And when we're at Sr. O'Brien's," she continued in a very sober tone, "you are not to leave the office, unless I tell you to. Do you understand that? If Sr. O'Brien suggests that you go with his secretary to get some ice cream or something, like Sr. Talon did in Lisbon, you are to say, very politely, that, no thank you, but you don't care for any. Do you understand that? You are not to leave me alone with him unless *I* tell you to."

I remembered the scene in Lisbon when Sr. Talon had suggested that I go with his secretary to get some ice cream, and Mother had said that I couldn't. This, of course, was the exact opposite of what had happened at Sr. Santos' photography studio, when Mother had told me to do as he said and wait in the waiting room. But I supposed that she was afraid that this Sr. O'Brien might try to take her diamonds away by force. Now I wondered if, perhaps, that was what had happened with M. Gordet. Had he tried to steal Mother's diamonds?

But somehow, I had the feeling that that had not been the case. If it had been, Mother would have referred to him as a thief. This *not a gentleman* business was more complicated than that. At any rate, tomorrow I would go to Sr. O'Brien's office with Mother and make sure he didn't try to snatch the diamonds.

I didn't get to saying my prayers that night, before falling asleep. It wasn't the first time this had happened in recent weeks. But this time, my experience with Irenka at the beach, had something to do with it.

The next day, I watched as Mother telephoned Sr. O'Brien's office and used her very limited Portuguese to explain her letter of introduction from Sr. Santos in Lisbon. As she best understood it, the secretary said to come right away and gave her the address. Mother immediately changed into one of the dresses she had bought for our boat trip, pinned on a little green, feathered hat with a green veil, and made me clean my nails with a brush. Then we set off in a taxi.

Mother and I had both expected the taxi to take us further into the city where one would think the offices of important businessmen would be, but our driver surprised us by driving along the beach until we were out in the country. Mother even leaned over the back of the front seat with the piece of paper that the address was written on, but the driver said, "Si, si," nodded his head, and kept driving. Mother lit another cigarette.

Then we were driving through a stone and iron gate and turning into a wide gravel driveway with flowerbeds on both sides. There was a large lawn ahead of us and a big stone house with many cars in front of it on a bit of a hill. Our taxi pulled up at the front entrance, where we had to climb some steps and then cross a stone patio to reach the front door.

A man in a black suit met us at the door. "Sr. O'Brien, Sr. Enrique O'Brien," Mother said, and the man nodded his head and proceeded to lead us across the marble floor of the foyer. Mother took my hand, and I didn't object.

The man stopped at a massive set of double doors that were open wide and motioned for us to enter. Now we found ourselves in the center aisle of a room where chairs had been set up as for a performance. Three women, dressed in black, sitting in the front row of the section on our left, were its only occupants. The middle woman of the group, considerably larger than her companions, leaned against the back of her chair with one hand seemingly in the lap of each of the other two. Her head was thrown back, and her black, curly hair, hatless and swept straight back from her upturned face, was in contrast to the pinned and lacquered hairdos that the two other women had under their little, black, veiled hats. At the end of the aisle that ran down between the two sections of chairs, huge sprays and wreaths of flowers surrounded what I took to be a long, gold-colored altar. This was no office, but some kind of church.

The two smaller women turned to look at us over their shoulders, through their black veils, as Mother stopped dead in her tracks. They kept looking, and then the large woman in the middle turned to look at us as well.

I felt Mother's hand pull me forward. We marched right to the altar, where I recognized a padded kneeler right up against it. I had never seen a setup like this, and I wondered if it might be Jewish.

Mother stopped just short of the altar. "We'll just say a short prayer and go home," she whispered.

I pointed to the kneeler. "I think we're supposed to kneel," I whispered back.

Mother knelt down, and I with her. She crossed herself, backwards again. I crossed myself the proper way and put my hands together. The smell of the flowers that surrounded us was overwhelming.

"Don't look inside," Mother whispered.

"Inside what?"

"Oh my God," Mother whispered under her breath, and I understood from her tone that wasn't in prayer. Finally with a slight movement of her head, Mother indicated the left end of the altar. For the first time I noticed that a lid was open at that end. I stretched my neck to see what it revealed.

"Don't look," Mother repeated. There was no way that I could have seen inside from my kneeling position anyway.

Mother had folded her hands and now, indeed, looked as though she were praying.

Then she crossed herself backwards again and stood up. I crossed myself and stood up with her.

Now she walked to the three women sitting in the front row. "Sra. O'Brien?" she asked.

One of the smaller women answered her. "This is Sra. O'Brien," she said, indicating the large woman.

Now Mother broke into Russian. "Senhora, I am so sorry for your loss. I didn't know. I have just arrived from Lisbon with my little son, and I have a letter of introduction to Sr. O'Brien from Sr. Rudolfo Santos."

I watched the Senhora's head, which had been tilted back again, slowly right itself and her closed eyes slowly open. It was like seeing somebody wake from sleep to full, wide-eyed attention. "Senhora is Russian," she said in that language. I saw that her large face had no makeup, while her two companions were made up to the degree Mother's friends had been in Poland before the war. Mother, herself, I now realized, as I compared her to these two women, wore considerably less makeup than she used to.

"No, Senhora. I am Polish, but my little mother is Russian."

"And Senhora, you have a letter from Rudolfo?"

"Yes, Senhora."

"May I see it?" The Senhora, who was totally alert now, held out her hand.

As Mother took the letter out of her purse, I began to understand what was under that open lid. I saw the light blue, silk padding of the lid and the padding along what I could now see of the interior sides, and realized that there must be a dead man in there. I raised myself on tiptoe to see inside and thought that, maybe, I saw a little bit of a forehead and some white hair.

Mother's elbow bumped my arm, and I automatically dropped from my tiptoes. I had seen people killed by the German planes, as we fled Warsaw, but I had never seen one laid out like this, and, suddenly, I had a deep yearning to see one.

"Ah Senhora," Sra. O'Brien was saying now, as she read the letter. "You and your little boy have suffered at the hands of the filthy Bolsheviks."

Words to that effect I had heard numerous times in the past few months, but never with such passion.

"You must have something to eat." Then she turned to the woman on her right and said something to her in Portuguese. The woman looked up at Mother, then stood up and walked quickly out of the room, her heels seeming to click even on the carpet.

"Please sit down next to me, Senhora, and tell me all about your escape."

As Mother sat down, I started to edge myself imperceptibly closer to the casket for a better look inside.

"Sit down," Mother hissed in Polish, and I had no choice, but to seat myself beside her. I had learned to understand Russian, first by listening to Mother and Grandmother talk together, and later from hearing Mother talk with the Russian officers before our escape. Now, for the first time, I realized that talking formally in Russian, as in French or Portuguese, one did not need to speak in the awkward third-person grammar that we did in Polish. Russian, French, and Portuguese all used the word "you" to address a person politely, while Polish only had the intimate version of the term, forcing you into third-person construction when you were speaking to someone you weren't intimate with.

Mother was telling Sra. O'Brien about our escape over the mountains, as I had heard her tell it numerous times before. I knew that she would tell her about me falling into the stream and her pulling me out, which hadn't happened at all, and that she *wouldn't* tell her about getting her leg stuck under a fallen tree branch frozen in the snow and how she would still be sitting there if it weren't for me. When she had first started telling the story that way, it had made me very angry, but now I had become accustomed to it, and I could even mouth the words along with her.

Then, the woman who had gone out came back in, and I quickly stood up to allow her to sit beside Mother.

Instead of sitting down, the woman stood, quite clearly waiting for Mother to give her back her seat.

But, by this time, Sra. O'Brien was holding Mother's hand, and Mother did not seem to see the woman. She was telling Sra. O'Brien about some priest blessing us before our escape, though I could not remember any such event, and though it must have been very hard for her not to see the woman standing right in front of her.

"Sit down, Vera," I understood the Senhora to say to the woman. I had picked up enough Portuguese in Lisbon to manage that.

Sensing an opportunity, I immediately stood up, and Sra. Vera sat down beside Mother, while I began inching my way toward the casket again.

Now a maid, with a little white apron and cap, came to us with a tray. The maid was black skinned with the flattened nose I had seen in my book, and I found her extremely pretty. There were little sandwiches on the tray and two cups. She offered them to Mother, who placed a sandwich on a plate and handed it to me. "Sit down and eat," she said in Polish

"I'm not hungry," I said.

"Sit down and eat," she repeated. Mother was smiling, but I could tell the smile was for the benefit of the senhora.

I took the plate and sat down on the other side of Sra. Vera. Mother took a sandwich for herself and one of the cups.

"Oh, you must eat more," Sra. O'Brien said, and Mother put another sandwich on her plate.

"And the boy," the senhora said to the maid.

The maid brought the tray to me, and I took a second sandwich. As she waited with the tray, I realized I was expected to take the remaining cup as well. I could smell the coffee.

I had had coffee once or twice before, and, with four spoons of sugar, it wasn't too bad. But this coffee was so strong that no amount of sugar would have made it palatable. I pretended to sip it. The sandwich was some kind of chicken salad, and it was all right.

I don't know how long we stayed sitting there, while Mother told our story to the senhora. Then the senhora said something to Sra. Vera, who stood up and, wordlessly, held her hand out to me.

I understood that I was supposed to go somewhere with her and shook my head. I had Mother's ring to guard.

"Stand up and go with her like a gentleman," Mother admonished me.

I stood up as ordered and placed my plate and coffee cup on my chair. But, while Sra. Vera was reaching for my left hand, I gave her my right instead. That meant that, as we passed the coffin, I was closer to it than she was. As we walked by, I stole a glance inside. What I saw I couldn't believe was a real dead man. He looked like a sleeping, wax doll, with makeup on his cheeks and powder all over the face. He had curly white hair, and he was wearing a tuxedo. There was a flower in his boutonnière. Brown rosary beads were wound around the sausage-like fingers of his clasped, pink, powdery hands.

Sra. Vera led me through several large rooms, some with people standing and talking in quiet tones, some empty, to a door that led out onto another stone patio in back. One or two steps—I couldn't tell exactly from my angle—led down onto a large lawn and, beyond it, a tennis court. Nobody was playing tennis, but a number of children were, evidently, playing a game on the lawn. A line of chairs had been set up, and the children marched around them to the music of a guitar played by a woman in a plain gray dress with a white collar. Her blond hair was in braids wound around her head, the way Kiki used to wear hers, and I guessed that she must be somebody's governess. She sat on a chair off to the side with her legs crossed to support the guitar. She played some lively tune with which I wasn't familiar. Kiki hadn't played any musical instrument.

The children were of various ages, two boys and a girl clearly older than me, some, two or three years younger. They were dressed in party clothes. One boy was in a blue velvet suit with shiny white buttons. Another had on a grownup style tie and jacket.

Suddenly the governess stopped playing, and the children all scrambled to sit down on a chair. It was then that I realized that every chair in the line was facing the opposite direction from that of its two immediate neighbors.

It turned out that there was one less chair than there were players, and, when the scramble for the chairs was over, one of the smallest girls was left standing. She seemed very unhappy, but the governess said something to her, at which point the girl brightened and ran over to sit on a long bench beside the musical governess. It was then that I noticed two other children already on the bench.

Now a man in a white jacket was removing one of the chairs from the row, so that there would, again, be one less chair than player. When the man and the chair were out of the way, the music resumed, and the remaining children continued their circular march. This time the governess played a different tune and sang along with the music in a clear, pleasant voice. Kiki used to say that she had a voice like a rusty gate.

I supposed I would be made to play this game. It was easy enough to understand, but I didn't like competitive activities. I liked make-believe. I liked pretending that we were soldiers marching in step on parade, with pretend rifles or musical instruments. I even liked it when we were all shooting at an imaginary enemy, encouraging each other and tending to make-believe wounds. I liked getting shot and falling to the ground holding my hand over a wound and gulping for breath as my life seeped out through the hole. But as soon as we were divided into opposite sides, shooting at each other and attacking each other, I hated the anger, even make-believe anger, that the opponents would direct at me. I would usually pretend to be shot right away and spend the rest of the game lying dead on the ground, or I'd gallop off to get reinforcements and not return till the battle was over.

During the one year that I had spent in school in Warsaw, before the war, when, at recess we made a "chain" by holding hands and weaving in and around our schoolmates, I would join in. But if we played tag, for example, I hated the sensation of being chased by someone and would always let them tag me, even though I could run faster than they—I found that I could run faster than all of my classmates—just to get it over with. Then, when I was "it," I would drag it out as long as possible, pretending that I couldn't catch anyone. Even in hide-and-seek, I preferred to be "it" and go looking for people than sit in my hiding-place, tense with the fear that I would be found.

As I had predicted, Sra. Vera led me up to the governess and said some things to her, most likely that I didn't speak Portuguese. I heard her tell the governess my name.

The governess stopped playing, and the scramble for chairs began. "Do you know this game?" the governess asked me in French.

I should have said that I didn't, but it was hard to resist saying that it wasn't difficult to figure out.

"Then why don't you join when I start to play again," she said. "Just stand over there with the others until I begin." Her French accent wasn't quite right, but her voice had a friendly, musical tone. Kiki's voice was often gentle, but it wasn't musical. I wanted to please this governess, and so I went to where the other children were, and, when the new song began, started to march with the others.

There was a system to playing this game that the other children didn't seem to understand. Since every alternate chair you passed was facing the wrong way, the trick was to delay in front of a chair that was facing your way, and rush past the one that wasn't. Following this strategy, I found myself in front of a chair facing the right way every time the music stopped. And in a little while, I and another boy, a little older than me, in a blue and white shirt, were the only two players circling one lone chair. The others were all either sitting on the bench beside the governess or standing behind it—all of them, of course, watching the two of us.

And then I had an idea. It was something I had seen in a movie in Poland, and everyone had laughed uproariously when it had happened. I didn't really care about winning the silly game, but these children and the governess, who certainly hadn't seen the Polish film, would find it extremely clever. What I had to do was to make sure that I was *behind* the chair, instead of in front of it, when the music stopped.

I couldn't make my delay too obvious, so I just had to hope for the best. And when the music stopped, I was, indeed, behind the chair, where I wanted to be. And as the other boy began to sit down, I yanked the chair out from under him.

He fell to the ground with utter surprise on his face, and I laughed and looked for laughter from the others. But they weren't laughing. Now the eyes of the boy on the ground began filling with tears, and I realized that I had hurt him. I hadn't intended to hurt him. I had been trying to be funny, and I continued laughing to show the others, on the bench, that it was a joke. But nobody else was laughing. The boy in the blue and white shirt was still sitting on the ground, his eyes full of tears now and looking totally bewildered.

The governess had put down her guitar and was walking over to us now, and I knew that I was in trouble. She squatted down in front of the boy and spoke kindly to him, touching his wet cheek with the back of her fingers. The other children were either looking at him with concern or at me with hatred. I was gripped by a feeling that I had had back in Warsaw, in the French school, when I had unwittingly done or said something that the other kids found offensive. Not being able to speak French, at the time, I had not understood what was going on most of the time, and I would, occasionally, find myself the object of anger and disdain. Except that this time I knew well what I had done to earn that hostility.

Now the governess was helping the boy stand up and brushing off his pants. She said something to the others.

They were yelling things at me or about me now that I didn't understand. And then they were crowding around him and the governess and saying things to him. One boy pushed me out of the way with his shoulder.

Then I felt the governess take my hand, and I realized that I was going to be punished.

She led me away from the group, and then stopped and squatted down to my level. "Why did you do that, Julien?" she asked me. Her voice was no longer musical, but it wasn't unkind.

"I... I... I w... w... w... was being f... f... f... funny," I said. "He wasn't r... r... really h... h... h... hurt, just s... s... s... surprised."

From the expression on her face, I realized that my stuttering had surprised her. The expression on her face grew softer. She reached out and stroked my head. "No, he wasn't hurt," she said, "but he could have been."

This possibility had never really occurred to me. The man in the movie hadn't been hurt. He had jumped right back up and chased the other man down the street. But I realized that I had done something terrible. My own eyes were beginning to tear up.

"You're sorry now that you did that, aren't you?"

I nodded my head.

"May I tell Roderico that you're sorry?"

The idea of this governess asking permission of me, really surprised me. Then I realized that she might not have known who I was. For all she knew, I might be the son of a count or an ambassador. But I nodded my head.

From somewhere she produced a handkerchief, a strange, very soft and scented handkerchief and wiped away my tears. Then she handed the kerchief to me. "Then let's go and tell him so," she said.

I tried to hand the handkerchief back to her, but she said to keep it. She took my hand, and we walked back to the group. She said something to Roderico, who wasn't crying anymore. But the other children were all crowding around him, as though *he* had done something clever.

"I told him that you are very sorry you did that—that you were just trying to be funny," she said to me, "and that now you want to shake his hand."

I was confused about the hand-shaking. You shook hands when you greeted someone or when you were saying goodbye.

Roderico held out his hand.

"Go ahead," the governess urged.

I reached out my hand as well. We touched palms. Much as I had been taught to shake hands firmly and look the other person in the eye, now I couldn't take my eyes off my own right shoe as it described little circles in the grass. I hadn't wanted to hurt him. I wished I hadn't. I had just wanted to do something clever. When people in the movies fell down, I now realized, there must be padding hidden, where the camera didn't show it, so they wouldn't get hurt. Why hadn't I realized that?

Then I sat on the bench next to the governess while the children played other games, until Mother came and got me for our trip home.

We had been given a long, black limousine and a chauffeur to drive us to our hotel, and Mother seemed very pleased with the day's developments. She asked me if I had had a good time, and I told her that I had. But my mind was on what I had done to Roderico. In Hungary I had tripped that man and, maybe, broken his nose. I didn't know why I had done that, but now I realized that I must have been trying to be funny then, too. I had seen grownups say and do things that made everyone laugh. In Hungary, the count used to make people laugh all the time. He would tell a story or do a trick with his napkin at the table or walk up behind a woman and grab her around the waist, surprising her, and everyone would laugh. And Mother had used to laugh at things M. Gordet would say, or some of the other men we went to dinner with. But when I tried to be funny, which was just something to *entertain* people, to make them happy, it always turned out bad.

There was something bad inside me. Maybe it had to do with my Jewish soul that I had been trying to turn Catholic. I was over that now—I knew now that you didn't have to be Catholic to go to Heaven—but maybe by trying to change it, I had damaged it, and that was why I couldn't speak like other people. There was absolutely nothing stopping me from speaking normally—it wasn't that I didn't know what I wanted to say, like some people kept suggesting, and I didn't have any kind of paralysis in my tongue or my jaw—I could move my jaw and my lips as well as anyone, and I could even curl my tongue, which Mother couldn't do. But some force inside me just would not let me speak normally. That had to be my soul.

And, maybe, I had damaged my soul by not wanting to be Jewish, which is what I was supposed to be. There was really nothing wrong with being Jewish, as long as you weren't around the Germans. If God allowed good Jews into Heaven, He must have forgiven them for what they had done to Jesus. God had intended for me to be Jewish all along, and I had been disobeying His will. That explained a lot of things.

It wasn't Kiki's fault that she had wanted me to be Catholic. She didn't know that good Jews went to Heaven just like good Catholics, and she was just trying to help me get to Heaven because she cared about me. She didn't realize that God wanted me to be Jewish.

You didn't *have* to wear a black hat and coat or grow your ear-locks long, like the men on the trolleys, if you didn't want to. Some Jewish men and boys wore those black beanies, because Jews were supposed to keep their heads covered all the time. That was kind of cool. I didn't have a black beanie, but I could get one. In the meantime, I had the scented handkerchief that the governess had given me.

I reached into my pocket, pulled out the handkerchief, and laid it over my head. I had seen women do that in church. Obviously God considered handkerchiefs to be an adequate covering. When He saw what was on my head and what was in my heart, maybe He would lift the stuttering. I had to be careful that the kerchief didn't blow off with the wind from the open windows.

"Yulian, what are you doing?!" Mother cried.

I wasn't doing anything except sitting there, but I knew Mother was referring to the kerchief. "G… G… God w… w… wants me t… t… to keep my h… h… head c… c… covered," I said.

"What are you talking about?"

The stuttering was still there. Well, it had been childish of me to believe that God would lift the stuttering just because I had laid a handkerchief on my head for all of two minutes.

"G… G… God made us J… J… Jewish because H… H… He w… w… wanted us to be J… J… Jewish. O… O… Otherwise H… H… He w… w… would have made us C… C… Catholic."

Mother's voice dropped to a whisper and became very harsh. "Don't you ever, ever say that in front of anyone, do you hear? We are Catholic, we have always been Catholic, and we will always be Catholic. Do you know what the Germans are doing to Jews?"

Of course, I knew about the Germans killing Jews back in Europe just for being Jews. But we were in Brazil now.

"Take that thing off your head now and give it to me before the chauffeur sees you," she hissed.

I knew that if I didn't, she would snatch it off. I handed her the kerchief. Mother squeezed it into a ball and put it in the ash-tray, as though I had contaminated it.

"B..B... But that's a good h... h... handkerchief," I protested.

"It's only a paper tissue. You throw it away after you've used it." I had never heard of paper handkerchiefs before.


I didn't say anything more for the rest of our ride. For the second time that day I had done something for which I had gotten into trouble, though, this time, God was on my side. Mother's reaction was one that I should have anticipated, based on past experience, just as I should have anticipated the fact that it would hurt Roderico when I pulled the chair out from under him. But I didn't. So, maybe it was God that was directing me to do these things. He had made me pull the chair out from under Roderico to alert me to what I had later realized about my soul, or, maybe Roderico had done something earlier that deserved punishment.

One thing I knew, I wasn't like other children. I wasn't one of a group. I didn't have friends. When I was in first grade in Warsaw, and everyone had friends, I didn't. I didn't even have any brothers or sisters. Maybe God had selected me to be His instrument, to do things for Him that He wanted done here on earth, like punishing Roderico and, maybe, even that man in Hungary. Maybe he had done some bad things, and God had made me punish him for Him. And the stuttering was my reminder of my mission. Maybe God would remove it as a reward for doing His bidding, or, maybe, He would leave it with me forever as a reminder. That certainly explained a lot of things.

Back in our hotel suite, Mother sat me right down on my bed and pulled up one of the chairs facing me, as though to block my escape. "Don't you ever, ever talk like that again!" she said.

"But I... I... I'm sure the ch... ch... ch... chauffeur didn't speak P... Polish," I argued.

"I don't want to hear the word *Jewish* from you ever again. In any language. Even in private."

"But wh... wh... what if I s... s... see a J... J... Jewish p... person w... walking d... down the s... street, or s... s... something?"

"Don't be impertinent!" Mother said.

I understood that I had a difficult path in front of me. God wanted me to be Jewish, but I couldn't do that in front of Mother—nor in front of people who might tell Mother. And not only was I supposed to keep my head covered, but there were certain things that Jews weren't supposed to eat, though I had no idea what they were. It wasn't going to be easy, but I wasn't scared. Instead, as God's secret agent, I had a whole new sense of purpose. I was here for a purpose. Not only that, but, as never before, I now had the sense of a Being who had singled me out for His special attention, a very powerful Being, a male Being.

That night, I remembered my prayers, something I had fallen quite lax with over past weeks. Actually, I realized, this would be my first time praying on Brazilian soil. For a moment I entertained myself with the idea that, since we were now in the Southern Hemisphere, where winter was summer and summer winter, it might be necessary to say your prayers backwards. This was, of course, just a joke between me and myself, but I regretted that there wasn't someone to share it with. Kiki would have laughed at it.

Then I realized that there was someone—there was Meesh, sitting there on the table, silhouetted on the wall behind him by the light coming from the street through the window. I had been ignoring Meesh lately. Now I explained my joke to him, and he found it funny. Then I told him about my recent thinking regarding God and being Jewish, but, although he didn't say anything, I had the strong feeling that this really wasn't his kind of material. Or, rather, that it was just too personal for me to share even with him. I told him to go to sleep.

I didn't know any Jewish prayers, but I expected that God would make allowance for that, as long as he saw my earnestness. What I did know about the Jewish religion was that Jews had a saint named Moses and that their symbol was a six-pointed star. When you did the sign of the cross at the beginning and end of a prayer, you said, "In the name of the Father, the Son, and the Holy Ghost," which I understood to mean that the one prayer was directed to all three of them. Alone in a hotel room in Budapest, some months earlier, I had corrected what I saw as a discrepancy by changing it to, "In the name of the Father, the *Mother,* the Son, and the Holy Ghost," and now I realized, quite brilliantly, that I could even incorporate both the name of St. Moses and the six-pointed star into the process by crossing, or rather *starring,* myself by drawing the six points of the star as I recited, "In the name of the Father, the Mother, the Son, the Holy Ghost, and St. Moses, amen." And, since I was alone at this point, I placed my pillow so that it rested against the top of my head, rather than under the back of it, forming a sort-of head covering. When I had finished my customary *Our Father* and the *Hail Mary,* and *starred* myself, I admonished myself to put a stop to the slacking off and go back to my previous routine of praying every night.

# CHAPTER V

BACK IN WARSAW, before the war, right near the park to which Kiki and I went every morning, stood a heroic statue of Poland's great warrior king, Jan Sobieski. Mounted on a splendid horse, wearing full armor, and with his sword in the air, this great general was as well known to Polish children as Paul Revere is to Americans. At the head of his Hussars, Jan Sobieski had lifted the siege of Vienna, and stopped dead the Tartar hordes overrunning Europe in the seventeenth century.

Whenever we stopped to gaze at this great champion, I would ask Kiki to tell me again about the great battle outside of Vienna when Polish Hussars, with great feathered wings mounted on the backs of their saddles, had charged the fearsome Tartars, the wings flapping noisily in the wind and terrifying enemy horse and rider alike. But one day, when one of my cousins and his governess were walking with us, my cousin, older than I by a full year, confided to me a little ditty which declared that Jan Sobieski had three doggies, a gray one, a brown one, and a blue one. While I was concerned over the propriety of saying such nonsense things about the great Polish hero and doubted that blue dogs even existed, I did appreciate the poetry, since the Polish word for *blue* rhymed with the word for *doggies* as well as the name *Sobieski*.

Poetry was something that I had been growing up with. Memorizing chauvinistic, patriotic poems and then reciting them in front of grownups, with grand, theatrical gestures, was something I had been made to do since I could remember. But my very favorite poem wasn't one of these, but a children's poem about a big, black locomotive that stands at the station with its collection of cars and passengers strung out behind it. The passengers vary from a car full of fat men eating sausages to figs and pigs to elephants and giraffes. It had a beautiful, pulsing rhythm that sounded like a chugging train, and it was written by a man with my own first name, Yulian Tuwim. Mother and Lolek had, actually, known him before the war, and I was even told that I had been introduced to him, though I couldn't remember that. I had learned this poem by heart, on my own, and would recite it in my head for my own pleasure.

But on that day, as Kiki and I walked home, after parting from my cousin and his governess, I found myself repeating the Sobieski poem in my head, and finally went on to compose a second stanza, stating that, after the king's death, his three doggies mounted the throne, first the gray one, then the brown one, and finally the blue one. My second stanza parsed and rhymed perfectly, and I remember experiencing not a little admiration for my creative achievement. Since I had not yet learned to write, I committed the entire poem to memory, but did not dare repeat it aloud for fear of being declared un-Polish.

Then, in the spring of the year that Mother and I sailed for Brazil, for some reason we had had to spend a few hours in the company of a Yugoslav border official who had entertained me by writing, for me, a little poem in Yugoslavian, a language quite similar to Polish. I had answered by picking up a pencil and piece of paper and composing a responding poem in Polish.

My facility with poetry writing seemed to impress Mother greatly and, soon after, as we witnessed the Yugoslavian custom of adorning children's collars with little brass bells at Easter time, Mother had suggested that I be moved to write a poem about it.

Not moved as much as Mother apparently wished, I had written a few humorous stanzas, which she dismissed as inappropriate and instructed me to start again, and compare the children to sweet little sheep with bells hanging from their collars.

I did as I was told, and Mother and I were both impressed with what I had done, though I preferred the first version. Nevertheless, Mother told me, then and there, that some day I might grow up to be a great poet, like Yulian Tuwim.

Then, a few days following our visit to the O'Brien's I was, again, put in contact with my poetic muse. Mother, it seemed, had an appointment to meet again with Sra. O'Brien the following week, giving us several days with nothing to do.

Mother had agreed to go to the beach with me, that first day, but, instead of putting on her bathing suit, she sat cross-legged on her bed, laying out her solitaire on a pillow and smoking cigarettes. She had said that we would go after breakfast, but it was well after breakfast, and she showed no sign of getting ready.

Every so often, I would hear the exclamation, "*merde!*" from the other room, telling me that she was stymied again and about to begin a new solitaire.

There was really nothing for me to do, while I waited. I had a harmonica that Carlos, the count's chauffeur had taught me how to play, but Mother wouldn't let me play it in her presence because it gave her headaches. And having the kind of conversation with Meesh that had covered many empty hours over the last few months, seemed a little awkward now, after the way I had cut him out of my thoughts the previous night.

Somehow, my mother must have sensed my impatience, though I had been careful not to make any impatient sounds, because I suddenly heard her call, "Why don't you sit down and write one of your poems!" through the open door.

"I'm not inspired to write a poem," I shot back, communicating, I hoped, the idea that the creation of poetry was fueled by divine stimulation, rather than parental mandates.

"Write one about how beautiful the beach is, curved like a crescent moon," Mother suggested.

There was, of course, no way that I was going to allow Mother to dictate in which direction my creativity would flow. If she wanted to see the Rio beach as a crescent moon, let her write her own poem.

And then I thought of the long, curving sidewalk, with its "S" shaped, black and white stripes, that ran along the beach and realized that the Polish word for *street* rhymed with possessive form of the word for *moon*, and a stanza forced its way into my resisting mind.

I would not, of course, write it down and endeavored to firmly lock my mind against any further suggestions from my inner muse, under these kind of circumstances.

When she finally called me to get ready and I made my way to the bathroom, where my bathing suit hung on a hook, I found Mother already in her bathing suit, a cigarette in her mouth, and shaving under one arm with her big Gillette razor. I had never heard of people shaving there, but Mother immediately told me not to look, which surprised me further, since I had watched her shave her legs numerous times, without any concern on her part. Then we walked to the beach where Mother lay down on the blanket and told me to build her a sand castle while she got some sun. I was relieved to see that she did not undo the straps on her suit, the way Irenka had.

Just like the time I had been there with Sra. De la Vega, there were several people playing with that strange feathered projectile that they slapped back and forth with their hands. This time they were hitting it over a net. After a while, the projectile, which I later learned was called a *pateka*, landed on a corner of Mother's blanket, making her jump.

A handsome, suntanned man came to retrieve the *pateka*, apologized profusely, and invited Mother to join their game. Mother answered in a mixture of Portuguese and Spanish, saying that this was her first day on his beautiful beach and that she had no idea how the game was played. The man said that it would be his very great pleasure to teach her, and he helped Mother to her feet and then demonstrated how the *pateka* was put into motion by a slap with the palm.

I was immediately concerned about Mother's diamond ring which, I feared, might come flying off during the game and be, immediately, swallowed up by the sand. I debated suggesting that she let me hold it, but, noticing how she was smiling at the man, decided that she would find any suggestion from me to be annoying and settled on just watching carefully for it to fly off. I saw Mother follow the man's directions, giving the *pateka* a blow with her palm. But instead of the usual *smack*, I heard Mother give a squeal of pain and immediately cover her face in embarrassment as the feathered projectile flew at a right angle to its intended path and landed against a small stack of papers in the hand of a very hairy-chested man, reading from the papers in a beach chair, under an umbrella. The papers flew in all directions, and the stunned man jumped to his feet and began chasing the escaping pages.

After clamping her hand to her mouth in embarrassment for a moment, Mother joined in the chase that she had caused, as, after another moment, did her *pateka* instructor. I joined in the chase as well, and did, indeed, recover what looked like two typed carbon copies on that very thin paper that they used for multiple copies, just before they blew into the ocean.

When I returned to the man's blanket with the pages, Mother was apologizing in her Franco-Spanish Portuguese, and the hairy-chested man, who, I now realized had a bush of thick, black hair above his longish face, was assembling his papers. "It's nothing, Madame," he said in French, then went on to explain that having a pateka knock the papers out of your hand was a hazard that any Copacabana beachgoer was prepared for.

Mother thanked him for his kindness over her clumsiness, then apologized to the first man for being so inept a pupil. It would be dangerous for everybody, she said, if she were to try playing the game with them, but thanked him for his invitation. Then she sat back down on our blanket.

A few minutes later, as Mother was beginning to apply suntan oil to my back, the hairy man came over and said, still in French, that if Madame and her son cared to join him on his blanket, he had a thermos of hot coffee, which was the best drink against the day's heat.

As Mother hesitated, he said that his name was Ernesto Segiera, that he worked for some ministry of the government, that he had just come back from the "interior"—whatever that was—that he was a widower, and that he had a son just about my age. This seemed to convince my mother, and in a moment she was settling herself in the beach chair that he had vacated for her, while I busied myself with the task of digging a hole in the ever-sifting sand.

"Unfortunately," the man apologized, his thermos bottle only had one extra cup, but Mother might want to share hers with me. Mother explained that I didn't drink coffee, but Sr. Segiera said that it wouldn't hurt me. His own son, who was my age, he said, had coffee every day.

I had had a taste of Kiki's coffee on occasion, coffee into which she put three spoons of sugar and a lot of cream. I had liked it, all right, since it reminded me of coffee ice cream, which I loved. Now I wasn't too happy about drinking from Mother's lipstick-stained thermos cup, but I knew that refusing to even taste the man's coffee would have been rude. Turning the cup to where it was free of lipstick, I took the obligatory sip. It was scalding hot, and it was bitter.

"Oh, it is too hot for him," Mother said, reaching for the cup.

I resented this. While it certainly was very hot, I was sure that I had given no outward sign of my discomfort, and Mother's assuming it to be too hot for me was an expression of her total disregard for my maturity. I deliberately took a second sip of the bitter and burning stuff.

"Why don't you go for a swim, *Julien*," Mother said to me in French.

I understood this as well. She didn't want me stuttering in front of Sr. Segiera.

"He needs to be very careful," the man said. Then he added, "I should go down and watch him." He began to get up.

"Oh, he's a very good swimmer, Monsieur," Mother said. I knew that the statement wasn't intended to compliment me as much as save Sr. Segiera the trouble of going down to the water with me.

"The undertow is tricky, Madame. Eventually he will become accustomed to it the way all the children do, but I will watch him until he gets used to it."

I remembered now how the water had tugged at my legs the last time. The hairy man stood up.

"Then I will come too," Mother said. The man reached for Mother's hand and helped her to her feet. Then, he and Mother stood with the water washing over their feet, holding their coffee cups and Mother smoking a cigarette, while I dove into the waves and let them tumble me back onto the beach.

After a few minutes, I saw that Mother and Sr. Segiera were no longer standing there, and later, when I returned to the blanket, they were lying on their sides, facing each other, and Mother was telling him about our escape from the Bolsheviks.

When we were back at the hotel, and Mother was shaking the sand out of our blanket, outside the bedroom window, over the hotel lobby, she was humming some tune. Mother had difficulty carrying a tune, and this one was unrecognizable. But I had never heard her humming to herself before.

That evening Sr. Segiera picked us up in a car that I recognized as an American Chevrolet, which had a dented front fender and torn seat covers. When he saw Mother hesitate before getting in, Sr. Segiera apologized for the car's condition, explaining that this was his own car, and that he had an "official" car which was in better condition. This seemed to make perfect sense to Mother and was something which I could ask her to explain to me later. Wearing a suit and with his black, wavy hair held down with some hair stuff and quite shiny, Sr. Segiera was actually quite good looking.

We went to a little restaurant with fishing nets on the walls. It was there that I was introduced to a kind of seafood that I had no idea existed. It wasn't fish, but meaty and delicious with a dipping sauce. Sr. Segiera was particularly interested in what it had been like living under Soviet occupation, before our escape, and I heard Mother tell him things that made it sound even worse than it had really been. But I was accustomed to that by now, and did not try to correct her, as I might have earlier. Sr. Segiera marveled at Mother's courage in her determination to escape in the winter snow, when everyone told her she was crazy to even consider it, and then he said, "You make me feel as though I'm right there in Poland with you, and my heart is beating with the excitement. May I please call you, Barbara?"

"Of course you may....*Ernesto*," she said. Then they picked up their wine glasses and clinked them together.

Then Mother went on to tell him the story about her letter of introduction to Sr. O'Brien, and they both laughed at our blundering into Sr. O'Brien's funeral. Mother also told him about the long talk she had had with Sra. O'Brien, who was Russian like my grandmother and who wanted Mother to come back in a few days and talk about doing work for her.

My ears pricked up at this last piece of information, since working for someone meant getting paid, though I had no idea what Mother could do for the senhora, since she couldn't cook or sew or type or even write in any language but Polish. Sr. Segiera said that he knew about Sra. O'Brien, though he hadn't met her, and called her "that crazy Russian," at which they both laughed.

Also that evening, Sr. Segiera said that this was the first time, since his wife's death, that he had wanted to go to dinner with a woman and that the only thing that had made it possible for him was my being along. Mother laughed a little and said that she would not have been able to go to dinner with him either, except for my presence, and then they both smiled at each other while I tried to figure out what my presence had to do with anything regarding this situation. I knew that it had nothing to do with guarding her diamonds.

The following morning, Mother settled down to solitaire and cigarettes and showed no inclination towards leaving our suite for any reason. "I'm waiting for an important telephone call," she explained. Since Irenka and Mr. K. lived just below us, and since Mother never wanted to hear from M. Gordet again, that just left Sra. O'Brien and Sr. Segiera. My hope was that it would be the senhora in regard to Mother's job, but my fear was that it would be Sr. Segiera.

I had seen Mother with many men, these few months, but there was something different when she was around him. For one, she didn't immediately explain to me that he could, maybe, buy a diamond or put her in touch with somebody who could. I was afraid that Mother was beginning to like Sr. Segiera. And if she liked him, and he qualified in her judgement as a gentleman, then the diamonds that were our bread and butter, as well as our passage to America, were no longer safe.

This, I was now realizing, was what women were all about. It was what made them different from us men, and that was why men were soldiers and doctors and lawyers and engineers and policemen, while women were only wives, mothers, governesses, and cooks. As Mother had explained, when a woman liked someone, she was likely to give him anything he wanted. If they were married to each other, that was all right because it still stayed in the same family. But if they weren't....

Of course, if Sr. Segiera was a gentleman, then he probably wouldn't ask Mother for her diamonds, which made me feel somewhat better. But what if she thought he was a gentleman, as she had thought M. Gordet to be, and didn't realize that he wasn't till too late?

But there was nothing more I could do about it now except be concerned, so I suggested that we contact Irenka to ask if she wanted to go to the beach with me, while Mother waited for her call. But Mother said that she might need me right after the call, when it came. This sounded ominously as though my fears regarding the senhor had proven correct.

Then, as though she had been reading my mind, though I knew that Mother did not have that power, and without looking up from her solitaire, Mother said, "You did like Sr. Segiera, didn't you?" She had said it in that way she had of saying something that I wasn't sure she even realized that she was saying it. Then, in a much more definite tone, she added, "You remember that he has a son your age, don't you?"

If this was supposed to make me look more favorably on the senhor, it wasn't working. My experiences with boys my age had not been successful. And it wasn't that I disliked the senhor. If he and Mother were to get married and keep the diamonds in the family, even though we wouldn't really need them anymore, since he would be supporting us with his earnings, that would be perfectly all right.

"H... e s... eems v... ery n... ice," I said. I hoped that Mother noticed that by dragging my words out, I wasn't actually stuttering. But I wasn't sure Mother had even heard me, because she was slapping the cards down hard, which meant that the solitaire wasn't going well.

I had become pretty accustomed to spending long hours in a hotel room, but that didn't mean that I enjoyed it. Now I tried keeping busy by practicing making my brass washer appear and disappear, but I had become so good at it, that that got old very quickly. I tried explaining to Meesh how different women were from men, but I had found that, since Meesh did not usually contribute to the conversation, talking to him was only fun when I felt a real need to talk to him, and not when I needed something to do. I even tried writing a poem, but, as with Meesh, with no inner need to write a poem at that point, that didn't go anywhere either. Finally, I did wrest from Mother permission to go into the bathroom, which was on the other side of the bedroom, and, closing both doors behind me, play my harmonica very quietly. Since the toilet did not have a lid that I could sit on, I dragged a chair in from the living room and passed several hours alternating between picking out tunes on the shiny instrument and remembering my beach experience with Irenka.

At lunch time I was dispatched to a little place across the street to bring back some sandwiches, and instructed to look both ways before crossing the thoroughfare. Then, in the afternoon, Mother allowed me to go down to the street again and walk around the block, as long as I didn't cross any streets, didn't dally, and came back up immediately. I was allowed to repeat this as many times as I wanted, so long as I checked in after each circuit. The phone call, however, did not come.

Then, on the day that she was supposed to do it, Mother called Sra. O'Brien, and they made an appointment for the next day, when the senhora would send a car to bring Mother to her house.

This time, Mother arranged for me to spend the day with Irenka, and I couldn't have been more delighted. Apparently, Mr. K. also had a meeting to go to, because, when Mother dropped me off at their suite on the floor below ours, he was tying his tie in the mirror in the bedroom, while Irenka, still in her bathrobe, was ironing his tan suit jacket in the front room. Over this, they carried on a conversation in very slow and labored Portuguese. From the fact that he was addressing her as *Senhora* and she addressed him a *Senhor*, I understood that they must be practicing the language and immediately realized that this was something that Mother and I could be doing as well.

Haltingly, Mr. K. was inviting Irenka, to ride to the top of Corcovado, the mountain that was at one end of the beach, and to look up at the statue of Jesus. Irenka answered, with a little more proficiency, that she would love to, as long as they could stop for lunch first, because she was very hungry.

Mr. K. didn't respond to this immediately, but I saw him turn to look something up in a book that lay open on top of the bureau. "It isn't possible," he finally said, "because you are too fat." Then he turned and winked at me. Irenka smiled a little, but did not laugh.

It, certainly, had to have been a joke, since you could not accuse Irenka of being fat by any stretch of the imagination. But I noted that Irenka had not found it at all funny. I waited for her to tell him that he was too stupid or something, but she didn't say anything. She went on ironing with what I thought was a sad expression on her face. I found myself feeling sorry for her. When Mr. K. took the jacket that she had finished ironing, picked up his briefcase, and kissed her cheek goodbye, I saw that Irenka didn't kiss him back. Mr. K. winked at me again, over her shoulder, before going out the door.

"So, Yulian, what should we do this morning?" Irenka asked me, when the door had finally closed behind him.

I was prepared for this question. All the previous night, after Mother told me that I would be spending the day with Irenka, as well as this morning, I had been filled with the desire to be beside Irenka on the beach again, when she undid the straps of her bathing suit. I considered it strange that, back in Poland, where one would, quite frequently catch sight of bare flesh, as people changed into a dry bathing suit, and where keen observation could have satisfied my desire many times, the desire had not been there. Only here in Brazil, where people did not change out of wet bathing suits on the beach, did this desire manifest itself.

"L… et's g… o to th… e b… each a… gain," I said. "M… aybe th… e w… aves w… on't b… e as b… ig, a… nd I'll b… e a… ble to t… each y… ou t… o s… wim."

"All right. I'll go put my bathing suit on. Do you have yours?"

To avoid my labored speech, I turned the top of my pants down a bit to show her my bathing suit underneath. Irenka went into the bedroom and closed the door behind her.

Now I reached into my pocket for the handkerchief I had put there. Kiki had taught me to tie a knot in each corner of a handkerchief and make a little cap out of it, to protect your head from the sun. This "cap" would do as my Jewish head-covering, and I slipped it onto my head.

But, in my mind's eye, I could see Irenka removing her bathrobe, walking naked across the room to where her bathing suit hung, and stepping into it. Then, surprisingly, I envisioned her standing over the bathroom sink with Mr. K's razor, lifting up one arm, and shaving under it. Fortunately, between my tight bathing suit and my outer pants, the fullness that I was now feeling under them did not show through to the outside.

She came out in the same suit, shirt, and sunglasses from the other day, and we headed for the beach. She had not asked about the kerchief on my head, and I was glad because I wasn't ready to explain it to her yet. I expected that she took it as protection from the sun. This time I put my hand in hers without the concern that it would make me seem childish. And what I seemed to feel back from her hand wasn't the mechanical clasp of a guardian, but the pleasure of a friend.

When we had sat down on our blanket, my companion produced a bottle of suntan lotion and proceeded to apply it to her shoulders, arms, and legs. Then she asked me to unbutton her straps in back, while she used her forearm to hold the top of her suit from falling down. Finally she handed the bottle to me and suggested that I apply the oil to my own skin, while she lowered herself onto her back.

She laid the loose straps carefully on her chest and stomach. But, while there was a little un-tanned bit of the side of her breast spilling out the side of Irenka's loosened suit-top, there was no sign of a nipple. And I found myself both disappointed and relieved. It would not have done to have my best friend seeing me seeing her. Actually, I now felt ashamed of my desires. Fortunately, while there had been a definite possibility that Sra. De la Vega had been able to read my mind that first day on the beach, I felt pretty confident that Irenka did not possess such powers.

"Do you want to lie down and tell me what you've been doing?" she asked me, and I promptly lowered myself to her level.

"We w… ent to a f… uneral," I said, glad to be relating on that footing again. Then I told Irenka about Mother's letter of introduction to Sr. O'Brien and the strange coincidence of our showing up just as he was about to be buried.

But what I really wanted to tell Irenka about was what I had done to Roderico. Lying on my stomach, I moved around so that my face was very close to hers. I could see the little hairs on her cheeks and over her lip and the black stuff she had put on her eyelashes to make them look thicker. Mother put it on her eyelashes too, but with Mother's you couldn't tell that those weren't the real lashes. From this close, I could see that Irenka's clumped together so you could easily tell that she had some kind of stuff on them. But now I closed my eyes and went ahead and told her about how

I quickly figured out the game with the chairs and then got the idea to do the funny thing I had seen in the movies.

As it had the other time, there was a delicious pain in telling Irenka something about myself that was embarrassing. I was whispering almost directly into her ear, even though there was little chance of any of our neighbors understanding Polish. And, with my eyes closed, it was almost as though there was no distinction between Irenka and myself.

Then, with my eyes still closed, Irenka was telling me about, when she was a little girl, taking her older sister's bead necklace and hiding it because the sister had scolded her for fidgeting at mass, and I could visualize the two little girls in their Sunday dresses and dearly envied little Irenka for having a sister, even one who scolded you for fidgeting in church.

Irenka went on to tell me about how her family were peasants growing beets in a field and how her aunt Rose, who worked as a cook for a family in town, had gotten her a position with Mr. and Mrs. Romanski, where Mrs. Romanski had been very kind to her and taught her to do hair and to speak good Polish, not the way the peasants spoke, and have good manners so that some day she could have her own hairdressing shop in the town.

Lying there on the blanket, with my face inches away from Irenka's and my eyes still closed, I could picture the good Mrs. Romanski and felt warmly toward her for being kind to my Irenka. In my mind, she looked something like my grandmother, but with blond hair, and she wasn't cross-eyed, like Grandmother. And she wore only a little makeup. Makeup because she was rich, but only a little, because she was more concerned about other people than about looking beautiful. Then, when Irenka had told me, again, about leaving Alicia, the cook, behind in the Romanskis' house when she and Mr. K. drove away in the Romanskis' car and how she regretted that she hadn't been more persuasive with Mr. K. to bring her with them, I decided to tell her about the conclusion I had reached in the limousine about God wanting me to be Jewish.

"God wants you to be Jewish?" Irenka said, as though not sure she had heard correctly.

"Y... es."

"Why would He want that?"

"I d... on't know," I said. "W... e c... an't e... xpect t... o u... n... der ... stand all of God's r... easons."

"If God had wanted you to be Jewish, Yulian, He would have had you born Jewish."

"I w... as b... orn J... ewish," I said. "M... y m... other a... nd f... ather are J... ewish, e... xcept th... at m... y f... ather is dead n... ow."

"Go on," she said, chiding me. And suddenly I could feel her hand on my head. Her fingers were feeling around the top of my head through the handkerchief. "So where are your horns?" she asked, laughing.

"M... y h... orns?"

"The little horns you were born with. If you had them cut off, there would be scars."

"M..y h... orns? C... ut off?"

"Jews are born with little horns, Yulian. Didn't you know that? That's how you can tell. And that's why they never take off their hats. Some have them cut off, but they always have scars that you can feel."

"Th... th... that's r... r... ridiculous!" I exclaimed, breaking into my customary stutter in my excitement. I opened my eyes and sat up. "P... P... People d... d... don't h... h... have h... h... horns!"

"Jews have little round horns, Yulian," Irenka was saying. "Yes, they do. My cousin Sonia knew a Jewish boy once, and he showed her. They're covered by their hats all week, but when they go into their temples on Friday nights, they take off all their clothes and dance around in circles all night. Sonia said that some of them even have tails. In my village, the Jews came in the middle of one night and stole a woman's baby, and nobody knows what they did with it."

I had never heard anything so ridiculous in my life. I understood that Irenka, having been born into a peasant family had not had much education and, like Kiki whose parents had been poor, didn't know a lot of things that my family did, but Jews with horns and tails dancing naked around, inside their temples, and stealing babies, was a preposterous concept.

"There was a Jew who came to the Romanskis every month with a grindstone on a wheelbarrow to sharpen our knives. Mrs. Romanski wouldn't let him into the courtyard, so he did it in front of the house. He never took his cap off, but I could see the horns making little raised bumps in his hat. And he sharpened the knives so they cut like some kind of magic."

I had no idea what to say to my companion. I had had no idea that there were people who thought that way, except, maybe, the Negroes in Africa. I remembered that book of mine with the several races of man portrayed, in order of superiority, and there had been no mention of people with horns and tails. If Jews really did have horns and tails, the fact would have certainly have been included in the book. There would have been a picture. But there hadn't been any. If I had had my horns cut off, when I was a baby and not remember it, there would certainly be something I would be able to feel on my head—I had fallen a few years earlier and got stitches in my chin, and I could still feel that scar. I remembered seeing my cousin Monica a few days after she was born, before the start of the war, and she had had no sign of either horns or stitches.

That a grownup could believe such nonsense was unthinkable. When I was younger, I had believed in witches and all sorts of monsters, and I could understand Irenka, while still a child, hearing this kind of thing from other children and accepting it, even finding a thrill in it, just as the report that in Africa there were people who ate other people, was something I had enjoyed believing. But the idea that my grownup Irenka actually believed things like this about me and my lineage was absolutely mind-blowing.

"Yulian, what's wrong?" Irenka asked, and I realized that my thoughts must have been showing on my face. I certainly did not believe Irenka capable of reading my mind.

"N... n... othing," I said. I was stuttering again.

"Are you angry about something?"

There may well have been some anger mixed with my disappointment. But who said that I had to tell *her* about it? "It's n..othing," I repeated, in better control of my speech.

The following day, Mother took me to see a Russian doctor who, Sra. O'Brien had said, could cure my stutter. The doctor, an old man, not much bigger than me, with a shiny, bald head, felt my jaw and my neck, with his little fingers, and said that, due to the malnutrition I had suffered, when we were living with the Bolsheviks, my speech muscles were underdeveloped. He had a machine, in a little black suitcase with a red light bulb, that could strengthen those muscles. He made me sit in a chair, holding two paddles, attached by wires to the machine, to the underside of my jaw.

The paddles tingled, the machine buzzed, and the red light blinked, while I had to chant the alphabet. I did this for half an hour, and I would have to come back once a week to repeat the treatment. He also prescribed that I eat more spinach to strengthen my blood and get more exercise. To my great embarrassment, he told Mother that my entire muscular development was not where it should have been. Swimming, he said, would be very good, but it was too dangerous to go out far enough in the ocean to avoid the breaking waves. So he recommended a public pool not far from where we lived.

Then Mother asked if he could put a plaster cast on each of my two pinkies because they were growing crooked. For the first time, I noticed that my pinkies were, indeed, the slightest bit banana-shaped, as they conformed to the shape of their adjoining fingers. This, the doctor said, he would be happy to rectify as well by breaking and resetting them. To my great relief, Mother opted to delay the matter till we were in better financial shape.

That night I had boiled spinach with my chicken. I hated boiled spinach. Kiki used to chop the spinach and scramble it with an egg, which made it palatable, but I couldn't expect the hotel chef to do that. The next morning we walked to the public swimming pool, and Mother bought a season pass for me and my "governess." I hoped that "governess" would mean Irenka—that Mother had made some sort of arrangement with her, and she told me that, indeed, she had.

Pleased as I was with this turn of events, I could not help being concerned over how much the season pass and Irenka's salary would be depleting our finances. When I voiced this to Mother, as we left the pool area, her response was that we have lunch at a café on our way back to the hotel.

This would be a further, non-essential expense. It was like the time in Lisbon, when Mother had gone out shopping for new dresses to wear on the ship.

The café had tables out on the sidewalk and very large menus, and Mother said I could order absolutely anything I wanted. I ordered a ham sandwich, and Mother only ordered coffee and lit a cigarette.

"I have a job with Sra. O'Brien," she announced, suddenly. I remembered her mentioning the possibility of one when we were with Sr.Segiera.

"Wh... at are y... ou d... oing?" I asked.

"I am helping her to write her memoir."

Well, this certainly took some pressure off our financial situation.

Then Mother said, "Well, I guess Ernesto doesn't like us as much as we thought he did, does he?"

The statement had taken me totally by surprise, and I realized that while this assuaged my concern over the security of our diamonds, I was actually disappointed, since I like the senhor.

"A gentleman would have called by now," she said.

"M..aybe he's v... ery b... usy," I said.

"You liked him, didn't you?" Mother said.

I shrugged my shoulders in response.

In the past, Mother would have admonished me for shrugging my shoulders, but recently she hadn't. I was pretty sure that the reason was that she didn't want people to hear me stutter. Or to hear me herself.


The very next day, when Mother drove off to Sra. O'Brien's again, in the black car, Irenka and I made our way to the pool, hand in hand. School being in session, there were very few people there. One muscular lifeguard sat in a chair raised several feet over our heads, reading a newspaper. In one corner of the shallow end, I proceeded to give Irenka her first swimming lesson.

I had seen enough swimming instruction in Yurata so that I knew what to do. Standing in chest-deep water, I showed Irenka the breaststroke arm action again. When she seemed to have mastered that, I held on to the edge of the pool and demonstrated the frog kick. Then I had her do the same. But when I demonstrated the arm action and leg action together, as I made my way across the pool and then told her to do the same, Irenka would not lift her feet off the pool bottom.

"J… ust j… ump f..forward and s… tart s… swimm… ing," I said, but she refused to try.

I remembered my own solo flight in the ship's pool. "J… ust t… ry it. Y… ou'll s… e it'll w… ork."

"I'll try it tomorrow," she said. "I've learned enough for one day."

It wasn't a matter of too much to learn. She had already learned it. All that remained to do was to put what she already knew into action. "B… B… But I t… t… tell y… y… you that it it w… will w… w… work!" I said, impatient with her timidity and frustrated by my own difficulty at expressing myself.

And suddenly there was a man standing there with us and saying,"Permit me, Miss," in Portuguese. He reached out for Irenka's hands, which she obediently gave him. Then he began pulling her forward, away from me, indicating that she should do her frog kick. She did as he directed, and he continued pulling her around by her hands. Then, when Irenka was on her feet again, the man put his hands on her waist and indicated that she should put both her arms and her legs into action, while he held her from sinking.

With this assistance, Irenka lay down in the water and proceeded to follow his directions. Except that, instead of the frog kick that I had taught her, her feet began to flutter up and down in the water.

"No, no, do the kick you were doing before," the man must have been telling her, though I couldn't understand or even hear everything he was saying.

I saw Irenka's arms stop their action and, as the man still held her waist, resume the proper kick. The man nodded his head in approval and said something else.

Irenka began her arm motion again, and her feet immediately went back to their flutter.

The man stood Irenka up again. Then he lay down and demonstrated the proper coordination of arms and legs in the breaststroke, as he swam a little ways away and then back to her.

I saw Irenka nodding her head, and then they resumed their position with him holding her from sinking. On his instructions, Irenka' legs began performing the proper kick, and the man seemed to approve. But the moment she started her arms moving, her feet resumed their flutter.

The man said something sharp and let go of Irenka's waist. Irenka immediately began sinking to the bottom.

"Oh! Oh!" I heard her cry, with the second *oh* cut in half by water entering her mouth.

I rushed as fast as I could toward her through the water, as the man reached down to pull her out. But Irenka's feet found the bottom before either of us reached her.

She was spitting water as she stood up, and I could tell by the tilt of the man's head that he must be apologizing. Irenka, I think, was apologizing as well. Finally, they shook hands, and she walked back to where I was standing, while he dove into the water and swam a splashy "crawl" to the far end of the pool.

"I'm so stupid," Irenka said. "I made him very angry."

"N... n... no, n... n... no, I... I... renka!" I protested, losing all control over my stutter. "Y... ou aren't!" But, at the same time as I was saying that, I was realizing that, maybe, there was something about my sweet Irenka that was very different from other grownups.


That evening, in bed, I re-thought our experience on the beach the other day. It was hard to believe that Irenka had actually had said the things about horns and tails. Could I have only imagined her saying them? Or did she really believe them? Even if I hadn't seen that my baby cousin had no horns and had not felt around my own head for scars, I would have known that the idea of horns and tails on people was preposterous. Just as I had known for years that there were no witches or goblins. I had known it not only because Kiki had told me so, but because it just wasn't reasonable. Oh, in moments of stress, I had doubted that conviction as I lay alone in bed, surrounded by provocative wall-shadows. But I was a child under stressful circumstances, and in the light of day, my certainty had always been restored. On the other hand, Irenka was a grownup who should have known that such things weren't possible. What she believed was a childish fantasy that she should have abandoned years before. She should have abandoned her fantasy years before I abandoned mine, even. And, yet, there she was.

There was, in my mind, an order, a system, into which things fit as they related to one another. And my new impression of Irenka was upsetting it. It didn't fit. Actually, this was just like learning that people *could* have horns or tails and having to readjust one's entire concept of reality in accordance. Now I was having to readjust my concept to the apparent fact that there could be grownups who still held childish beliefs, beliefs that I had long ago grown out of, and that my Irenka, who couldn't speak French or coordinate her hands and feet in the breaststroke, was one of them.

Her former employer, Mrs. Romanski, had taught Irenka to speak good Polish, and she had done a good job, because Irenka didn't speak anything like the peasants I had heard speaking before our escape. Maybe I could teach Irenka to speak French. Yes, I had learned most of my French from Mademoiselle, whom Mother had hired as my governess in Lvoof, just before our escape. She had taught me while we went for our walks or played Gin Rummy, simply by speaking French to me. I could do the same with Irenka. And suddenly, the idea of my teaching Irenka French had restored my faith in her. And I was so excited by the prospect of lying on our beach blanket with Irenka and teaching her to speak French, that sleeping was out of the question. In fact, even lying still was no longer possible, and I got up and pulled an armchair to the window, where I would wait anxiously for the sun to come up.

"Oh my God, Yulian! What are you doing there?" It was Mother's frightened voice waking me up in the armchair by the window. It was still dark, except for the streetlights outside.

I didn't have a proper response to Mother's question, so I closed my eyes and pretended to stay asleep.

I felt Mother's hand on my forehead, feeling for a fever. Then I felt her take my hand. "Come back to bed," she said, quietly now, and pulling gently on my hand. I realized that she must think that I had walked there in my sleep, the way I had heard my Uncle Benek used to do in Poland.

Keeping my eyes closed, I let Mother pull me to my feet. She was holding both of my hands now.

I had had bouts of crying in my sleep, since the start of the war and woken up in the middle of the night, to be told that I had had bad dreams, though I couldn't remember having them. It was a small step now for Mother to believe that I walked in my sleep as well. I had to press my lips between my teeth to keep from grinning, while I let Mother walk me back to my bed.

"My God," I heard her whisper under her breath, as we crossed the room. It was one of those expressions I had heard escaping from Mother on occasions, without her seeming to be aware of it.

Maybe I shouldn't have done this. I didn't want to frighten Mother. But I couldn't very well tell her now that I had only been fooling. I let her tuck me back into my bed and pretended to drop off into deep, untroubled sleep.

# CHAPTER VI

THE FOLLOWING MORNING, the big car came to take Mother to Sra. O'Brien's again, and Irenka and I waved goodbye to her from the sidewalk, as we set out for the beach. Irenka had expected to be going to the pool again, for my prescribed exercise, but I had suggested that we save that for the afternoon, so that I could start in on the French lessons. Of course I hadn't told her yet what it was that I was planning.

"Tadek is all beaten up this morning," she said, as I put my hand in hers. I was about to respond with an automatic expression of sympathy, but realized that her statement required some clarification, which was certain to come by itself, as well as that there had been a detectable tone of glee to Irenka's statement. I waited.

"He got into a fight with some people in a bar last night, and now he can barely see out of his eyes," she finally went on. "And if he thinks I'm going to care for him, he can think about something else. He even ruined his good suit."

I had never actually known any grownup who had been in a fight. I, of course, knew about soldiers fighting with guns, and I had seen boys get into fights at recess in the school that I had attended for a year in Warsaw, so this took a moment to assimilate. "W... hat di... d th... ey f... ight about?" I finally asked, my curiosity aroused.

"He didn't tell me, and I don't want to know," she said.

I took this as the end of discussion on that subject, though she had raised a new question, and, reluctantly, let it go. We walked the rest of the way in silence.

"H… ow w… ould y… ou l… ike to s… peak F… rench?" I asked, once we were settled on our blanket.

"I can't. I don't know how to speak in French," Irenka said.

"I m… ean, h… ow w… ould you l..ike me to t… each you so that y… ou c..an?"

"Do you speak French?" There was real surprise in her voice.

"I do."

"You swim, you speak French, and you do magic tricks. What else do you do? Do you dance?"

Suddenly I was embarrassed. But I laughed. "I d… on't d… ance," I said, "but b… efore we es… caped f..rom the R… ussians, I h… ad a g… overness who s..poke F… rench to me, and I c… an do the s… ame w… ith you."

"But I won't understand anything you say."

"W… ell, I'll t… ranslate it f… or you. But s… ome w… ords you w… ill un… derstand j… ust f… rom wh… hat I'm t… alking ab… out, or d… oing." The thought now descended on me that, maybe, my friend Irenka just wasn't very smart.

"Like how?" she asked. She sounded really interested now.

"L..ike, if I t… ell y… ou th… at I'm g… oing to s… it on the b… lanket, and y… ou d… on't know the w… ord for b… lanket, but y… ou s… ee me s..it d… own on it, th… en y… ou w… ill know th… at the w… ord m… eans *b… lanket.*"

"Oh, so it'll be like a game."

"Y… es."

"So go ahead and say, *I'm going to sit down on the blanket,* in French."

"*Je v… eu m… 'assoir s… ur le…* " I began, but stopped. The fact was that I didn't know the word for blanket, though Sr. Segiera had used it a few days before. Taking a step to the side and moving off the blanket, I added the word *sable*, as I seated myself on the warm sand.

Irenka repeated the entire sentence with surprising accuracy. "That means *I'm going to sit down on the blanket,*" she said.

"N… no d… d..don't you s… see m… me sit d… d… down on the s… sand?" I was beginning to lose my patience.

"Oh, so you were trying to trick me."

"No, I j… ust d… idn't know the w… ord for *b… lanket.*"

Now Irenka laughed, and I found that I couldn't be mad at her.

"Say something else," Irenka urged.

"*Je m… e l… eve,*" I said, getting to my feet, and heard Irenka repeat the statement almost flawlessly.

"I stand up?" she said.

I nodded my head. Then I went ahead and gave Irenka several similar statements, which she repeated with equal accuracy. By the time we headed home for lunch, Irenka was able to say a number of things in French, most of them on the first try, and to remember them minutes later. I certainly did not remember my own learning experience as having been that easy, but I put it down to her being a grownup. On the other hand, I did find that I had to alter my earlier assessment of her intelligence.

After lunch, at the swimming pool, Irenka informed me that she had instructions to see to it that I did a lot of swimming, while her own swimming lessons she had decided to put on hold for the moment.


The telephone was ringing when I unlocked the door to our suite, and I rushed across the room to answer it before the caller hung up. Had I been less concerned over the chance of losing the call, I might have given myself some advance warning of the caller's probable identity and prevented the long pause after Sr. Segiera said, "*Basia*?" mistaking my voice for Mother's.

"It's *J... ulien*, Monsieur," I finally said in French.

"Ah, *Julien*. You recognized my voice. How are you?"

"I a... m f... ine, M... onsieur. H... ow are y... ou?" I responded automatically, as I had been taught. But I had little interest in the state of his wellbeing. Rather, I was concerned over the restarting of his and Mother's friendship and debating the possibility of not delivering the inevitable message to Mother. If she didn't know that he had called, she would decide that he wasn't a gentleman and the diamonds would be safe.

"I have just flown back from 'the Interior' in an airplane," he said. "Would you like to see a picture of my airplane?"

I had no idea what "the Interior" was, but it didn't matter. I instantly had a mental picture of Sr. Segiera's head in a leather helmet and goggles, sticking out of the open cockpit of a silver biplane, and the question in my mind was whether he had been the pilot, himself, or whether there was a second head. I had never known anyone who knew how to fly an airplane! For that matter, I didn't think I knew anyone who had ever flown *in* an airplane.

"Y... y... yes, M... m... onisieur," I said, seeing my scheme go up in smoke.

"May I please speak with your beautiful mother, *Julien*?"

"Sh... she i... i... isn't h... here, M... monsieur," I said. I realized that I was lapsing into my stutter again.

"Then, when she gets home, *Julien*, would you please tell her that I will pick you both up at nine o'clock—no, that would be too late for you—I will pick you up at seven thirty for dinner."

I said that I would. I wanted to ask if he would be bringing the picture of the airplane with him, but didn't want to go through all that stuttering. Somehow I was much more conscious of my stutter on the telephone, than when speaking in person.

"G… oodbye M… onsieur," I said, making a great effort to curb the stutter. Then I hung up.

There was, of course, another good thing about the senhor taking us out to dinner: the menu in the hotel restaurant was limited and the food not very interesting. I wondered whether he would be bringing the picture with him, or whether he meant it for another time.

Because I didn't have a watch, I wondered how long it would be until seven thirty. Yes, I was sure that he would bring it. To tell me that he had the picture and then not bring it, would be a cruelty that was not in the senhor's character. Even though I knew that it could not possibly have any effect on the actual outcome, there was a feeling inside me that, if I were to take a piece of paper and draw the image that I wanted to see, that of only the senhor's helmeted head sticking out of the opening on top of the fuselage, it might, somehow, influence reality. But, while I could see the airplane and its pilot so clearly in my head, I had absolutely no talent at drawing and, if there had been any truth to my supposition that the picture could affect reality, what I produced would have resulted in Sr. Segiera's piloting a sausage.

"Look what Sra. O'Brien gave me, mother said, when she came in, a little breathless because the elevator wasn't running. Under her arm, Mother had a leather-bound notebook that was about four times as thick at the spine end as at the other. Laying it on the table, Mother opened it to reveal two, shiny metal rings, sticking up in the air. When she pulled one of the rings apart, the second one snapped open as well, and you could lift the pages right out. "See, you can add pages when you want, or change the order, or whatever you want," she said. "The paper comes separately, with two holes in it, and you just clip the pages in."

We both marveled over this invention, with Mother even letting me snap the rings open and closed several times. "I'm helping the senhora write a book," Mother said. "She was born in Russia, you know, during Tsarist times. You know what 'Tsarist times' means, don't you?"

I did. The count, with whom we had stayed for a while in Hungary, was also Russian and had lived there before the Communist Revolution. I tried to read what was written in Mother's handwriting on the first page of the notebook, and it didn't at first make any sense. Then I realized that it was supposed to be Russian, but wasn't in that crazy Russian alphabet, but the regular one. Mother, I remembered, didn't know how to write in Russian.

"Y... ou're w... riting it in R... ussian with P... olish l... etters," I said.

"Yes, we're writing it in Russian, and then Sra. O'Brien will have somebody translate it into Portuguese."

I had serious doubts that a Russian-to-Portuguese translator could understand Mother's writing. There were sounds in Russian for which the regular alphabet didn't have letters. I expressed my doubts to Mother, who laughed. "Don't worry about that, Yulek," she said. "You and I will be in America before the book is finished. But, in the meanwhile, I'm getting paid. Look."

Mother took some money out of her purse. "Look at that, Yul. Your mother is a working woman," she said and began to laugh at the idea. "We'll go to a real restaurant for dinner tonight and celebrate."

Then I had to inform her that there were other plans.

"What, he thinks he can ignore me like that, and then just call up when he feels like it and say to be ready at seven? Ha!"

"S... s... seven th... th... thirty."

Mother picked the pillow off my bed and flung it across the room. "If he ever calls again, you are to just hang up on him, do you hear?" She paused to light a cigarette, and I could see her hand shaking. "Just hang up. Don't say a single word—don't let him say anything. Just hang up the moment you hear his voice!"

I could see pitfalls in this strategy. What if it was someone else who sounded like Sr. Segiera, and I hung up on him? But I said, "He s... said that he j... ust c... ame b... ack fr... om s... omewhere in an a... irplane."

But Mother was already laying out a solitaire on the table, and she did not respond.

"When they call from downstairs to say that he's here," Mother said, after a while, as though it were the solitaire she was talking to, "tell them that I'm not here, and he can't come up."

"B... ut they know y... ou're h... ere. They s... aw you c... ome in."

"They will understand."

"W... hat w... ill they u... nderstand?"

"People say they're not in all the time, when they don't want to see someone. Hotels understand that."

"W... hy d... on't we j... ust go to d... inner be... fore he c... omes?"

"Because, when he sees the desk clerk speaking to you, he'll know that we are here and just don't want to see him."

"B... ut th... at's l... ying."

"All right, then, we just won't answer it. The desk clerk will tell him that we are in, but just aren't answering the phone. He'll understand."

I had been instructed not to answer the phone before, when I was alone at night. Now I realized that that had been lying too. Or was it just failing to tell the truth, which wasn't as bad?

When the phone did ring, Mother and I looked at each other. I had always found not answering a ringing telephone to be very difficult. After a few rings, it would become like an itch that badly needed scratching. Maybe it would have been better to do as Mother wanted in the first place and tell them that she wasn't in.

Mother did not seem to be bothered by it. In fact, she seemed to be smiling a little, as she continued playing her solitaire.

Finally, the ringing stopped. "We'll give him a few minutes to leave, then we'll go out to dinner," Mother said. "Go comb your hair."

I was in the bathroom, combing my hair with a wet comb, which was the only way I could get my cowlick to stay down, when I heard a knock on our front door. "Flower delivery for Mme Barbara!" a man's voice that I did not recognize was saying.

Hurrying back to the living room, I found Mother standing a foot or two from the door, biting on her lower lip. Seeing me come in, she pointed to the door and whispered, "Open it, Yul." She stepped back to her table, as I stepped to the door.

I opened the door. Behind a large bouquet of red flowers, stood Sr. Segiera, dressed in an all-white suit, his finger to his lips, requesting my silence. "Flowers for the beautiful senhora," he said in that same make-believe voice.

Mother stepped forward to receive them. "Ernesto!" she cried out, when she recognized him. Then, "No, no! You can't do that! Get out!"

"But Barbara," he said in French, in his own voice, "I just got back from the Interior this afternoon."

"No, Ernesto! I don't want to see you! Get out! Go away!"

"I couldn't call you because… "

"Gentlemen don't behave this way!" Even speaking French, she used the English word *gentlemen*, just as she did in Polish.

"Barbara," he seemed to be pleading, "there was a messenger waiting in front of my house when I got home after our dinner, telling me that there was a problem I had to fix in the Interior, immediately. It was too late to call you, and there are no telephones there."

"Just go, Ernesto. Get out and take your flowers with you." Then she slammed the door shut, crushing the flowers, I was sure, against Sr. Segiera's white suit.

"Look out the window and tell me when he leaves," she said to me. Surprisingly, the anger was all gone from her voice now.

Leaning out the window, I saw the top of a very long and shiny black car, parked in front of the hotel lobby. A man in some kind of military uniform leaned against a fender, smoking a cigarette. Suddenly the man flicked the cigarette away and opened the rear door. Sr. Segiera, in his white suit, but without the flowers, came out of the lobby, crossed the sidewalk in hurried steps, and ducked inside the back seat.

"He's g... one," I said, as I watched the car pull away. With the senhor went my photograph of him piloting the airplane, which I was now sure must have been in one of the pockets of his white suit. But, with him, also went the fear of Mother's growing to like him to the extent of giving away our diamonds.

Mother had a definite smile on her face now, which I assumed to express her victory. "I think Sr. Segiera likes us," she said, "don't you?"

# CHAPTER VII

THE FOLLOWING DAY, we began a morning routine that we would follow for a while. At eight thirty, Mother would drop me on Irenka's floor, then continue on down to the street level, where Sra. O'Brien's car would be waiting to take her to her job.

More often than not, Mr. K. would still be asleep behind the closed bedroom door, and Irenka would explain that he had had a late-night meeting. Occasionally, I would find him in his bathrobe, in a chair by the window, reading a newspaper. Sometimes he would call out a Portuguese word, and Irenka would go look it up in the little book in the bedroom and then give him the Polish translation. Often, she would already know the word and translate it immediately. It was quite clear that Irenka was picking up the language much faster than the rest of us. The first time that I saw Mr. K. seated there, I did notice a bit of a swelling under one eye, presumably from the fight that Irenka said he had been in a few days before.

Mornings, Irenka and I would usually spend at the beach. We were both developing deep tans and had no fear of sunburn. We continued Irenka's French lessons, which I soon came to view as similar to throwing fish to seals at the zoo. Each word or phrase that I gave her, Irenka would make her own, right on the spot, and I would soon hear it as an integral part of her vocabulary. Soon, with my own, limited vocabulary, it became difficult to come up with new words, and so we began a game of role playing a variety of situations. Sometimes I might be a chauffeur and she a lady on her way to the theater, or she would be a lady buying meat, and I a butcher. The problem, though, was that it was always I who had to think up the situation and to, even, prompt Irenka in her role.

One day, we were both invited to join a *pateka* game, much the way Mother had been invited that time that we met Sr. Segiera. And my friend proved as incompetent at the game as Mother had, so that we soon had to retire to avoid further embarrassment.

This didn't seem to bother Irenka any, and, when we got back to our blanket, she laughed and said, "Oh, I am so terrible at games," with which I had to, privately, agree.

One morning, when I was a policeman and she was a lady who had had her purse stolen, Irenka switched, suddenly, to Polish and said, "I don't want to play right now."

We continued lying on our stomachs, our faces turned toward each other, and I could see Irenka's lips moving slightly, as though she were trying out different words. Finally, she said, in Polish, "Tadek didn't come home again last night."

I immediately searched my mind for a prior such incident, that the *again* would refer to, but came up blank.

"He was gone all day yesterday, all the night before, and now all of last night," she said. I hadn't known about either day or the night before.

"D... o y... ou th... ink he was h... it by a c... ar?" I asked, conscious of how important it was for me not to stutter under these circumstances.

"I hadn't thought of that," Irenka said.

It hadn't been my intention to suggest this new option, but simply to determine if this was the direction of her concern. "I'm s... ure th... at is n... ot wh... at h... appened, and th... at he will c... ome h... ome soon," I assured her.

And I turned out to have been right, because he was there in the suite when we returned from the pool that afternoon. "Hello, my two fine friends," he said, when we came in. His tone was more jolly than I had ever heard from him before. "I've just made a big hay-load of money," he said, using the colloquial Polish expression for a large quantity, "and we're going to celebrate. We're all going out to dinner tonight!"

"We have to check that with Yulian's mother," Irenka said, without much enthusiasm over his accomplishment.

"We'll bring her too," he said.

"You go right upstairs now," Irenka said to me.

"Sh... ould I a... sk M... other... " I began, but stopped when I saw Irenka shaking her head. Mr. K., I realized, must have had too much to drink and was just talking nonsense.

It must have been a week or so after Sr. Segiera's aborted visit that the desk clerk handed me a letter as Irenka and I returned from the swimming pool. In the afternoons, when it got very hot and it bothered Irenka a lot, though it didn't me, we would go to the pool for my muscle-building exercise. I would swim back and forth, the length of the pool, while Irenka sat in the shallow end and kept cool. We had given up on the swimming lessons, at least for the time being. Every once in a while, some man would approach Irenka, often with an offer of a cool drink or just conversation, or, sometimes, even swimming instruction, but she would explain politely that she had to keep an eye on me, and was not permitted by my mother to talk to people.

But this time, as we passed through the lobby, I heard the desk clerk go, "Pssst!" and turned to see him holding an envelope in my direction. The envelope only had the words, "Mme. Barbara," on it, and must, I deduced, have been delivered by hand to the hotel. I took it upstairs and laid it on the table, never suspecting that it would be from Sr. Segiera, since he had the telephone to use and could not have known that I was instructed to hang up if he called.

When Mother came home and saw it, she did not open it right away, but sat down at the desk and played absently with the envelope, as though trying to decide what to do with it, before even finding out who it was from and what it said. She even tapped her chin with one corner a few times.

"D... on't you w... ant to f... ind out who it's f... rom?" I asked.

"It's from Ernesto," she said, as absently as she had been tapping her chin with it. I supposed she was debating whether to throw it in the trash without opening it. Finally, I watched her strike the end of the envelope lightly on the table to slide its contents to that end, then tear away a narrow strip of envelope at the other end to release the contents. She read it, smiled, then tore the letter up into little pieces, before throwing it into the wastebasket.

"What d... id he s... ay?" I asked, even though I knew full well that it wasn't polite to enquire into other people's correspondence.

"He says he is sorry, and it won't happen again."

"S... o will you s... peak to him n... ow, if he c... alls?" I dearly wanted to be relieved of the burden of having to hang up on him.

"First he has to send flowers," she said.

"S... end f... lowers? He al... ready b... rought you f... lowers, r... emember?

"That was before he said he was sorry. Now he has to send them again—send them, not bring them."

"How w... ill he know th....at th... at's what y... ou w... ant him to d....o?"

"He'll figure it out."

And the next day, there was, indeed a telephone call soon after Mother came home. "Hello, *Julien?*" I heard Sr. Segiera say, and, with Mother watching me, immediately hung up.

The phone rang a second time, and I performed my duty again. We waited for a third ring, but it did not come, and I was much relieved.

The next day, however, the telephone rang before Mother came home. "*Julien?*" I heard Sr. Segiera say. His voice was quiet, as though he didn't want Mother to hear him, as though this were private between him and me.

"She s... ays she w....ants f... lowers," I blurted out. Then I hung up the phone.

That same evening, a huge bouquet of flowers was delivered by a man in a military uniform, probably the same one I had seen holding the car door open downstairs.

"They're very beautiful," Mother said to the delivery person, as she took them from him, though she did not smile. "Please tell Sr. Segiera that they're very beautiful and thank him." Then she closed the door. "You see?" she said to me. "He figured it out."

"S... o n... ow will y... ou s... peak to him?"

"Yes, the next time he calls, I'll speak to him."

I was much relieved.

The next day I was eager to tell this whole story to Irenka, but when we got to the beach, I decided that, due to her intellectual limitations, she might not understand. And, frustrated by not being able to tell her, I didn't feel much like role-playing in French either. But I did come up with a very interesting pastime, which was to observe the contours of Irenka's bathing suit and imagine what she must look like underneath. And since the only experience I could draw on was Mother, with her hands covering the crucial parts, or the quick glimpses I had caught at the beach in Poland, my imagination had a difficult task, and the images tended to be fuzzy. Then, when I was back in our suite that afternoon, following our session at the swimming pool, I told Meesh all about the Sr. Segiera business. It was the first conversation I had had with Meesh for some while, and I felt good, as we talked.

And Sr. Segiera did call soon after Mother came home, and I told him that she was, indeed, home and would talk to him.

First, though, Mother lit a cigarette, while the receiver lay on the table. When she finally picked it up, Mother said, "Hello, Ernesto," with a big sigh, as though speaking was a big effort. "Thank you for the flowers, they are lovely." But her tone was as though she were telling him that she hadn't had a good night's sleep, or something. Then she listened for a long time, while he talked. I watched a smile grow on her face as she listened, but it disappeared instantly before she said, "Very well, but not tonight. I'm busy. Call me again tomorrow." She didn't say *goodbye*.

When she had hung up, Mother seemed very pleased. "He was called suddenly to the Interior and couldn't call me," she said, though he had told her that before, when she had slammed the door on him. "He's taking us to dinner tomorrow."

I took the occasion to ask what the Interior was, and Mother explained that Brazil was a very big country, but all of its cities were on the coast. The Interior was that part of the country that was away from the coast, and it was all jungle with wild animals and wild people. This immediately set off, in my mind, a movie in which Sr. Segiera, in his flying helmet and jodhpurs, dodges from palm tree to palm tree, as naked, black-skinned people go about their normal business of dancing, spearing lions and giraffes, and eating them raw.

The next evening, Sr. Segiera wore his white suit again and brought Mother another bouquet of flowers.

"You're late," Mother said, as she took them.

The senhor looked confused, and when I glanced at the clock, I saw that he was, indeed, half an hour late. "I'm sorry, Barbara," he said. I could see how sorry he was, and felt sorry for him. I didn't think it was very nice of Mother, when he had just brought her flowers.

"Let's go. I'm starving," Mother said, and headed for the door. When she got there, she stopped, and Sr. Segiera stepped up quickly to open it.

He had come for us in the long black car I had seen from our hotel window the other evening. It was called a *Lincoln Continental,* and, unlike the count's limousine in Hungary, this car was sleek and very modern looking. I got to sit up front with the chauffeur, the same man who had delivered the flowers the other evening. The maitre d' at the restaurant, dressed in a tuxedo, knew Sr. Segiera and led us to a table that was reserved for us.

Unlike the previous restaurant, where there had been fishnets and boat things on the walls, this one had gold, silk drapes, white tablecloths almost to the floor, and a little orchestra playing slow music on a little stage. I could see that Sr. Segiera was being extra attentive to Mother. He held her hand when she got out of the car, held her chair at the restaurant, and was very eager to light her cigarette for her. Mother accepted these attentions politely, but I did not see her smile at him. When he spoke, she listened and nodded her head to show that she really was listening, but she did not say anything that wasn't in answer to his questions.

Sr. Segiera did have a photograph of his airplane, which he gave me as soon as we were seated and said that I could keep. But it wasn't a biplane with open cockpits, only a monoplane with the wings above the cockpit, which was enclosed, so that you couldn't see if anyone was sitting in it or not.

"Say *thank you*," Mother said, when he handed me the picture, although there wasn't the slightest chance that I wouldn't have said it on my own. But I knew this to be something that Mother did quite automatically, probably without even knowing she was saying it.

Some people were dancing, but Mother told her companion that she had had a long day of work with Sra. O'Brien and was too tired to dance. When the senhor asked what she did for Sra. O'Brien, she told him, as she had told me, that they were writing a book together. And when he asked what sort of book, that was when Mother finally began to talk to him. We had eaten most of our appetizers by then, which may have revived Mother some, because she began to tell Sr. Segiera that when she had first met the senhora, she had told her about the book that she was planning to write when we got to America, and that the senhora had said that she had been planning for a long time to also write a book about her own experiences, but couldn't get started and probably needed an energetic, younger person like Mother to work with her. Then she told him about writing it in Russian, but not knowing the Russian alphabet and writing the words out using regular letters. They both laughed at this, and, from then, on she was as friendly to him and he as relaxed, as they had been that first night. Mother even agreed to dance with him.

At one point, I was amused to see Mother pick up the senhor's hand and examine his fingernails. "A European gentleman," she told him, "would not have his nails cut so short."

"Sometimes, Basia, I have to work with my hands, and they break."

"A gentleman can work with his hands, but he finds a way to keep his nails from breaking. He might wear gloves. And you shouldn't have your hair cut off that way in back, but tapered gradually."

"I will talk with my barber."

The next day, on the beach, I did tell Irenka about the restaurant and Mother being too tired to smile or dance until the snails that she ate gave her renewed energy so that she had told Sr. Segiera all about the book she was writing, and even danced with him. And about her telling him how to cut his nails and his hair. Irenka told me that Mr. K. had been gone all night again.

It was two or three days later that Mother came home from Sra. O'Brien's, an hour later than usual and wearing a strange, green kerchief on her head. She explained that the senhora's son had offered to drive her home in his open sports car. Mother had said, *no thank you,* explaining that she had nothing to cover her hair with, at which point he had brought her one of his mother's kerchiefs. Then he had insisted on stopping somewhere for a drink, and Mother had said, *all right,* because she didn't want to hurt his feelings. He had wanted to take her out to dinner as well. When she said that she had a small son, waiting for his supper at home, he asked if there wasn't somebody she could leave me with, to which she said, *no.* So he had, finally, driven her to the hotel, with Mother promising to make some arrangements in the future so that she could go to dinner with him. Then we both laughed over the fact that, unlike Sr. Segiera, this man had not suggested bringing me along, and Mother was glad because she didn't want to go out with him anyway.

The next day started out warmer than usual, and Irenka suggested that we go to the pool in the morning, and then an air-conditioned movie in the heat of the afternoon. The heat in Rio didn't bother me as much as it did Irenka or Mother, but I loved movies. I particularly loved the anticipation as you stepped into a darkened theater, about to be transported into another existence.

In Portugal, Mother had taken me to see a movie about a cow-boy who played the guitar, drew his gun faster than anyone else, and captured bad men with his lasso. But Irenka didn't want to see a cowboy movie, but the one with the handsome actor named *Gooper*, whom she had seen before. I wasn't excited by the prospect, at first, but we saw on the placards outside the theater that it was about soldiers fighting Arabs in the desert, so that made it all right.

The movie was in English, of course, which neither of us understood, and had Portuguese subtitles, but neither Irenka nor I could read them fast enough. But the story had horses and camels, and I recognized from the round, box-like, white hats that the soldiers wore, that they were in the Foreign Legion. Irenka didn't know what the Foreign Legion was, and I had to explain it to her in whispers. But she cried when the handsome soldier was killed and his friend covered him with a French flag, then poured gasoline on him and set him on fire. I found it sad too, but I knew it was all make-believe, and, besides, I didn't want Irenka to see me cry.

Coming out of the cool theater into the hot afternoon was terrible, even for me, and we had to stop and catch our breath after taking only a few steps on the sidewalk. But we decided that the excursion had still been worth it, and decided to do it again, even when the day wasn't too hot. Then I explained to Irenka how people didn't have to give their right name to join the Foreign Legion, so that a lot of the soldiers were crooks hiding from the Law or husbands trying to get away from mean wives, and things like that. And, finally, I told her about Sra. O'Brien's son wanting to take Mother out to dinner, which she didn't want to do, but also didn't want to upset her employer.

That Saturday, Sr. Segiera took us to the beach, but not the big beach near our hotel. It was a little beach somewhere else and practically empty, except for large boulders and logs that had washed up from the ocean. It took a while to get there, and he brought us there in his own car, not the Lincoln Continental, with the chauffeur, but the much smaller and older Chevrolet, that he said was his own.

And he had surprised us by arriving exactly on time. Mother had told me, that morning, that he would probably be late, since it was customary in Brazil to be late, but the senhor had been right on time.

And he had also brought me a present. As I got into the back seat, I saw an airplane sitting there. It wasn't the same kind of airplane as the one in the photograph that he had given me, but a sleek fighter plane, about thirty inches long, with green and brown camouflage markings and the target-like insignia of the British Royal Air Force, which was, at that time fighting German bombers over London.. "That's for you, Julien," he said, over his shoulder, as he started the car.

"Oh my God, it's an airplane," Mother exclaimed, turning around. "You shouldn't have, Ernesto. Julien, say *thank you*."

Ordinarily, Mother's prompting would have been totally superfluous, but this time the gift had, literally, taken my breath away. "Th... th... thank y... y... you, M... m... monsieur," I stammered.

"Every boy needs an airplane," the senhor said to Mother.

"Oh, but Ernesto..."

"It isn't expensive, Barbara. It's cardboard, and if it crashes, he needn't worry about it."

"You mean it actually flies?"

"Oh, yes. You'll see when we get to the beach."

"Oh my God. Did you hear that, Julien, when we get to the beach, Sr. Segiera will show you how it flies." Then, in Polish, she added, "You should kiss him."

That was a command that I had no intention of following, but, since we were under way, at that point, and some time would elapse before it would even be possible to do what Mother had said, I was sure the directive would be forgotten. In the meanwhile, I held the beautiful plane carefully in my hands visualizing myself throwing it into the air and watching it glide to the ground, like the paper airplanes I had seen the older boys fold and fly in Poland. Except that this one was much bigger and actually looked like an airplane.

With my attention on the airplane, it took me some time to notice that the back of Sr. Segiera's head looked very different now. Instead of his hair being cut off in a straight line at his neck, it had been tapered gradually, just the way Mother had told him. I wondered what his nails looked like.

When Sr. Segiera finally stopped the car on a road with a nearly-empty beach on one side and some houses on the other, I carefully extracted the airplane from the back seat and waited patiently by the side of the road, while the senhor opened the trunk and began to remove some beach things, including a wicker picnic basket.

"Julien, don't just stand there. Help Sr. Segiera," Mother said, but the senhor said, "He has to hold the airplane. That's his job. I can handle the rest."

"Well, here, let me," Mother said, taking the basket from him. "Oh, what do you have in here?" she exclaimed, apparently surprised by the weight. Then we made our way over some grass and, finally, onto the sand.

"Help Sr. Segiera," Mother said to me, as he laid out the blanket, and began to open the beach chairs.

"It's *all right*, Barbara. It's *all right*. Let him hold on to his air-plane," he said, and, suddenly, I was aware of a feeling that I had not experienced before. Sr. Segiera was telling my mother not to tell me to do things. I had had people telling me to be nice to my mother, to be obedient, to not bother her when she said she had a headache, to help her because she didn't have a husband taking care of her, and one man in Spain had even grabbed me by the elbow and marched me to the bathroom, when Mother told me to go wash my hands, but no one had ever told Mother not to tell me to do something. And I suddenly had a great feeling of affection for this man.

Mother laughed and sat down again, though I doubted the sincerity of her laugh.

"Let's go, Julien," Sr. Segiera said, starting back up to the street. "Bring your airplane."

"Oh, you're going to make it fly," Mother said, standing up.

"Just Julien," the senhor said.

"I can't come?" she said, very surprised.

"Just us men. You'll see it when it's up in the air."

Mother sat down again with another laugh that didn't sound totally sincere.

I had been standing there watching the exchange, and now ran to catch up to the senhor. As I ran, I could actually feel the air-plane in my hand already wanting to fly. Then Sr. Segiera stopped, turned to me, and said, "Go ahead, wind up the motor."

"M... m... motor?" I said.

Sr. Segiera now laid his hand on my shoulder and, with the other, turned his finger in a circle, indicating, I thought, that I should turn the propeller. "The rubber band," he said. "The rubber band inside." He said it, as though expecting me to know what he was talking about. Then, I guess seeing the expression on my face, he explained, "The propeller is attached to a rubber band. You can wind it up."

Suddenly I grasped the situation. I had seen other rubber band-powered toys before and understood the principle. If you wound the propeller one way and let go, it would turn the other way by itself. I had just never imagined that rubber bands big enough to handle this job existed. I began winding.

"No Julien, the other way."

"I'm s....s... orry, M....m... monsieur," I said, embarrassed at my mistake. I wound the other way. "H... ow m... uch do I w... ind it, M... onsieur?" I asked, gaining control of my stuttering. I was afraid of winding the rubber band too tight and breaking it.

"More," he said.

I continued winding until he said to stop. "Now set it down on the road," he said.

Holding the propeller so that it didn't unwind, I set the airplane down on the paved street and looked at my mentor.

Sr. Segiera now raised both thumbs. I didn't understand his signal.

"That's a signal to pull the wood blocks from under the wheels," he said. "Let it go."

With trepidation, I let go of the propeller. It began to spin. I felt it pulling forward against my hand. Then I released the airplane.

The plane began to roll forward along the pavement, gathering speed. Then I saw it lift about a foot off the ground and, when the propeller stopped spinning, settle back to the pavement.

I ran after the airplane, as it rolled to a stop. I picked it up and brought it back to where Sr. Segiera was standing. "It f... lew!" I said.

"Yes. Now if you wind it a little tighter and then launch it from your hand, it will fly even further. A lot of the energy is spent just getting off the ground, you know."

I began winding the propeller again. I could feel the resistance building to the point at which I had stopped the last time, and kept winding beyond it.

"That's good," Sr. Segiera said. "Now just...." and he mimed throwing the airplane lightly.

I did as instructed, and the plane took off into the air. It climbed quite high above the ground, but then I watched in horror as its right wing dipped and it banked toward the beach and the water.

I ran after it, ready to dive into the water after it. The plane crossed the strip of beach, but out over the water a breeze seemed to blow it back, just as the propeller stopped and the plane began its descent. One landing gear and one wingtip hit the sand, and the plane nosed over, with its tail up in the air, practically at my feet.

Picking it up with a heavy heart, I was relieved to find that the only damage was a little nick out of the wingtip. Sr. Segiera was jogging towards me now, and I covered the injured wingtip with my hand. "N... n... no d... d... damage, M... m... monsieur," I said, stammering furiously. It wasn't the injury to the plane, which was only cosmetic, that I didn't want him to see, but the blemish that it seemed to imply in our relationship.

I did not fly my airplane again that day, fearing for its safety. As Sr. Segiera and Mother sat in their beach chairs and talked, I ran along the empty beach, holding the plane overhead and feeling its wanting to fly.

Sitting again in the back seat of Sr. Segiera's Chevrolet and holding the airplane in my lap, as we drove home, with the light growing dim outside, I, once more, played in my mind the scene of the senhor telling Mother that she couldn't come with us to fly the airplane. "Just us men," he had said, and Mother had gotten that surprised look on her face and then sat back down. *Just us men—Julien and me.* And then he had laid his large hand over my shoulder.

But neither was I totally unaware of the fact that this had not upset Mother very much, that she had spent the whole afternoon talking, and laughing with Sr. Segiera, and, that she was, quite clearly, getting to like him, as I had feared earlier. But the emotions that I, myself, was now feeling towards Sr. Segiera kept that fear in a back corner of my mind, where it could not interfere. My feelings were reaching out to this very nice man to the extent that those diamonds on Mother's hand did not seem to matter anymore. What mattered was that we should see him again soon, that he should lay his hand over my shoulder again, and that he should have that *us men* expression on his face once more.

When the senhor stopped the car in front of our hotel, he and Mother whispered something to each other and then touched their puckered lips together. It was the first time that I had seen Mother do that with anyone, and it gave me a strange feeling.

# CHAPTER VIII

THE FOLLOWING DAY, Sr. Segiera had to work, even though it was Sunday. So I was surprised to see Mother putting on one of the dresses that she wore around company. "Sr. O'Brien is taking us out for lunch, in the mountains," she said. Sr. O'Brien I took to be the man who had brought Mother home in his open car, with the kerchief on her head, some days earlier.

"W….ill w… e be g….oing in his o….pen c….ar?" I asked hopefully.

"I don't know," Mother said. "But I'm not taking any chances," she added laughing, as I saw her take one of her large kerchiefs out of a drawer.

"I th… ought he d… idn't w… ant me c… oming al….ong," I said.

"I told him that the only way I would go with him would be if you came along as well. I don't really want to go with him at all, but he is Sra. O'Brien's son, and she is important to me."

"Isn't he nice? Is he a gentleman?"

"Oh, he's quite nice and seems to be a gentleman, but he's very young."

"H… ow y… oung is h… e?"

"He's probably my own age, but I feel a lot older than him."

This was a new concept for me, the idea that people could feel older or, I supposed, younger than their actual age. Mother, I knew, was just twenty years older than me, which made her twenty-eight. I wondered what twenty-eight felt like in comparison to, say, thirty. I wondered what seventy felt like, and a hundred, which was what people were supposed to live to if nothing happened to them along the way. What did it feel like to be a hundred and know that you're not going to live another year? I felt a shiver go through me at the suggestion, and decided to think about something else.

The desk clerk rang to say that Sr. O'Brien was here, and Mother said we would be right down. Then she lit a cigarette and sat down to smoke it.

"You s... aid w... e'd be r... ight d... own," I said.

Mother smiled. "A lady never comes 'right down,'" she said. "The gentleman should always have to wait a little. If Andre doesn't know that yet, this will be good education for him. Remember how Ernesto, I mean Sr. Segiera, didn't know how to treat a lady until we taught him?" I remembered the lesson "we" had administered to Sr. Segiera regarding his not calling Mother, when he was someplace that he couldn't call her from.

Then I leaned out of the window to see Sr. O'Brien's open car down below. I had never ridden in an open car before. What I saw down below looked like a piece of white ribbon with a red pocket in the middle, laid on the pavement in front of the hotel. A man in a blue jacket and white pants was sitting within that red pocket. On the top of his head, surrounded by thick, dark, curly hair, was a bald spot.

"I s... ee his c... ar," I said. "It's all w... hite, with r... ed s... eats."

"Don't look," Mother said.

"W... hy n... ot?"

"He might see you."

"He's g… oing to s… ee me wh… en we c… ome d… own."

"I don't want him to see you looking out the window."

This was getting much too complicated. I pulled away from the window and waited for Mother to finish her cigarette. Then I watched her put on and adjust her kerchief, in front of a mirror.


Sr. O'Brien's car had a tiny back seat. It was big enough for me, but I wondered how a grownup was meant to fit into it. Mother had said, "Good morning, Andre. I'm so sorry you had to wait," and kissed him on the cheek. Sr. O'Brien had curly brown hair, in the center of which, I knew, he had a bald spot. He also had a round face, and a little bit of a belly under his double-breasted blue jacket. The jacket had brass buttons, like a military uniform.

"It was no trouble at all," he said. His hand felt even larger than Sr. Segiera's, when we shook hands, and he smiled at me with a big grin. "Call me Andre," he said to me, and I felt, right away, that he was very friendly. Also, he spoke French better than Sr. Segiera. But that was because his family was very rich and he had probably had a lot of private lessons.

I was, actually, kind of pleased at having made that deduction. It was further evidence that I was smarter than other eight-year-olds, and I suddenly realized what it felt like to feel older than your age. I wondered how old I felt like. Could it be ten? I had always wanted to be ten. I sat up a little taller in the little red seat and swung my knees to the side, as though I didn't have enough legroom, the way Kiki had always had to put her knees to the side because they didn't fit under the little table in our room.

Then, the car, which had been rolling at city-traffic speed, reached some open road and sped up. I felt a blast of wind on the back of my head and my hair blowing forward on my face.

This was surprising—I would have expected the wind to come from the front. Why was it coming from the back? Here was a problem for my ten-year-old mind to solve. But I couldn't get my mind around it. Well, maybe it was a fifteen or even twenty-year-old problem.

We drove for a while, over some winding, mountain roads, and finally stopped at a restaurant with tables on a second-floor deck. I waited for Mother to get out so that I could push the back of her seat forward and get out myself, but the moment he had helped Mother to stand, Andre reached both hands into the rear seat and lifted me right out of the car.

"Oh Andre, he's heavy," Mother protested.

"Not for me," Andre said. "I lift twice, three times his weight every day."

Mother laughed.

Mother laughed a lot of times during that lunch. She and Andre both laughed, because Andre told a lot of jokes, most of which I didn't understand. But Mother also laughed when he wasn't telling a joke, and I realized how differently she was acting than with Sr. Segiera. With Sr. Segiera they talked about serious things—or, at least, their voices were serious, while Andre told jokes and "funny" stories, all of which Mother pretended to find *very* funny.

Several times, just as Sr. Segiera had done the day before, Andre turned his attention directly to me, asking me whether I had been to such-and-such a place yet or seen such-and-such a movie. The only one I could say, yes, to was the movie that Irenka and I had seen about the Foreign Legionnaires.

"Wasn't it great when the only man left alive in the fort puts all the dead soldiers up on the walls, so the Arabs think the fort is well defended and don't dare attack?" Sr. Andre said.

"Ow, that's awful," Mother said. "You shouldn't encourage him to see movies like that." But I agreed with Andre.

When Mother went to the ladies' room, Andre said to me, "Did you hear about the dog that found a glove in the pasture?"

I had no idea where I was supposed to have heard of it, or why it was newsworthy.

"He brought it to the cow," Andre said, "and asked, 'Madam, did you lose your brassiere?'"

I must have turned bright red, at his use of the word. I, instantly, looked around to see if anyone was within earshot. But it was a funny story.

Then, when Mother came back, she seemed to sense that Andre and I had been talking, because she immediately told him that my stammer was the result of "malnutrition," but that the doctor that Andre's mother had recommended was curing it. To my surprise, Andre laughed at this. "You mean Baresky?" he said.

Mother said, "Yes."

"Baresky's no doctor," he said with another laugh. "He's a tailor from St. Petersburg with a black box, with which he'll promise to cure anything. He's offered to grow hair on my bald spot."

I never had to go back to that doctor.

Driving back, Mother made Andre drive slowly, because they had had a lot to drink. In the back seat, I couldn't hear much of their conversation, but I could hear Mother laughing frequently. She kissed his cheek again, as we said goodbye, and I saw Andre try to kiss her on the mouth, but Mother slipped her face away, with a little nervous laugh.

In the elevator, I saw the smile drop from Mother's face and her eyes close. "I have a splitting headache," she said. "I can't drink."

Mother had two types of "splitting headaches." One kind was when she wanted me to leave her alone, the other when she had had more than one glass of wine to drink. This was the second kind. I had learned to tell them apart, but this time I could well have seen it coming.

"Wh....y didn't y....ou j... ust p... ut y... our h... and o... ver y... our g... lass?" I asked. This was something I had seen her do many times before.

Mother turned her head, very gently, from side to side. "Because," she said through tense lips, and I realized that it hurt her to speak and was sorry that I had asked. "I was afraid that Andre would....drink that whole bottle by himself....and drive us off a cliff."

Suddenly I felt a great admiration for what Mother had done. "I w... ill g... et y..ou a wet c... ompress as s... oon as we g... et to our ap... partment," I said.

Mother began to say, "Thank you," but the elevator stopped on our floor with a lurch, and I saw her cringe.

"D... on't o... pen your eyes," I said. "G... ive m... e y... our h... and, a... nd I w... ill l... ead y... ou."

"Thank you," she said, smiling weakly. "My knight in shining armor."

Ordinarily that expression would make *me* cringe. Every previous time she had said that, I had found it to be a naked plea for sympathy, usually in preparation for a request. This time, however, I was certain that it was sincere, that it was my offer that had led to it. I took Mother's hand in mine anyway, and led her into our suite. When she had lain down on her bed, I removed her shoes.

"Oh, thank you, Yulian," she said.

Walking on tiptoe, I went to the bathroom and returned with a wet washcloth, wrung out thoroughly, the way she liked it, and laid it over her eyes and forehead. Mother thanked me again.

Then, as I began to tiptoe into the other room, Mother took my hand and, with very feeble pressure, indicated she wanted me to sit on the bed beside her. "There is something I have to tell you," she whispered.

I sat down and waited.

"I have to tell you something," she said again.

"Y... es?" I said.

"Sra. O'Brien... Andre's mother... Sra. O'Brien says you should be in school."

Mother could not have surprised me more, or more unpleasantly. I had known that school would eventually come back into my life, but I had not expected that to happen until we reached America. What was the use of my struggling with Portuguese reading and writing, if we would be going to America any time now? "B... b... b... but a....a... aren't w... w... we g... g... going to Am... m... merica anymore?" I blurted.

"Yes, we're still going to America, but the senhora says it isn't good for a boy your age to be spending so much time on the beach with Irena, and she's right. You should be with children your own age."

"B... B... but...." I began, but realized that I had no argument against this logic. I knew very well that there was something perverse in some of my feelings towards Irenka. How Sra. O'Brien had found out, was beyond me.

"Tomorrow... we will go... and enroll you in the school her children went to."

"A... a... andre?"

"Yes, Andre and his sister Isabella."


The following morning, Mother's headache continued. It was unusual that it did not disappear overnight, but I had known it to happen. As we rode to the school in a taxi, Mother kept her eyes closed and a hand to her forehead. When I tried to ask the name of the school, she shushed me.

It wasn't till we were in the principal's office, that Mother could muster enough energy to return to her more normal self. There, she told the principal, in French, that we were Polish on our way to America, that we had escaped over the Carpathian

Mountains into Hungary, walking eleven hours in the snow after our guide had abandoned us, and that I could speak French but very little Portuguese and that I had a very bad stutter. She also said that she was a close friend of Sra. O'Brien, whom she was helping with her memoirs and would be writing her own book once we reached America.

The principal, a man with gray hair and wearing a gray suit, said that he knew both Sr. and Sra. O'Brien very well and had been very saddened by the senhor's death, but he knew that the senhora had an exciting story to tell, and Mother's sounded equally exciting. He and Mother smoked several cigarettes each and drank coffee, as Mother gave him more details regarding the exciting elements of our story, giving me a chance to make certain assessments of this school, based on what I could see through the office window.

Right off the bat, I realized that this school was an improvement over my old French school. Instead of the grim, multi-story, brick, factory building with steel stairs and pitted, wooden floors of the French school, this one was a series of single-story buildings of some brightly painted, cement-like material and connected by breezeways. The buildings wound their way around a courtyard, where I could see some children, apparently enjoying outdoor recess.

Another improvement was that the pupils wore a uniform. In Warsaw I had looked forward with great anticipation to wearing the blue uniform with long pants, brass buttons, and peaked, military caps that students wore. They even marched in parades, and for several years I had visualized myself marching along our street, one of hundreds of students, all dressed alike, all in step, all belonging together. It was with unimaginable disappointment that I had learned that my French school's uniform would not be the same, military style outfit. Instead, with incredible embarrassment, I would walk to school with Kiki in the school's black smock, white Peter Pan collar and a beret. Kiki's explanation that, apparently, that was the way schoolchildren dressed in France, had not mended even the slightest dent in the car-wreck of my dreams.

The uniform these Brazilian children were wearing, was, in fact, a compromise between the two. Certainly not a black smock, it also lacked the brass-button panache of the Polish version. It consisted of tan shorts and jacket, a blue shirt, and an enameled badge over the left breast. While not military, it was definitely the uniform of an institution, and I felt a sudden longing to wear it and be thus made identifiable as a full fledged member of that institution. Some day, I believed, I would become a boy scout, which was a world-wide institution, and after that, I would be a soldier.

My thrill at finally fulfilling my dream of wearing a uniform I need not be ashamed of, had made me forget the one, universal negative that stained all schools. Whatever uniform a school might or might not prescribe, it was at bottom, a collection of children. And children were always trouble. Suddenly, I realized that by this time tomorrow, I would be among those pushing, shoving, and laughing children with no idea regarding what they were pushing, shoving or laughing about, or what was expected of me. Suddenly, I found myself longing for the long days of security in our hotel suite, racking my brains for something to do.

Perhaps sensing my anxiety, the principal had two items of good news to add. One was that there was another Polish boy in the school, a Stefan Stepnanski also from Warsaw, who could be my friend and help me out with any language issues.

"Oh my God," Mother said. "Stepnanski from Warsaw? I knew the Stepnanskis, if it's the same family. The father was a doctor, Michael Stepnanski, and *her* father was Bolek *Terasocki*. They had a son Julien's age. He was at your birthday party, Julien."

There had been a lot of children, that I didn't know, at that birthday party. Mother had bought toy rifles and tall *Ulan* hats for everybody, and there was a picture from the party in the paper. Mother was in the middle of the picture, wearing an *Ulan* hat, canted over one eye, and aiming a rifle, surrounded by children doing the same thing. Kiki had shown it to me. Except that I wasn't in the picture.

The principal acknowledged that Stefan's father was, indeed Dr. Michael Stepnanski. The Stepnanskis, he said, had been fortunate enough to leave Poland before the war began. Mother said that that was, indeed, good, because Stefan could help me find my way around. I had reservations about this, but kept them to myself.

The other bit of good news was that the school operated a bus that would pick me up right at the hotel every morning and return me there every afternoon, so that I wouldn't have to walk.


My concern over relating to my schoolmates was pushed to the back of my mind, as I was fitted for my uniform, at a downtown store and supplied with two white "T" shirts, decorated with the school logo over the left breast, which the saleslady said I would need for gym class. But I was greatly disappointed when Mother told me I could not wear the uniform until I started attending school the next day.

In fact, on the bus back to our hotel, we had a debate over the issue, in which I was quite proud of my logic. If, as Mother implied, I was not authorized to wear the uniform until I had actually begun attending classes, even though the principal had already entered my name and assigned me to a class, then I had no right to don the uniform the following morning either. If Mother's argument were correct, then I would have to bring the uniform on the school bus, in its cardboard box, and not put it on until class started. But Mother's headache returned at that point, and she didn't have a chance to see the powerful logic of my argument.

We ended up spending most of the rest of the day with Mother doing her solitaire and me keeping the terror of tomorrow at bay by imagining myself marching down the street in front of our hotel with my classmates in our tan uniforms, on some Brazilian holiday. An additional benefit, that occurred to me, was the fact that this was the same uniform that Andre had worn at one time.

The next morning, Mother and I stood in front of our hotel, waiting for the school bus. In my hand, I held a pencil box, the same blue as my uniform shirt, and one of the "T" shirts that the woman in the store told us I would be expected to bring to class. Mother's hand rested possessively on my newly-uniformed shoulder, and no wiggling of that shoulder seemed to dislodge it. Mother surprised me by her perception of my concern. "The other children will respect you more when they see me with you," she said. Every instinct inside me told me that greater respect for me was not the result that this image would produce. But I had no choice, but to stand as tall as I could, with my shoulders back, and present as impregnable a figure as I could to my new schoolmates.

Then a bus of the same color as my uniform, with the same logo as on my badge painted on its side, and its interior filled with children dressed just like me, pulled up in front of us, and I prepared to climb on board with firm step and my chin raised.

"Give me a kiss," Mother said. Kissing was not part of our normal repertoire. Mother never suggested kissing before she left for Sra. O'Brien's, but, for some reason, she felt the need to bless the start of my adventure with this display of affection.

"You are embarking on a new career," she said, as the bus driver waited with his door open and the engine chugging, "and I want you to do it with your head high and a firm step."

This was precisely what I had intended to do, but now that resolve felt, somehow, definitely deflated. Nevertheless, I hurried onto the bus, before the driver could get angry at me and drive off. As I made the turn towards the rear of the bus, I pretended not to notice that my mother was waving at me.

There was an empty seat beside a girl dressed in the feminine version of our uniform. It was, probably, my unconscious sense of relative security in the company of girls, that made me seat myself beside her. This immediately set off a flurry of loud Portuguese words and hand gestures from my intended seatmate, conveying the idea that I should not be doing that, followed by similar expression from our fellow passengers.

In an instant, my shoulders slumped forward and any sense of impregnability that I may have salvaged from Mother's good-bye left me. Desperately, I looked around for another empty seat and heard the driver yelling something at me. The other passengers quickly picked up the driver's message and endeavored to drill it into my mind through ruptured eardrums. It took several repetitions before I understood that the bus could not move until I sat down. I found another empty seat beside a boy, further back in the bus and seated myself, braced for whatever unpleasantness might come from that quarter.

My new seatmate, some years older than I and quite large, was reading a book, and, blessedly, took no notice of my presence beside him. Unfortunately, I soon discovered an unpleasant odor emanating from his direction. I dearly wanted to move to another seat, the next time the bus stopped, but could imagine another barrage of Portuguese questions and protests, and just satisfied myself with making a mental note of the large boy's appearance, for the purpose of not sitting beside him again.


My teacher, a stocky woman with red hair, a long chin, and a very tight skirt, had, evidently, been well primed for my arrival. The moment that the principal's secretary led me into her classroom, the teacher greeted me with a smile and an extra loud and distinct, "Good morning, Julio. My name is Sra. Fernanda. Did you understand that?" I assured her that I did. Sra. Fernanda did not offer to shake hands. Then she instructed a boy in the desk directly in front of her own to move all his belongings to a desk in back, and directed me, my pencil box, and my "T" shirt to the newly vacated one. From her own desk, she produced two notebooks, a blue one and a red one, and, smiling at me, lifted my desktop, deposited the red notebook inside, and laid the blue one on top of the desk.

With me thus settled, Sra. Fernanda began a monologue to the class that was too fast for me to understand, except that, from the words like "Poland" and "Hitler," I gathered that she was explaining who I was and why I was there. Then, switching gears, she turned to me and explained, very slowly and quite loudly, that Stefan Stepnanski was somewhere and would do something later. She asked if I understood, and I, again, said that I did, guessing that this Stefan must belong to another classroom and I would be introduced to him some time in the future.

Much to my relief and delight, my classmates seemed to take no notice of me. When I saw them writing in their blue notebooks, I had my own open on my desktop, and when they switched to the red one, I did the same. And, when they turned them in at the end of the lesson, I also handed in my blank one.

At recess, the boys all seemed to join in a game of tag, while the girls stood in little groups and talked. A man teacher, who seemed to be in charge of this activity, urged me to join in the game of tag. I pretended not to understand him, even when he mimed by tagging me and running away, and he, finally turned away to deal with a fight that was developing between some older boys.

I wasn't introduced to Stefan Stepnanski, until classes were over that first day. Stefan was older than me, but I shook hands with him and greeted him in Polish. Stefan turned away without a word, after our handshake, and went to rejoin his classmates. That was fine with me. On the bus going home, I was one of the first people on board and found a seat next to a window. Nobody came to sit beside me, and that was fine with me as well.

The following day, Sra. Fernanda wiggled herself onto my chair, right beside me, opened a book she had brought, and proceeded to coax me to read from it. They were easy words, and I worked my way through a couple of paragraphs, trying hard not to stutter, by drawing my words out very carefully. Sra. Fernanda probably thought it was the letters that were giving me trouble, not realizing what would happen if I tried to speak faster.

I wasn't comfortable sitting right up against this teacher. There was a roll of fat above her belt, showing through her dress and a very slight odor coming from her, which wasn't exactly unpleasant, but somehow distressing to me.

The story in the book was clearly about a boy, a girl, a dog, and a ball. I knew most of the words, and the ones that I did not, were easy to guess. "Do you understand?" Sra. Fernanda asked when I had finished half of the page. It was at that moment that a plan occurred to me, and I shook my head extending my palms in a gesture of total ignorance.

"You did not understand any of it?" she asked. I repeated my previous reply.

The senhora drew in a breath and pointed to the name *Jose*, in the first line. She enunciated it, just as I had done, then pointed to the boy in the illustration. "Jose," she repeated, tapping the boy's stomach.

"Jose," I repeated after her. Then I tapped my own stomach and said the word once more.

"No, no, no, no," she said, in surprise. She drew an imaginary line around the entire boy. "Jose," she said.

I drew an imaginary line around my entire body and repeated the name, "Jose." I had played this trick before, on a Soviet officer who was trying to teach me Russian words pertaining to a glass of very hot tea and had had a terrible time keeping a straight face. I had the same difficulty now, keeping myself from bursting into laughter by sucking in my lips.

Sra. Fernanda shook her head. She traced my outline with her finger and pronounced "Julio."

I performed the very best imitation I could of finally grasping her meaning. I smiled with happiness and tapped my own chest. "J... ulio," I said, proudly. "J... ulio."

Sra. Fernanda smiled a smile of disappointment. What she had on her hands, I was sure she was thinking, was not just a language problem, but a dunce. I smiled back sweetly.

Now, Sra. Fernanda pointed to my chest, and said, "Julio," which I repeated proudly. Then she pointed to the illustration, being sure to touch the boy's chest. "Jose," she said.

"Jose," I said. Then, to prove how well I had learned my lesson, I pointed to my own chest, without her prompting, and pronounced, "Julio," then back to the boy with another, "Jose."

"Very good, very good," Sra. Fernanda said. I beamed in the glory. Realizing that she needed to return to the class, Sra. Fernanda urged me to continue reading the book by myself and began handing the red notebooks back to the students.


I could not wait to get home and tell Meesh about how I had fooled the teacher. But, as I had suspected might happen, I found little satisfaction in my monologue. It was Irenka that I needed to tell my story to. She would understand and laugh. I went down and knocked on Irenka's door.

"Oh, Yulian," she said, opening the door a little and looking at me. She seemed quite surprised to see me. "What is it?"

"I h... ave s....ometh....ing to t... ell you," I said.

"What is it?" she asked, not opening the door any wider.

"Is s... omething wr....ong?" I asked.

"No, no, come in." She opened the door wide for me to come in. I saw that Irenka was dressed in a bathrobe, which would not have surprised me had it been my mother, but I didn't expect to see other people dressed in bathrobes at that time of day.

"What is it?" Irenka said, sitting down on the chair. I had the strong feeling that she wanted me to say whatever was on my mind and leave.

"I... t's ab....out what h....appened in scho.....ol,"

"Yes?" I could tell that she was only pretending to be interested. I told her my story as quickly as I could. While I was telling it, it occurred to me that in her present mood she might not find it funny and reprimand me instead. But she didn't. She did laugh, though not with the enthusiasm I had hoped for, and I went back upstairs. I knew that grownups, particularly women, had moods when they didn't enjoy things the way they did at other times.


There was a boy named Gustavo in my class, who was, clearly, the fastest runner of all the boys. He had reddish hair, cut so short you could see his scalp, and freckles, and his skin seemed stretched tight over his face, and when they played tag at recess, no one ever seemed able to tag him. I could tell by the grin on his face, as he evaded his pursuer, that he thought he was pretty good. That look on his face annoyed me. I had been the fastest runner in my class at the French school in Warsaw. It had been the only positive element of that entire school experience, but the title had clearly been mine. And now, to see Gustavo think he was so great really incensed me.

So I slowly began to work my way into the game of tag. The first day, I stood close to where the others were playing and followed closely with my eyes, with a look of intense interest on my face. But this did not result in an invitation to join, so the following day I proceeded to walk across the playground several times, hoping to get tagged. But I had been tagged, while walking across that playground on the first day, and ignored it, so I wasn't really surprised that no one bothered tagging me now. But it was just a small step from walking across to actually jogging along behind the others, and pretty soon I was running around just as though I was an actual participant. And, finally, on the fourth day of my efforts, I felt myself being tagged on the arm.

Immediately, I set out after Gustavo. I saw him at the other end of the playground and made straight for him. The other boys scattered at my approach, and I could have tagged several of them quite easily. But it was Gustavo, with his close-cropped, reddish hair, freckles, and tightly stretched skin, who was my prey.

I was almost on top of him before Gustavo realized my intent. I had slowed down, because tagging him while he stood still would not have served my needs. For an instant, there was a startled look on Gustavo's face. I felt immediate gratification and burned that look into my memory. The surprise turned into a grin, as Gustavo dashed off to my right. I followed. I let him get a few steps ahead of me before shifting into my top gear.

Realizing now that this was a contest between Gustavo and me, the other boys stood still and watched, and, in the corner of my eye, I could see that even some of the girls were looking.

Gustavo reached the other end of the playground a few steps ahead of me, but I could see that I was catching up. Gustavo turned to his right, and I could have cut across and taken a short-cut, but that wasn't what I had in mind. I made the same right turn that he had, and in three more steps I had him. I was close enough to reach one hand out and tag him, but I ran another few steps and tagged him with both hands, right in the middle of his back. Gustavo's arms flayed to his sides, and he took two more steps and stumbled to the ground.

I stood over him, breathing hard, with my hands on my hips, as Gustavo sat up and began to cry over a skinned knee.

I had done it again. I had hurt a boy, without meaning to.

I looked around for one of the teachers to come and make us shake hands. But then I felt my shoulder gripped hard. I thought it was a teacher, but it turned out to be Stefan Stepnanski. He and three other boys, all bigger than me, suddenly pushed me up against the wall of the school building, and held me there, while Stefan began punching me in the stomach.

"W... w... why are y... y... you d... d... doing this t... t... to m... m... me?" I stuttered in Polish.

"Shut up, Jew!" Stefan answered, in Polish.

# CHAPTER IX

I HAD CAUGHT GUSTAVO, tagged him harder than I should have, seen him cry over his skinned knee, and been punched in the stomach a number of times by Stefan, while his friends held me against the wall. Then we had gone back to class and, finally, I got on the bus. But I didn't remember any of this clearly, the way I usually remembered things that had happened that same afternoon, but hazily, as though it had happened a long time ago, or even in a dream. I couldn't remember anything about what had happened in class, after the recess, or on the bus, up to that moment.

Now we were stopped in front of our hotel, and I was fully awake—though I hadn't been asleep—and I had a terrible headache, though I didn't remember anyone hitting me in the head. My stomach hardly hurt at all. But I was very afraid.

I didn't know what it was that I was afraid of. My classmates and Stefan and his friends were all angry at me for pushing Gustavo. Maybe Sra. Fernanda would find out and punish me. But my classmates in Warsaw had been angry at me as well, and I had been punished before. There was something more. But the bus was stopped in front of our hotel now, and I had to get off.

It wasn't till I was up in our suite, waiting for Mother with an anxiety for her return that I had not felt for some time, that I remembered. Stefan had called me a Jew.

Suddenly, I was filled with an unfamiliar dread. It was the first time in my life that anyone had called me a Jew, and I could now recall the hatred with which I had heard the word directed to others. "Jew" wasn't just some letters making a word—it was an expletive, an expression of loathing, an utterance spit out through protruded lips and a nose scrunched up as though the word itself smelled bad.

Stefan, whose parents knew us in Poland, had lashed out at me with that hatred. When we had been introduced originally, he had just not wanted to talk to me, but when he saw me doing something bad, that hatred had come out, and he had attacked me with it.

I wondered if he had told others that I was Jewish. Would other boys be grabbing me, whenever I made some mistake, or even for no reason at all, and beating me? I could understand now why Mother had said not to ever mention the word "Jew." What if grownups were to find out as well? Not all grownups hated Jews— many people in Poland had known we were Jewish and not done anything mean about it—but some people, like the Nazis, actually went around killing Jews.

Suddenly, I was aware of a whole new kind of fear. I had held fear for witches and goblins, when I was alone at night in a strange hotel room—fears that somewhere in my soul I knew were, at bottom, products of my own, childish imagination. But the fear I felt now was a grownup fear that felt totally real. It wasn't fear of any specific hurt—not another beating by Stefan and his friends or punishment by Sra. Fernanda—but of something much greater, something that applied not just to me, but to a larger group to which, I now realized, I belonged.


Mother came home and said that we had to hurry downstairs to the restaurant, where I would have my supper right away, because, later, she and Sr. Segiera were going out to dinner, somewhere, without me. I wasn't afraid to stay alone, was I? she asked, and I said that, no, I wasn't. If I were, she would ask Mrs. Kosiewicz to come and stay with me till I was asleep.

I said that, no, I wasn't afraid. I had stayed alone in hotel rooms in Hungary, Yugoslavia, Italy, Spain, and Portugal, and I had been terrified by the witches and goblins that I, myself, had created out of shadows on the wall, cast by the doily or the towel that Mother laid over a lamp in an effort to fashion a night-light for me.

It had been a strange ritual. It would usually begin as a game, with my wondering what there was that could possibly scare me and looking around for a shadow that one could imagine into an old woman, looking at one from behind a tree or some horned, long-snouted apparition that could be called a goblin. Of course there weren't any. These were just doily shadows. Kiki had taught me that witches and goblins didn't exist. And then, a breeze might flutter the doily, and a shadow would move. I might catch the motion out of the corner of my eye, or I might see a form I had not noticed being there before, and, instantly, my blood would turn to ice and my game to terror. Suddenly, I would be overtaken by totally unreasonable fears of monsters assembling on my walls to pounce on me.

But, this evening would be different. This evening, I had the feeling that I was beyond that now, that, as a result of this afternoon's happenings, I was, now, impervious to such phantasmagoria, and I welcomed the opportunity to confirm this hypothesis. And, as for Irenka staying with me, I just felt that her naiveté—though the word naiveté, itself, was not in my vocabulary—on the entire subject of Jewishness would not be conducive to my present frame of mind.

To my relief, it turned out that my original hypothesis had been, indeed, correct, since neither witch nor goblin made an appearance that night. I had, of course, skewed the test somewhat, by closing my eyes the moment I was settled in bed and not opening them until the following morning.

When Mother had first returned from work, the evening before, and hurried me down to the hotel dining room, I had been debating how to tell her about that afternoon's happenings, or if I was even going to tell her at all. But the following morning, after my victory over the witches and goblins and the maturity status that it implied, I decided that any relief she could give to the situation would not be worth the pain of the disclosure.

In the first place, she might have become very angry at my even mentioning the word *Jew*. And, in the second place, sharing a fear with Mother just did not seem like a constructive idea. Mother, who had, after all, embarked on our perilous trek over the Carpathian Mountains last February, against all advice, and who had instructed me to just jump into the pool on board ship, when I did not know how to swim, held little tolerance for fear.

I put on my uniform and boarded the school bus, knowing full well now that, though I wore the uniform, I did not and never would fully belong to the entity that the uniform represented. And that what I was a member of was a realm that belonged nowhere, held no rights, and was welcome at no table, except its own.

And then I saw Gustavo come to school with a large square of gauze taped to one knee and a bandage around the heel of his hand. I recalled how painful it had been when I had skinned my own knee and hand, falling on the sidewalk in Warsaw, and knew that that was what I had done to Gustavo. That it was I who had pushed him to the ground and made him cry. I could see his face as I had seen it the day before, his mouth stretched wide in sobs, as the tears ran down his face, encircling his bleeding leg with his arm, and looking up at me for explanation.

I had done this to Gustavo for no other reason than the fact that he could run fast. That was all that he had done. He had done nothing to me. He had been playing an ordinary game with his friends, and I had chased him down and pushed him to the ground. Gustavo had sat there on the ground, crying from the pain that I had caused him.

I wanted to wipe the image of him sitting there, crying, from my mind. He kept looking up at me, sobbing and snuffling his runny nose.

I wished that Sra. Fernanda had done what the governess at Sra. O'Brien's had and made me shake hands with Gustavo and tell him that I was sorry. That had seemed to prevent what I was feeling now. There had been a certain pain to saying I was sorry for something I had done, but it wasn't anything like this.

Of course, I could always walk up to Gustavo, offer my hand and say that I was sorry—I knew the Portuguese expression for that. I could push my way through the other boys who were crowding around Gustavo and do that. But I knew that I couldn't do that. Besides, I wasn't sure that, without a grownup's assistance, it would work.

I was sure they were talking about me, right now, and about what a bad thing I had done, and they were right. And they were saying how bad I was, and that was all right too. I knew that I was never going to be one of them, and I didn't care what they said about me. In a little while I would be going to America.

Except that the picture of Gustavo clutching his knee in pain and looking up at me kept coming back. I kept as much distance between Gustavo and myself as I could. All day, I found myself glancing out of the corner of my eye for anyone approaching me with violent intentions. But none did. I tried to make myself as unobtrusive as possible. When the others were writing in their notebooks, I opened mine and drew pictures in it. Drawing was not something I did well or particularly enjoyed, but it meant wagging my eraser-tipped pencil, while the others did the same with theirs, and, thus, not drawing attention to myself by my idleness. During recess I stayed as far from their game of tag as possible and, in gym class, I made sure that I didn't dash from one end of the hall to the other any faster than my classmates, or throw the rubber ball with any more accuracy or catch it with more consistency. It seemed as though the school day would never end.

And the bus crawled at a snail's pace on the way home. I could not wait to take off the uniform, in which I now felt an impostor and intruder, and go downstairs to talk to Irenka. Maybe telling *her* how sorry I was, could help me get the image of Gustavo out of my mind. I would not, of course, tell Irenka about the Stefan business, which was quite separate and outside her range of understanding, but whispering to her about how sorry I was for what I had done to Gustavo might be almost like telling Gustavo. I remembered the delicious intimacy of lying on our stomachs on the warm sand and telling each other things we wouldn't say to anyone else. I knew that there wasn't time to go to the beach now, but we could sit close together in chairs in her living room, or maybe even lie on her bed, and talk.

Irenka was very happy to see me this time. "Oh, Yulian, I'm so sorry about not being very interested in what you said the last time," she said. "I wasn't feeling very well that day."

I told her that was all right. That there were days when Mother didn't feel very well, too. Irenka was mending the elbow of a white shirt, and it reminded me of Kiki.

"How is school going?" she asked.

I pulled a chair close to where she was sitting, sat down, and then lied, telling her that school was going fine. But that was all right, because in a few minutes I would be telling her the truth.

"I saw you waiting for the bus in your uniform yesterday," she said. "You looked really nice in it."

I was wearing my uniform when I'd come to see her the other day, but she didn't seem to remember that. "I h... ave s... omething I h... ave to t... ell y... ou," I said, before the conversation could get too far afield.

"Oh, what's that?" I could tell by her tone that she was expecting me to tell her something fun, and felt guilty.

"It i... sn't g... ood," I said.

"What is it?" Suddenly, Irenka's voice was full of concern.

I dropped my voice to a whisper. "I h... urt a b... oy," I said.

"You hurt a boy?"

I told her about watching them never being able to catch Gustavo and how that had annoyed me because I had always been the one that the others couldn't catch, and how I had joined the game and caught Gustavo, but pushed him too hard so that he fell and skinned his knee and his hand.

"Oh, that's nothing," Irenka said. "Boys are always falling down and skinning their knees. You should have seen my brother coming home from school with his knees."

"But I m... ade G... ustavo c... ry."

"Well, skinned knees hurt. Haven't you ever skinned a knee and cried?"

"Yes, b... ut...."

"He'll be back in school tomorrow, playing tag. You'll see."

"A... ctually it h... appened y... esterday, and h... e w... as b... ack t... oday." I had even seen him playing tag, I realized.

"There, you see?"

Irenka didn't understand. What I saw right then was Gustavo sitting on the ground again, hugging his knee in pain, and looking up at me. My own pain was no less than before. Maybe even more.

"Now tell me, have you made any new friends?" she asked.

"I h… aven't m….ade a….ny f… friends." I would have bet that she didn't remember my telling her, that other time, about making Sra. Fernanda think I was stupid.

"Because you don't think you can speak Portuguese. But you can, and you won't learn unless you try. Would you like to practice with me? I'll pretend that I'm one of your classmates." I knew that Irenka had learned a lot more Portuguese than I had, and now she seemed quite eager to play our old role-playing game.

"No," I said. I surprised myself with my abrupt answer. But I knew that it had been a mistake to try talking with Irenka about the things that bothered me. I realized that my response had surprised Irenka as well. "Would you like some tea?" she asked.

"I h… ave to g… et b… ack I h… ave h… omew… ork to do," I lied.

That lie surprised me too. I had been taught that God didn't allow lying, but now, for some reason, that did not seem to matter. What mattered was that I had to get back to our suite.

Gustavo's face, looking up at me from the ground, kept haunting me for the rest of the day. Except that, strangely enough, each time it appeared now, in place of tears running down his cheeks, there would be blood pouring from his nose. Then I would remember that the blood had been on his knee, not his nose, and would try to correct the picture. But, somehow, the bloody-nose image kept coming back.

There was no mention of the Gustavo incident or the Stefan incident the following day or the day after. But the image of Gustavo on the ground with his bloody face kept coming back, and pretty soon I no longer bothered correcting the picture, but only tried to get it out of my head as quickly as possible. I found that if I thought of a certain Polish marching song, I could replace the image with one of soldiers marching down the street in Warsaw. Pretty soon, I would catch myself actually humming the tune under my breath.

Then, about three or four days later, at lunch, which we ate at long picnic tables on a roofed-over, raised platform without walls, I was just about to step off the platform, eating a banana, when someone pushed me from behind. I landed painfully on my knees and my elbows on the ground below. When I looked around, there was no one near me.

I did not cry or even grimace, except for the very first seconds—I, instinctively, didn't want to give anyone satisfaction. It wasn't till one of the teachers had helped me to stand up and taken me to an office where a woman with a white dress, white shoes, and black hair began to wash my wounds, that I felt tears filling my eyes. There were pieces of dirt that had to be picked out with a folded cloth, and the woman was saying something in Portuguese, which I supposed had to do with the fact that the washing was necessary to ward off infection.

I bit my upper lip to keep from making any sound, and I think the woman said something about my being very brave, which, at another time would have pleased me immensely, but now seemed to make no impression.

I returned to class with dressings on both knees and both elbows, and I could see the other kids pretending that they didn't notice me come in. Sra. Fernanda asked if I was all right, or something like that, and I nodded and resumed my seat. Then a girl, several years older than me, came into class and handed an envelope to Sra. Fernanda. The senhora motioned for me to come up and take the envelope, and, speaking slowly and extra loud, instructed me to give the envelope to my mother. Then she asked me if I understood, and I nodded that I did.

When Mother read the note, with my help because it had been written in French, which Mother spoke fluently, but could read only with difficulty, we found that it explained that I had been careless and tumbled off the platform, but my injuries had been cleansed and disinfected by the school nurse. I confirmed that this was all correct.

And since this was Friday, with no school the next day, the note also instructed Mother to check my scrapes for infection the following day and apply some kind of medication. But for this task, the next day, Mother called Irenka to come upstairs and perform what was needed. Irenka and I went into the bathroom, where I sat on the edge of the bathtub, while mother remained in the front room with a cigarette. As Irenka squatted at my feet, ministering tenderly to my knees, I could see deep down the top of her dress. But, somehow, the view did not excite me anymore.

One time, a few days later, I was eating some kind of sweet fruit that we had been given for dessert, a fruit I had never tasted before, when a boy, playing tag, knocked it out of my hand, as he ran by, and the boy chasing him stepped on it. I picked it up, so as not to be admonished for littering, and threw it into the garbage.

Surprisingly, even to me, at the time, I did not feel angry at this act. But it wasn't as though I welcomed the punishment, but, rather, that I didn't care.

That was the last of any kind of torment that I received, except, possibly, for the large rubber ball that hit me in the side of the head, at recess a few days later, though that could, actually, have been an accident. During recess, I would stand, leaning against a particular section of the wall of our classroom building, my face lowered in caution, and wait for recess to end. Then I would walk back to class, making sure I would be the last through the door, to avoid being tripped from behind.

On occasion, Mother would ask me how I was doing in school. Fortunately, probably because my stuttering so annoyed her, she tended to only ask questions that I could answer with a simple yes or no, and in that manner I told her that, yes, I was making friends and that, yes, I had met Stefan, and that the teacher was nice to me and spoke slowly and that I was, indeed, understanding more and more of what went on in class.

The image of Gustavo on the ground, with his bloody face, still kept coming back, still causing me great pain, and I would chase it away with the Polish marching song and the image of marching soldiers.

Sra. Fernanda had begun spending a few minutes with me every day, teaching me the multiplication tables, and giving me arithmetic problems to do while she taught the class. A few times, one of the boys, or even the girls, would approach me in an obvious effort to engage me in conversation. Had this happened earlier, before the Gustavo and the Stefan incidents, I would have welcomed it. But now, even though I understood that my offense had been forgiven or forgotten, I had no desire for friendship with these people.

# CHAPTER X

EVERY FEW WEEKS, when her session with Sra. O'Brien ended early, Mother would pay a visit to the American embassy to find out where we stood in terms of being allowed to come into that country. I didn't ask what they were telling her, because I was no longer excited about going to the land of skyscrapers, cowboys, Mickey Mouse, and watches that you could buy for a dollar in a pharmacy—any more than I was excited by anything. Mother had said that in America, I would soon learn to speak English like an American, join the Boy Scouts, have a two-wheel bicycle, maybe a dog, and earn money by delivering newspapers on my bicycle, like the boy in the film. But I knew that, in America, I would still be a Jew.

Mother had noticed my loss of an appetite, and taken me to a doctor recommended by Sr. Segiera, this time, but he had found nothing the matter. He had asked whether I participated in gym class at school, which I said I did, and whether I played games at recess. To this second question, I said that I played some, which was only half a lie, and the doctor said that I probably just wasn't getting as much exercise as I had been when I used to go to the pool with Irenka. Or maybe school was a bit of a strain on me, what with the language problem and my being a "new boy." He slapped me, playfully, on my behind and told Mother not to worry. Then Mother asked him about my stutter, and he said that I would grow out of it.

Of course, what Mother did not learn and what I didn't tell the doctor, was that, one or two times a day, I would visualize Gustavo sitting there on the ground and looking up at me through the blood on his face. And what was strangest of all, was that I had begun seeing little Gustavo wearing a beard.


It seems that Sra. O'Brien must have been paying Mother just enough to cover our living expenses, including my school, but, probably, not enough to pay our passage to America, whenever America might let us into the country, or to live on, once we got there, until Mother could write her book. Those twin diamonds on Mother's hand were supposed to take care of all that. But those twin diamonds still *were* on Mother's hand. The senhora had not been interested in buying even one of them, herself, and she had not introduced Mother to anyone else who was interested.

I suggested to Mother that she try to sell them to a jewelry store, but she explained that they would not pay her as much as they were really worth, since they had to make a profit when they resold them. I realized that, in the past, I would have been quite proud of being able to understand that economic concept, without any further explanation, but I had no more appetite for pride of accomplishment. On the other hand, Mother further explained, if we did get our permit to sail to America, and she hadn't sold at least one of the diamonds, she would then take my advice and sell one of them to a jewelry store, just to pay for our passage. But, again, the idea of my advice being taken, in no way excited me either.

I was well aware that my mood must, certainly, have been evident to Mother, in addition to my appetite loss, and that the doctor's admonition not to worry was growing thinner and thinner.

So, one afternoon, she surprised me by coming home early and announcing that she was bringing me along to the American embassy with her. There, I would see the biggest flag I had ever seen, maybe, even, the biggest in the world, for all she knew, hanging over a staircase and that I would meet a man who had lived in Hollywood, where they made movies, and where he had, actually, appeared in cowboy films.

I had been sitting at the table, writing down a parody on a patriotic Polish hymn that I had thought up on the bus. It poured scorn on a certain Polish government leader, generally believed to be responsible for Poland's lack of preparedness for the Nazi invasion, and produced an acidity in my mouth that gave some welcome relief to the mass of my mood. I was quite aware of this effect and, when I heard Mother's proposition, became aware of a certain curiosity. It was, definitely, not curiosity to see the huge flag or the former cowboy actor, but curiosity over how, seeing the cowboy with my own eyes, would affect me. It seems that I had stepped outside of myself and was, now, observing my own responses, in this strange, disinterested state that possessed me.

The American flag, hanging over the staircase, was, indeed, huge, but seemed to have no affect on my emotions. As for the cowboy actor, we were, actually on our way back down the stairs when I reminded Mother of her promise.

"Yes, yes, I forgot," she said, stopping on the stairs and starting back up. We walked back down the hall that we had passed along a few moments ago and finally stopped at an open door to a room in which several men, in shirtsleeves, worked behind identical metal desks.

"Do you see that blond man at the second desk by the window?" Mother whispered. "No, no, don't point. Just look."

He had on an unbuttoned, brown, pinstriped vest, as he bent over a typewriter. "That's him," Mother whispered. "He used to wear a cowboy hat and ride a horse, shoot a gun, throw a lasso, and all those things in movies."

I didn't think he saw us looking at him. But I wondered why anyone who had done all those things would want to stop and operate a typewriter in an office. And then I wondered whether he really was who Mother said he was, or whether she had just made the whole thing up to get me to come with her. In the few months that Mother and I had been together, I had learned that Mother was just as likely to make up a story as to tell the truth. Before our escape, while dealing with the military authorities she had said that my father was a senator, that her own father was a general, that I was sickly, and that she had been a teacher of French. She had done this in order for us to survive, and I appreciated that now, though I hadn't then. But then, in Hungary and later in Yugoslavia, when she didn't like my behavior, she had told me that there was a ship in the harbor that was picking up all the Jewish children to take them to safety in Palestine, and that she was going to put me on that ship. The first time she said it, I found it hard to believe that she would do that, and the next time I was certain it wasn't true. But the idea of being put on that ship with all those other children was so horrible to contemplate that I would put my arms around her neck and promise to behave, just to stop her drawing the image.

It was too early for supper, when we came out of the embassy, and Mother suggested that we walk back, instead of taking a bus. The exercise would do us both good. We walked leisurely past stores, offices, and restaurants, looking in display windows. "Would you like to see me wearing that on my head?" Mother suddenly asked, pointing to an outrageous feathered entity on a stand in a hatter's window. Kiki and I had used to laugh at hats that we considered outlandish, both in store windows and on women's heads, and Mother's keying into this familiar game gave me a very warm feeling. I found myself laughing, and Mother laughed with me.

The next window held office equipment, and I pointed to a calculator, with its long handle and rows of buttons, and asked, "Would you like to see me wearing *that* on my head?" and we both laughed again. Then we were both looking for something else to make a joke about, until Mother pointed to a plate of simulated meat and vegetables in a restaurant display. "Now Yulian, you must eat every one of your vegetables before you can get up from the table," she said, in a mockery of her own stern tone.

Mother had never done that before. She had never made fun of her own self, and now she had just lifted the entire weight that I had been carrying, right off my shoulders. Suddenly, I was laughing and happy, as I could not remember having been before. Suddenly, I was feeling about my mother as I had never felt about her before. Impulsively, I took Mother's hand, and we both stepped, with long strides, around the restaurant's railed sidewalk seating area. Except that the sight of the food display had made me hungry. It was the first time I had felt hunger for quite a while.

Suddenly, we heard a woman's voice shouting in the unmistakable, sibilant, clipped tone of the Polish language. I remember recognizing the tone before comprehending the words. And those were, "Mrs. Basia! Mrs. Beautiful Basia!"

I turned immediately toward the caller, dropping Mother's hand in the process. Mother didn't turn immediately. She stood there for a moment, as though deciding whether it was she being addressed.

A woman was standing at one of the tables, waving her hand, and repeating the exclamation. "Mrs. Basia! Mrs. Beautiful Basia from Warsaw!" A man was sitting at the table with her.

Mother turned slowly to face the woman. She shaded her eyes from the sun, with her hand. Then, hesitantly, almost reluctantly, she began to walk back, towards the restaurant.

"Fela," the woman prompted, "Fela Brodnik and my husband Bolek from Marszalkowska Street, *please missus*." She used the awkward, formal form of address as, we approached. She was older than Mother and much heavier, with graying dark hair. The couple had drinks on the glass-topped table.

Mother's face turned into a smile. "Of course, Mrs. Brodnik. Missus was a friend of Christina Pjasienski, am I right?"

They were shaking hands at this point. "Yes, but poor Christina is still in Warsaw....if she's alive at all."

Mother's face changed instantly. "So many people have been lost," she said.

"But we've heard of what missus did," the man said, "carrying your son on your back, over the Carpathian Mountains."

Mother had, certainly, not carried me. Mother couldn't even lift me. But I had heard our story distorted in that direction before.

"The whole Polish community, here in Rio, knows about what missus did," the woman said. "We were all hoping that one of us would run into missus, and we did. So many Polish people come to Rio."

"We hope to be in America soon," Mother said.

"Missus has a visa?"

"Yes, I have a friend with the Polish embassy in Washington. But we're waiting for an entry permit."

"Missus is fortunate."

"Michael Kwapiszewsi—maybe missus knows him. He's from Warsaw."

"I know the name, please missus," the man said. "But missus has had such an adventure."

"Life under the Bolsheviks was unbearable," Mother said. "They were so cruel. But, fortunately, they were also stupid."

"We were in Belgrade when it all began," the man said. He looked older than his wife.

"We knew something was going to happen, please missus, and, when Bolek had to go to Belgrade on business, I insisted on going with him," the woman said.

"But, please missus, missus should sit down," her husband said.

"Yes, please missus," the woman said. "Please, please."

"Well, only for a moment. It's late, and my son must have his supper."

"What is your son's name?" Mr. Brodnik asked.

"He is Yulian. Shake hands with Mr. Brodnik, Yulian."

I shook hands with the man, as Mother sat down. Then I walked around to the empty chair and sat down as well. I hoped we would end up eating something here, instead of at the hotel, particularly now that my appetite seemed to be back.

"Missus must tell us her story," the man said, "but first, how about a small vodka?"

"No, no. No thank you, mister."

"A sherry, perhaps?"

"No, please mister, nothing thank you."

"Some hot chocolate for the boy?"

"Yes, he would like that."

Hot chocolate probably meant that we wouldn't be eating supper here, but I liked hot chocolate. Mr. Brodnik called the waiter over and ordered one for me. "Now, please missus, from the beginning." He pulled his chair a little closer to the table. "A cigarette?"

Mother took a cigarette from the pack he offered and let Mr. Brodnik light it for her. "Well, I was in Durnoval," she began, "with my sister-in-law, Edna Tishman and *her* sister-in-law, Paula Herbstein—perhaps mister and missus know them—and their two children, when the Bolsheviks came, and we were living in a hovel, sleeping on the floor, standing in long lines to buy food, the children with legs like matchsticks and sick all the time. We, mothers, couldn't bear to look at them."

Mother had left out the fact that Sonia's governess, Miss Bronia was with us as well, and that it was Miss Bronia who did all the cooking and the sewing, and took care of me when I was upset about my separation from Kiki. I knew that Mother hadn't forgotten about Miss Bronia, but that her story sounded better if it looked as though she and my aunts did everything. She had also said that we were in Durnoval when the Russians came, which wasn't true either, since we were on the farm at that time and didn't get to Durnoval until a few days later, but that was all right, since it didn't make any difference to the story except simplify the telling of it.

And I also understood Mother's not correcting Mr. Brodnik when he thought Mother had carried me on her back, over the mountains. That was just the way Mother was.

Mother went on to tell about the commissar who, she laughingly said, fell in love with her and offered to marry her and teach her to drive a tractor on his parents' collective farm, which Mr. and Mrs. Brodnik laughed at a little, as well, and then about the hired guide who was supposed to carry me over the mountain, but abandoned us. She did not, specifically, say that she carried me, which was probably because I was sitting there, but neither did she say anything to suggest that she didn't. She also said that I fell into the stream, and she had to pull me out, which was totally untrue as well, but she had told it that way so many times, that she probably believed it. I turned my attention to counting the iron pipes that held the awning over our heads and noticing how they were joined together so that the awning could be retracted.

Then a man whom the Brodniks knew, but mother didn't, stopped by, and Mrs. Brodnik told him that this was Beautiful

Basia from Warsaw, who had escaped from the Bolsheviks, on foot, over the Carpathian Mountains that February and was just in the middle of telling her story.

The man said that, yes, he had heard about the escape and was so glad to meet Mother in person, and wanted to hear her story. He pulled up a chair from another table, and sat down to listen. He was a small man, older than the Brodniks, with a large head of gray hair that needed a barber, thick, gray eyebrows, and stained fingertips. The fingers on his left hand were yellow from cigarettes; the ones on his right were stained black. He had on a very old brown suit that someone had mended, and he kept shrugging his shoulders, as though he were cold and trying to wrap the jacket around himself. His stained fingers kept drumming on the table. The longer that he sat there, the faster the drumming became until, finally, after listening for only a few minutes, he got up, explained that he had to go, kissed the ladies' hands, and left.

Mrs. Brodnik explained that he had been a journalist in Poland, but, not knowing Portuguese, he had only been able to get a job as a printer's assistant here in Rio. He earned very little money, and his wife had hanged herself in the stairwell of their apartment building a few months earlier. I felt terrible sadness for the poor man and for his dead wife and wondered whether she had hanged herself because she didn't want to live in poverty or whether she did it so that he wouldn't have to share his small salary with her. I didn't know which I should hope for it to have been. If it was the first, she had done something very selfish and very cruel to her husband. If it was the second, then it was so terribly, terribly noble and sad.

I shuddered at the thought, and Mrs. Brodnik said, "Oh, the boy is cold," which wasn't true. "Bolek, give him your jacket."

Mr. Brodnik stood up immediately and removed his jacket.

"I... am n... ot c... old," I protested. I didn't like the idea of wearing the man's jacket.

"Put it over his shoulders," Mrs. Brodnik instructed, and her husband draped it over me. I really, really didn't like wearing his jacket, even just draped over my shoulders. I didn't know why. I wouldn't have minded wearing Irenka's jacket, but I realized that I wouldn't have liked Sr. Segiera's jacket or Andre's either. I tucked my elbows close to my sides to make as little contact with the material as possible.

Mother had finished telling her story, but the Brodniks had questions. "The boy needs something to eat," Mrs. Brodnik then said.

"Yes," Mr. Brodnik agreed and called the waiter over. He ordered me a ham sandwich.

"Can he eat a ham sandwich, please missus?" Mrs. Brodnik asked Mother, and Mother told her that I liked ham.

I wondered whether the Brodniks knew we were Jewish. Would they be so nice to us if they knew? I recalled hearing a conversation between Kiki and my cousin Fredek's governess, in which Fredek's governess said about somebody, "But he isn't Polish—he's a Jew." Then I wasn't really Polish either. Jewish was a religion, like Catholicism, not a nationality. Kiki had been Catholic *and* Polish, but I was just Jewish. So in America, I wouldn't be American either, but just Jewish—exactly the same as I was now.

Then the waiter brought me the ham sandwich, but I wasn't hungry anymore.

I worked at the sandwich, because I didn't want to hurt Mr. Brodnik's feelings, while Mother was still answering the Brodniks' questions, and the Brodniks were telling Mother who, of her Warsaw acquaintances, might be in Rio. Then Mrs. Brodnik asked Mother if she could come back in two days and tell the story all over again to the other Polish people in Rio. She would get the word out tomorrow, and anyone who wanted to hear it would come to this restaurant, which was also a café and a regular meeting place for Polish people.

Mother said she would be happy to, and they agreed on a time. Mother made me thank Mr. Brodnik for the use of his jacket and for the sandwich, and we walked back to our hotel.


I didn't want to go back to the restaurant/café with Mother, two days later, but she said that I had to. The walk would be good for my appetite. And she also said that it was perfectly all right for me to speak among the Polish people. Back in Portugal, Mother had told me that I should speak as little as possible, when we were with other people, supposedly so I wouldn't say anything that might alert any German spies to our presence. We had been told by a man from the Polish embassy in Budapest that the Nazis did not want us to reach America, where Mother planned to write her book. But I knew that the real reason that Mother did not want me to speak in front of other people was because of my stammer. And the real reason why she said it was all right for me to speak in front of the Polish people was because my stammer was going to be a part of her story.

So I went and saw fourteen people, including the Brodniks, sitting around some tables that had been pushed together, and all the people stood up and applauded as we walked into the café area.

Mother hugged some of the people, she cried a few times, laughed once, and both laughed and cried at the same time once. All this took some time, and I suddenly felt a pair of woman's arms around my neck. Turning around, I found myself looking up at a woman I did not recognize.

"Little *Yulechek*," she said, using the extreme diminutive of my name, "you don't remember me, do you?"

"N... o, p... lease m... issus," I said.

"You and your governess came to our apartment, one time when our little grandson, Yanechek was staying with us, and you played t....t...." Suddenly she was crying. She hugged me tight to her large chest, having to bend over to do so.

I understood that something must have happened to her grandson, in the war, or maybe she just didn't know what had become of him, and this was terribly sad, and I wished there was something I could say to comfort her. I raised up on tiptoe so that, at least, she wouldn't have to bend as far.

"I'm sorry," she said, between sobs. "I'm so glad you and your beautiful mother got out all right. Will you sit beside me?"

It didn't much matter to me where I sat, and if it gave this woman comfort for me to sit beside her, that was the least I could do. I nodded my head.

"Here, you sit here," she said, pulling out a chair, "and I'll sit here."

I sat down. The others were still standing and talking.

"Would you like something to eat or drink? Maybe some ice cream?"

I wasn't interested in ice cream, but even if I had been, I couldn't take anything from this poor woman who had lost so much. "N...o th...ank y...ou, p....lease m...issus," I said. .

"Oh, you poor, poor boy!" she exclaimed. "What has happened to you? You didn't speak like that in Warsaw. What did the Bolsheviks do to you?"

I shook my head. "It w...asn't th...e B...olsh...eviks, p...lease m...issus. I d...id s...omething b...ad in H...ungary."

"Something bad? What are you talking about? Who told you that you did something bad? How could you do something bad? Nonsense! I will talk with your mother."

Mother was just starting to tell our story again, and the woman stopped talking aloud. "When she is finished," she whispered, "I will have a talk with her."

Mother was telling about driving out of Warsaw, during the bombing, in the back of the truck that was from my stepfather,

Lolek's factory, in the middle of the night. I felt the woman's hand reach for mine. Of course I let her hold it, though it was a little awkward, with my arm against the wrought iron arm of her chair. She bent down to me, "Wouldn't you like a nice cup of hot chocolate?" she whispered.

I remembered the chocolate from the other evening, and I had enjoyed it. But I couldn't accept it. I made a huge effort to say, "No thank you," without either stuttering, or dragging the sounds out, because of how it upset her, and pretty well succeeded.

But the woman shook her head with a sad expression on her face, and I realized that my refusal was upsetting her. Maybe I should have accepted. Maybe my accepting her offering would actually make her happy. Maybe my accepting would not be taking something away from her, but, actually, doing something *for* her. I resolved to say, yes, to her next offer.

A few minutes later, the woman leaned down to me again and whispered an offer of tea. I accepted, and soon two cups and a little pot of tea were placed in front of us. My tea needed sugar, and the sugar was out of my reach. But my table companion seemed to be quite relaxed now and involved in Mother's story, and I wouldn't have disturbed her for anything in the world.


I had been hoping that Irenka, preferably without Mr. K., would be at the café as well, since she was also Polish, but I did not see her. Following school, the next day, I went to tell Irenka about the cafe, and that it was a meeting place for Polish people, since she seemed to be alone a lot of the time now. There was no answer to my knock, which surprised me because that had never happened before. Irenka had been there every other time I had knocked, and, now, I was very disappointed. But as I turned to head back up the stairs, the elevator door opened, and Irenka stepped out.

"You were coming to visit me," she said.

"Y… es. I w… anted to t… ell you s… ometh.…ing."

"Oh, what would that be?" she asked, but I could tell by her tone that her mind was elsewhere.

"I'll t… ell you wh… en we g… et i… nside."

"Oh, I can't let you come in. Tadek is very sick, and I wouldn't want you to become infected. Your mother would kill me. Tell me out here or save it for another time."

"Wh… at does he h… ave?"

"Oh, the doctor has some long name for it, that I never heard of."

So I told her about the café being a place where Polish people went, and she might meet some friends there, the way Mother did, but I didn't want to go into the details of Mother's story telling, standing out there in the hall. Irenka thanked me, and then shooed me up the stairs, before she would unlock her door. If it had been all right to wish for Mr. K. to get sick enough to die, I think I would have done so.

Apparently, Sr. O'Brien, Andre, kept asking Mother to go out places with him, because she would come home, sigh, roll her eyes, and tell me that *he* had asked her out again. I didn't see what Mother's problem was. Sure, Andre was different from Sr. Segiera, but that did not make him bad. He took us out to eat and told funny stories, which Mother did laugh at.

Once every two weeks or so, Mother would accept his invitation, though he asked her more often than that. Each time she would tell me that it was only because she didn't want to spoil her relationship with Andre's mother. Then she would, always, bring me along.

Since Andre was very rich and, also, the son of her employer, I doubted that my presence was really for the purpose of guarding

Mother's diamonds. Mother would usually explain my presence, to him by saying something to the effect of my being very delicate and that, with what I had been through, I could not be left alone. She also explained my stutter to him as the result of our scary escape over the Carpathian Mountains into Hungary, evidently forgetting that, earlier, she had said it was due to malnutrition. Neither explanation was, of course, true, since I didn't begin stuttering till we left Hungary for Yugoslavia. But accustomed, by now, to being represented as either physically or emotionally delicate, I did not raise an objection.

I had never heard Mother explaining me that way to Sr. Segiera. Of course, Mother and Sr. Segiera did a lot of talking that was out of my earshot. They went out without me a lot of the time, and, even when I was along, they would often put their heads close together and talk in low voices, I supposed about things that I would have no interest in.

It was funny, but Sr. Segiera didn't tell jokes, the way Andre told jokes, some of which I could tell were intended to amuse me, and he didn't allow me to call him by his first name, and he usually took us out in his old Chevrolet, rather than his chauffeur-driven Lincoln Continental, but I really liked Sr. Segiera better, as, I was sure, Mother did too.

One time, I noticed, with some amusement, that Sr. Segiera's fingernails had all grown to the length that Mother prescribed for gentlemen. On the other hand, I also realized, that Mother no longer smoked in his presence.


One time, when Sr. Segiera had to fly to the "interior" again, Mother said that Andre was taking us for a motorboat ride. Now, I knew that that should have gotten me excited. Back in Poland, last summer, Kiki and I would watch the long motorboats skimming along the water, and I would long to be in the cockpit of one of them, cutting through the water with the wind blowing around me and the waves swishing by. But, right now, nothing excited me, including the prospect of a motorboat ride.

Mother had, evidently, picked up on my mood, as we waited for Andre to arrive. "It's a motorboat ride to an island," she said. "You'll love it." And as we rode down the elevator, she coaxed, "A big smile now. You know, if you think you're going to have fun, you will."

That was a ridiculous thing to say, and as we bumped along the wave-tops, Mother turned in the front seat, holding the kerchief around her hair, and said in Polish, "If you embarrass me today with that long face of yours, when Sr. O'Brien is trying so hard to entertain us, you will be very sorry. Just pretend you are having a good time. Look at me—I have a smile on my face. What does a smile cost? It costs nothing."

And, here, she was right—a smile did cost nothing—but, somehow, I could not form my face into a smile, even if I had wanted to. Instead, I pressed my lips tightly together, and Mother turned away with an angry shake of the head. "I don't know what's wrong with him," she shouted to Andre, above the noise. "He's been like this for weeks now. I've taken him to the doctor, and there's nothing wrong with him. He's just decided that he's going to give me a hard time."

"Well, you know, Barbara, that's how boys are," Andre said.

And then, I suppose maybe out of habit, and forgetting that I had learned to speak French in the last few months, she said, "I don't know what I'm going to do with him anymore. He's not like other children. The school principal tells me he doesn't play with the children in school. He's gotten into fights, knocked another boy down, and come home with skinned knees. He has no appreciation for all I've done for him. And then he does this just to upset me."

And later that day, as we sat on the island, having watched a Negro man, dressed only in shorts, tie his two ankles together and climb a palm tree, to throw coconuts down for us, and I had a little glass of cocoanut milk sitting in front of me, that I didn't want to drink, Mother whispered to me, "Andre has just told me that the ship that picks up Jewish children to take to Palestine is in the harbor, right now. We can take you to the ship straight from here." It was a familiar ploy, but, even though I knew she was lying, the mere idea of it had always been very painful for me. "You'll never see me again," she continued, as she had on other occasions, knowing how that would upset me, "but you'll be able to play with all the other children."

She had first said it in Budapest, where there were ships tied up in the Danube and in Dubrovnik, which was right on the Adriatic Sea and in Barcelona on the Mediterranean, and even in Madrid, where there was no harbor.

I knew how to put a stop to it. In the past, I had to put my arms around her neck and told her that I loved her and didn't want to be away from her. Even though I knew that there was no ship, I would do that, and we would be done with it. This time, however, there was no force in the world that could make me perform that charade. "Go ahead," I said, turning my back to her. I immediately regretted turning my back because I couldn't see the expression on her face. But I didn't hear her say anything more.

On the way back from the island, Andre made the boat go really fast, with its bow out of the water and banging against each wave. Mother held the kerchief around her head with one hand, clutching the side of the cockpit with the other, with her teeth clenched, but still smiling every time Andre turned to look at her. And, for the first time that day, I found something to smile about.

Sr. Segiera was away, all that next week, and I suggested to Mother that we go to that café, when she comes home from work, because she might meet more of her Warsaw friends. My real reason was that the ham sandwich I had had there the first time was a lot better than the food they served at the hotel. I could munch it, while the grownups talked, and she would not be urging me to eat. Mother agreed, and we did meet a couple there that Mother knew from Warsaw. They also had American visas and were waiting for their turn to be allowed in. The man and woman had left Poland just before the war began, because they were sure it was coming, and had arrived in Brazil some months before we did. The only news they were able to give Mother about what had become of mutual friends was the report that one of those friends had been arrested by the Nazis and sent to a concentration camp. This made Mother cry, and it made me feel guilty about my ham sandwich. If I had been willing to put up with hotel food, Mother would not have learned about her friend. I did not suggest going there again.

That Saturday, Sr. Segiera was back from the interior, and Mother informed me that the following day, Sunday, the senhor would be taking us to the country to meet his mother and his son, Paolo.

I wasn't thrilled by the news regarding his son. If he paid attention to me at all, he would want to wrestle and prove that he was stronger than me, or race, in which case I would win and he would be angry, or play some sort of game where I had to be the bad guy and get punished in the end for being bad. Or he would have some friends with him and they would make fun of the fact that I couldn't speak much Portuguese or didn't know any of their games. Or I might just hurt someone again.

But then, Mother sat me down on my bed and explained that I had to be very nice to Paolo because he was crippled and couldn't walk. She said that he had been in a car accident two years ago, in which his mother was killed and his legs got all smashed up.

I had known two people who couldn't walk. One was my grandfather, who had been very old and paralyzed from the waist down, and I always had to be very quiet around him. The other was my Uncle Mortikai, who had only one leg, and I was told to feel sorry for him and be extra nice to him, bring things to him and so on, to compensate for his loss. And, of course, you weren't supposed to look at a crippled person's deformity, or whatever, or to ask questions about it, but just act as though they were completely normal—but, at the same time, feel very sorry for them because they weren't, and, of course, be extra nice to them.

The next morning, Sr. Segiera picked us up again, in his old Chevrolet, to drive into the country. On the way down to meet him, Mother asked me why I wasn't bringing my airplane. I hadn't brought it because I didn't want it to get damaged and had no plans to ever fly it again, but I knew that Sr. Segiera wouldn't approve of that, so, instead, I said that I didn't want Paolo to feel bad by running after it, when he couldn't, and Mother stroked my head affectionately.

It was a long and boring ride. Mother said to look at the beautiful mountains, and to think about the good time I was going to have, playing with Paolo, but mountains didn't interest me, and I dreaded the idea of having to play with a crippled boy, whom I didn't know, and in a language I wasn't all that comfortable with. When Sr. Segiera finally tooted his horn as we pulled into the driveway of a small house, I felt an immediate tension at the prospect of the imminent meeting.

Before we could get out of the car, a woman, whom I immediately recognized as the senhor's mother came out of a side door and hurried towards us. She had the same black hair as Sr. Segiera, except parted in the middle and pulled severely back, the same thick eyebrows, and the same longish face. As she ran towards us, Sr. Segiera walked around the car and was helping Mother get out. Then he and his mother put their arms around each other and hugged.

I was just wondering whether the crippled Paolo was able to come outside, when I saw him wheeling around from the back of the house, in his wheelchair. He almost bumped into his grandmother's legs, as he released the big wheels on his chair and raised his arms toward the senhor, before the chair stopped rolling, and insisted on being hugged as well—in what I thought was a shocking breach of courtesy. Sr. Segiera immediately released his mother and lifted the ill-mannered boy right out of his wheelchair, wrapping his arms around him in a big hug. Suddenly, I was overcome by a great envy. No one had ever swept me up off the ground and into their arms, like that. But I satisfied myself by feeling sorry for the grandmother, as she had to step to the side, while that went on, and turn to shake hands with my mother, without her son introducing them.

Sr. Segiera tossed his son up into the air and caught him several times. Paolo was laughing, I supposed at the way that he had succeeded in pushing his grandmother aside for his father's attention, or, maybe because he could see my envy showing on my face. I was very surprised that the senhor and his mother permitted such rude behavior. More importantly, I was concerned how I was going to fare, for the rest of our visit, at the hands of this aggressive and self-centered playmate.

Then, still holding his son with one arm, the senhor turned to, finally, introduce my mother to his own, speaking slowly in Portuguese. Then, he introduced Mother to Paolo, and I heard Mother say, "Oh, he is so sweet." And, finally, the senhor reached his free arm out to place his hand on my shoulder. With Paolo still against his chest, Sr. Segiera's hand on my shoulder felt very differently than it had that day at the beach. "Paolo, this is *Julio*," he said, using the Portuguese pronunciation of my name and still speaking quite slowly and distinctly, "Julio, this is my very big son Paolo."

As far as I could tell, Paolo was no bigger than me. He had, the same dark hair as his father and grandmother, but a rounder face. He reached his hand out, from the perch on his father's arm, and we shook hands, while I worried how firmly it was safe to grip his.

Then the senhor said, "Paolo, Julio is new in Brazil. He and his mother used to live in Poland when the war—that you know about—began last year. When the Bolsheviks occupied where they were staying, Julio and his mother did a very courageous thing and escaped over the mountains."

I could not help feeling a little better after that introduction.

"Julio is still learning to speak Portuguese," Sr. Segiera continued, "so you'll have to speak slowly and clearly to him. So why don't you go and show him your room now." And he carefully set the boy back down in his wheelchair.

Gripping the two big wheels of his chair in his hands, Paolo pulled them in opposite directions, and the chair spun right around. Without a word to me, my host began wheeling back towards the back of the house, at a speed which would have required my running, if I had had any interest in keeping up-which I didn't. I finally caught up to Paolo, as he had to slow down for the slope of the wooden ramp that led to the back door of the house.

I wondered if I was expected to push the wheelchair up the incline. But he reached the door without my help, and we were in the kitchen.

I followed Paolo's rush through the house until we reached what I immediately recognized as his room. There was a photograph on the wall of someone kicking a soccer ball and another of his father, in a big cowboy hat, riding a horse, and I immediately felt that tang of jealousy again, as I thought of the only photograph I had of my own, late father, which was just the head of a balding man, wearing a tie. And, on one wall, there was a photograph of the same airplane that was in the picture the senhor had given me, except that the door was open, and Paolo was sitting inside.

Then I noticed a shelf full of books with brightly colored covers, something black on a bureau top that must have been a camera, and the radio on the table beside his bed. I was sure Paolo never had to look very hard for ways to occupy himself. And finally, what I hadn't noticed until Paolo picked it up off his bed, was a cat. It was orangy brown, with a bright orange spot on its forehead and had been snuggled up against a pillow, looking like a stuffed toy. But it turned its head to lick its side, as Paolo held it in his arms.

"Her name is Lila," he said, enunciating very slowly and holding her towards me.

Evidently, he wanted me to hold her, and that totally surprised me. I had never held a cat before, but more than that, I had not been expecting any gesture of that sort from my host.

I reached out with my hands and, carefully, received her. She was a lot lighter than I had thought, and I had no idea an animal could be that soft. I cradled her in the crook of my elbow, like a baby. I stroked her head with my free hand, but Lila seemed to ignore my caress and took this as an opportunity to lick her own belly. Suddenly, I found myself laughing at this, and Paolo began to laugh as well.

I would have been happy to just sit in a corner and stroke Lila all day, but saw that Paolo had taken a box off a shelf and looked as though he was waiting to show it to me. It was a flat, wooden box, about the proportions of a cigar box, but several times bigger. It had some abstract design painted on the cover and sides.

I went to hand the cat back to him.

"Just drop her," he said.

I wasn't sure that I had understood correctly.

Paolo must have noticed the look of uncertainty on my face, because he laughed and repeated the statement. He accompanied his words with a gesture of releasing something to drop to the floor.

Carefully, I did as directed. Lila landed, lightly and noiselessly, front paws hitting first, and immediately proceeded to continue her grooming. I could not help laughing again, and my host, again, found it funny as well.

Then he took the cover off the box. Inside there was a series of compartments, separated by wooden partitions. At first I couldn't understand what the unrelated objects in the compartments were all about. One was a very pretty seashell, another, an even prettier butterfly. There was a long, curved tooth and a piece of flat, triangular rock with sharp edges. Then I realized that this must be a collection of things Paolo had found.

My scan of the collection was suddenly stopped by an eye, looking at me out of one of the compartments. I had heard of people who had lost an eye having it replaced with a glass one, and I guessed that that was what I was looking at—and what was looking at me—and immediately wondered how Paolo had come into possession of such an object. Paolo saw me looking at it, said something I didn't understand, and laughed. I laughed too. It really hadn't occurred to me that the eye was funny, but I was beginning to like Paolo.

Then Paolo said something quickly, which I didn't understand, and wheeled himself back towards the door. I would have preferred to hold Lila some more—she was back up on the bed, now, snuggling against the pillow where we had found her—but Paolo was already wheeling himself out of the room, and I had to run to keep up.

In the back yard, there was now the smell of meat cooking, and I could see the three adults standing beside a little stone chimney, that stood right on the ground, with smoke coming out of it. I had never seen a chimney like that and assumed there was an underground room below it, like the root cellar I had seen on the farm in Poland, before our escape. But Sra. Segiera was, apparently, cooking something right on that chimney. Nor had I ever seen anyone cooking out of doors. But the senhora had a kind of paintbrush in her hand, and she was brushing something onto a piece of meat, as they talked. But I didn't get much chance to examine this more closely, because Paolo wheeled right through the back yard, to where a path had been cut through the high vegetation under the trees. The path twisted and turned to get around trees and to avoid upgrades and downgrades. I understood that it must have been made especially for Paolo's wheelchair.

The wheelchair could not move as fast here, as it had before, and I was able to keep up at a walk. Then, suddenly, we were at the edge of a stream. Somebody had built a square wooden deck, about the size of a small room, out over the water, with a railing around three sides. Paolo wheeled out onto this platform, rolling right to the railing at the far end. He motioned for me to come to the railing with him. I saw him lean forward and look into the water and looked down as well. Paolo didn't seem to find what he was looking for and wheeled to his right along the railing. "There he is!" he finally said, pointing down into the water. I looked down too and saw sand and rocks under the water. There were some green plants growing around the rocks and wiggling in the slight current. And then I saw a fish.

I had never seen a fish in the water before. Except before the war, when Marta, our cook would bring a live fish home from the market and put it in the bathtub until it was time to cook it. But here was a fish, about the size of a man's shoe, standing still, next to a rock, his mouth and his gills opening and closing.

Paolo said, "His name is Pedro," and I was about to ask how he knew that, when I realized that Paolo must have named him that, himself. Then he said, "Some day I'm going to catch him and eat him," or something close to that.

Then Paolo turned towards me and put his finger up to his lips, as though for silence. Except that I wasn't saying anything. He lowered his face in a mysterious look, and with his finger still to his lips, looked left and right. I got the impression that he was about to tell me a secret, which I wasn't supposed to repeat to anyone. Then, using his hands, he pulled each of his feet off the chair's footrests and lowered them to the deck.

Again, he raised his finger to his lips and swung his eyes left and right. Finally, he put his hands on the railing and pulled himself up to a standing position. Balancing himself carefully, he lifted his hands an inch or so above the railing. I saw him totter there, and held my breath. Then, as he began to lose his balance, he grabbed the railing again and dropped into his chair.

And, smiling this time, Paolo put his finger up to his lips again, in a sign that I clearly understood now. I nodded my head, assuring him that I would keep our secret.

# CHAPTER XI

RIDING HOME IN THE DARK, I was physically tired, for the fist time in a long time, from all of the time that Paolo and I had spent outside. We had played catch with a rubber ball, that I was very careful to throw within Paolo's reach, and which he caught with one hand, every time that it *was* within his reach. I, on the other hand, trying to catch the ball with both hands, had it bounce off my hands, much of the time, producing laughter from Paolo, as I chased it across the yard.

Mother and Sr. Segiera were whispering, in the front seat, probably thinking that I must be asleep. When we had first gotten into the car, I had heard Mother praise Paolo for how well he dealt with his affliction, how cheerful and active he was—words that I supposed I was meant to overhear. Now they were whispering. But I was far from asleep. I was going over my day with Paolo and longing deeply to have a life like his—a cat to sleep on my bed, a fish I could name—while I schemed to catch and eat it—a secret to share with friends, a father who rode horses and picked me up and hugged me. And I longed for a disability that I could deal with. I appreciated how difficult it must have been for Paolo to learn to stand on his crippled legs, and I longed for something in my life that I could devote energy to overcoming.

I did, of course, have my stutter, but there was no way, that I knew of, of overcoming it. It wasn't something that I could secretly practice a little bit of, and then an imperceptible bit more the next day, and the day after that, and the day after that, until those imperceptible bits added up to a difference that I could surprise somebody with. It wasn't so much for the praise. Even if, for some strange reason, I couldn't show it to anyone, I would still know that I had done it.

I wrapped my arms around myself, closed my eyes very, very tight, and longed for a wheelchair that I could teach myself to whip around the way Paolo did and to practice standing up out of, as he had learned to do.

My thoughts were interrupted by a deep purring sound, and I opened my eyes. Sr. Segiera had his right arm around Mother's shoulders, and she was nibbling his ear. The sound, I presumed, had been an expression of satisfaction from the senhor about having his ear nibbled. Mother gave a little, throaty laugh.


I heard Sr. Segiera whisper to Mother that he would carry me inside, but I let them know that I was awake. "Thank Sr. Segiera," Mother said to me, and I extended my hand from the back seat and stammered out a *thank-you*. Mother leaned toward Sr. Segiera's cheek with puckered lips, but he wrapped both arms around Mother's chest and pulled her to him. Mother resisted just a little, and they kissed just like they do in the movies. Embarrassed, I opened my door, and walked across the sidewalk into the hotel.

Then, as I walked into the single-story addition that was the hotel lobby, there sat Irenka, in an armchair, a red suitcase and a carton on the floor beside her. She was wearing sunglasses, and stood up as soon as she saw me. But she headed not to me, only towards Mother, and burst into tears before she reached her. She was considerably taller than Mother, but Mother put her two hands on Irenka's shoulders, as though to keep her from falling down.

I watched Irenka telling Mother something, though I was too far away to hear much of anything. I did hear her address Mother with, "Please Missus," in several places, and I saw Mother maneuver her to a chair and, actually, push her into it.

"Yulian, get Mrs. Kosiewicz a cup of tea," Mother said, as she squatted in front of the, still crying, Irenka.

"Th... th... the r... r... restaurant is c... c... closed," I stammered.

"Oh my God!" Mother said, "can't you do anything? Go ask the desk clerk."

I couldn't imagine the desk clerk going into the closed-up kitchen and putting on a pot of tea, but I explained to him that Mother had asked me to ask him for a cup of tea for the lady who was crying, though I didn't know what about. He looked in Irenka's direction, then, to my surprise, said, "Yes, just a moment," and disappeared into the office.

In a while he was back with a mug, with a teabag string hanging out. I thanked him and conveyed it to where Mother was, still squatting in front of a sobbing Irenka. She was assuring the younger woman that she had a powerful friend in the government who would have Mr. K. found and arrested, that Mr. K. would not be able to hurt her again, and that all she had to do was to smile and be happy. What I would learn later, to my great delight, was that, while I was waiting for the tea, Mother had told Irenka that she could move in with us, since she had been evicted from her own suite for, long-term non-payment of hotel bills.

In the meanwhile, I stood behind Mother, holding the mug, its handle hot in my hand, waiting for her to take it from me, while Irenka, with Mother's filmy, green kerchief to her face, was saying, "Missus is so kind to me. I won't be any trouble, and I will help with Yulian and Missus' wash and Missus' hair."

Then, without turning to look at me, Mother snapped, "Oh, put it down, Yulian!" as though I had been pestering her about what to do with the tea, which I had not done.

I put the tea down on the coffee table, and Mother picked it up and handed it to Irenka. "Here, please Missus, drink this."

Irenka took the mug and brought it to her lips. "Oh, it's hot," she said.

"Then Missus should blow on it," Mother said. Then, softening her tone, she said, "Missus should just take her·time. There is no hurry. Has Missus eaten?"

Sobbing and sniffling, Irenka explained that she hadn't eaten since she had half a roll for breakfast the day before.

"Oh my God!" Mother said, using the same words and tone she used when I had done something stupid. "Yulian go and..... no, I had better do it." She got up. "You stay with Mrs. Kosiewicz," she said, then marched to the desk clerk.

I saw her asking the clerk for something, and I could see by his hand motions that he was telling her that he couldn't do whatever it was she was asking. She spoke some more, and he gestured some more, and, finally, he stopped gesturing and went into the office behind him. He was out, moments later, with a key, which he handed to Mother.

Mother now crossed the lobby and proceeded to unlock the glass dining room door. Then she was in the dining room and out of sight.

"W... what is Missus doing?" Irenka asked, Mother's green kerchief still to her face.

"I... I... I d... d... don't kn....ow," I said, trying hard to control my stutter.

I saw a light go on somewhere beyond the dining room doors, which Mother had left ajar. "I th... ink sh... e is g... ett... ing y... ou s... ometh... ing to eat," I said. Then we both waited, our eyes fixed firmly on the glass doors.

In a few minutes, Mother emerged a plate in her right hand, the left hand to her mouth. On the plate, she had a slice of bread, considerably thicker at one end than at the other, covered with an equally uneven slice of ham. On the left hand, a trickle of blood flowed down toward her wrist.

"Oh, Missus has cut herself!" Irenka exclaimed, getting quickly to her feet. From somewhere on her person she now produced a white handkerchief. Her tears gone, Irenka took hold of Mother's hand, and removed it from her mouth. "Oh, this is bad," she said, examining Mother's index finger. "We must wash it."

With Irenka still holding her hand, Mother said, "This is ridiculous. Yulian, grab Mrs. Kosiewicz's suitcase." She was trying to wrap the handkerchief around her finger, but Irenka wouldn't let her. Irenka did the wrapping and instructed Mother to hold her hand up over her head. Then she took the suitcase from me, I took the sandwich and the tea, and we all trooped to the little elevator.


That first night, I had had to sleep with Mother again, while Irenka slept in my bed. On previous occasions, when I had had to share a bed with Mother, there had been no alternative. This time, however, there was. There was no reason why it couldn't be Irenka, who slept with Mother. In Barcelona, when Mother had run into Mrs. Paniewicz, a Warsaw friend, in a café, she had invited the lady to stay with us in our hotel room and share her bed to save money. Mrs. Paniewicz had stayed with us until we left for Lisbon.

So, this time, I decided to implement a plan that I had thought of some while ago, but had had no opportunity to apply earlier. It took some courage to do this because I knew how angry Mother would become at the irritation, but when I woke up in the morning, instead of lying very still, until Mother woke up, as I was supposed to, I rolled over, shuffled my feet under the blanket, and even emitted a slight groan, all the time pretending, of course, that I was still asleep.

As I paused between moves for the sake of realism, I entertained myself with the fantasy that my action resulted in *Mother's* switching places with Irenka, for the next night. Then, Irenka and I could pull the sheet over our heads and whisper, as we had on the beach. And, if Irenka wore the kind of loose fitting nightgowns that Mother did, one of her breasts might, occasionally, slip out while she slept.


Irenka was still asleep, when Mother and I got up and I got ready for school. We tiptoed around the living room, and Mother whispered to me that Irenka had not been able to sleep for many nights, because of worries.

In school, I had a difficult time keeping my mind on the problems that Sra. Fernanda had assigned me, while my imagination created fantasy situations in which my new suite-mate became as accustomed to my presence as Mother was and allowed herself to move about the premises without positively securing her private parts.

As it turned out, my original plan did, actually, succeed, while my fantasies appeared to turn out to be exactly that—namely, fantasies. When I arrived back at our suite, Irenka was there to greet me with an apple and a piece of toast with cheese—we had not owned a toaster before, but now, we apparently did. She thanked me for the use of my bed and informed me that it was mine again, since she would be sharing Mother's bed from then on. As for the fantasies, however, I couldn't help noticing a new and more formal attitude towards me, on Irenka's part. While I could not identify any decrease in friendliness, there was something in her demeanor that shattered any expectations of increased intimacy. Evidently, she and Mother had discussed matters, and formalized certain agreements that were to govern our three-sided relationship.

Irenka had supper with us in the hotel dining room that evening. When Mother discovered that she was out of cigarettes, Irenka immediately said, "Please Missus, I will get some for you."

"This is craziness," Mother said. "We can't go around *please-Missussing* each other all day. My name is Barbara, and you're Irena."

"Oh, please Missus," Irenka said, evidently quite overcome by Mother's gesture. "Missus is so kind."

"*Barbara*," Mother said.

"*Barbara* is so kind."

In a move that gave me a deep sense of satisfaction, Mother laid her hand over Irenka's. "We will be friends, Irena, not mistress and servant," she said.

"Oh yes…, Barbara." Then she immediately got up, accepted some coins from Mother, and went out to the lobby for mother's cigarettes.


Irenka continued living with us and sleeping in Mother's bed with her. When I came home from school, there was a snack for me, even when Irenka wasn't there, herself, and, that first weekend, when Mother and Sr. Segiera went somewhere overnight, it was Irenka who went to the beach with me and to a little restaurant around the corner from the hotel, for supper. But, though, at Irenka's request, we had another French lesson, our relationship there was as different as it was at the hotel.

When Sr. Segiera came by our suite to pick Mother up for some outing, Irenka would serve him a cocktail, then keep him company, while Mother put finishing touches on her makeup in the bathroom. Because her Portuguese was much better than either Mother's or mine, she could speak to Sr. Segiera in that language. And, on the occasions that I was included in an outing with Sr. Segiera, Irenka came along as well, though she always sat in the back seat with me.

Where I had, first, been excited by Irenka's coming to live with us, I soon grew quite bored with this new arrangement. Not only had my fantasies been dashed, but I felt that I had, actually, lost a friend. Irenka had become Mother's friend, which made her ineligible to fill that special role that she had filled for me before. And with that loss, I felt myself descending again into what I now recognized as a state, for which I had no name, because the word *depressed,* or even the word *state* was not part of my vocabulary.

"What is the matter, Yulian?" Irenka would ask, when she saw me laboring over my after-school banana. In the days before she had become Mother's friend, I would, probably have made some effort to describe my feelings to her, but sharing my feelings with Irenka now, was as difficult as expressing them to Mother. I assumed that Irenka must have, later, discussed her observation with Mother, who, I was sure, had said that I was subject to such moods.


I soon realized that my moods must have been a discussion subject with Sr. Segiera, as well, because, one day, Mother informed me that, the next day, Saturday, the senhor was going to take me up in his airplane. In my head, I could hear the discussion between Mother and Sr. Segiera, as one of them suggested that what I needed was to spend more time with a man.

Some months earlier, during our few-days' stay in Rome, I had done something, which, I now recognized as very dumb. I had found my way to the roof of our hotel, from which I had thrown pebbles onto passing cars. Someone had reported it to the hotel, and a uniformed employee had caught me red-handed. Mother's reaction, when I had been turned over to her custody, was to take my act as a direct attack on her. Later I had come to understand this attitude to be quite reasonable. Italy, under Mussolini, was a Fascist country, allied with Germany, and our only reason for being there was that Mother knew the Polish ambassador, who, she hoped, could negotiate, for us, a visa to Spain or Portugal or, even, South America. But with the Nazis trying to stop us from reaching America, attracting attention to our presence in Rome, particularly by dropping pebbles on people, was not helpful to our security. Mother's response had been to tell me that, if my father were alive, he would beat me.

Months before that, in Hungary, Mother had wanted the Count, on whose estate we were staying, to teach me to hunt, and, in Spain, when Sr. Sabastian had bragged about having been a fencing champion, she had said, "Oh, I would so love for Julien to learn fencing from you."

Weeks before this proposed outing with Sr. Segiera, the prospect of flying in an airplane with him would have thrilled me beyond measure. But now, like everything else, the image of the flight as an enjoyable experience just refused to crystallize in my mind. When Sr. Segiera came to the hotel to take me to the airport, Mother told him that she had a "terrible" headache and would stay home. Since she had made no mention of the headache before his arrival, I understood that Mother had other reasons for not coming along. She did, however, ask Irenka to go, but the senhor said that, actually, nobody was coming, except him and me.

Then Mother said, "Do you really think this is a good idea, Ernesto?" and he said, "Yes, I do. Paolo has been up with me, and loved it, and I think it will be very good for Julien. He will love it too."

Mother, then, turned to me and asked, "Are you sure you want to go?"

That was a strange question, since no one had, yet, asked me whether I wanted to, in the first place. And it wasn't that I *didn't* want to—the idea just didn't excite me. But for Sr. Segiera's sake, because he had invited me, I didn't want to disappoint him, and I planned to give every sign of enjoying myself. "Yes, very much," I said, surprised to find how big an effort it took to seem excited.

Since it was just the senhor and I in the Chevrolet, on the way to the airport, I got to sit in the front seat, which, again, should have been exciting for me. Sr. Segiera was wearing the kind of faded blue pants and checkered shirt that cowboys wore in the movies. His sleeves were rolled up just to his elbows, and his forearms had more hair on them than I had seen on anyone before. "Paolo says he had a very good time with you, Julien," Sr. Segiera said. From somebody else I would have taken this as just some of the politeness that well-mannered people expressed to each other, but I could not imagine anything but the truth coming out of the senhor's mouth.

"I h... ad a v... ery g... ood time w... ith P... aolo, M... onsieur," I said. I remembered the secret that Paolo had shared with me. I wondered if the senhor knew about it. Then, for the senhor's sake, and, in a way, for Paolo's as well, I pushed on into unknown territory. "I th... ink P....aolo is v... ery b... rave, th... e way he d... oes th... ings with h... is wh... eelchair, M... onsieur," I said. I had never made that kind of statement about another boy before. It felt grown up.

"Yes, I think so too. But, I think you're also very brave, the way you struggle with your speech, Julien."

Nobody, nobody had ever said anything like that to me before. I was very embarrassed. If the senhor was expecting a verbal response, he wasn't getting any. I was much too confused.

After a minute or two, he said, "You and Paolo could be good friends, you know."

I wanted to tell him how much I agreed, but I was not about to open my mouth. I nodded my head vigorously, though I wasn't sure that he saw me.

"Paolo, you know, goes to school, just like you do. It's not a special school or anything, and the boys play football after school" he went on, "Paolo helps the teacher who's in charge of the football. Your mother tells me that you're a very fast runner."

At his mention of my running, the picture of Gustavo appeared again. I shut my eyes tight, grimaced, and shook my head in an effort to dispel it.

"What's wrong, Julien?" the senhor asked.

"N… othing, M… onsieur."

The senhor seemed satisfied by my answer. "You and Paolo can go fishing in the stream behind his house," he continued. "Paolo has a fishing pole with a reel to wind the line in, and you could have one of your own too."

What Sr. Segiera was doing was trying to make me want Mother to marry him. I would live with Paolo and his grandmother, and Mother and Sr. Segiera would come and visit us. I thought that I would like that. I nodded my head and smiled.

"And I'm sure that, after a while, your stutter would go away."

That was wonderful news.

"It's all in your mind, you know," he went on. "You have the power to make it go away, except that you, first, have to find the key to that power. Do you understand what I'm saying? There is something in your mind, something you don't understand, and I don't understand, and your mother doesn't understand, that wants you to stutter, because of something that happened to you in Hungary. But, just as soon as you figure out what that something is, you can tell it to stop. It's as simple and as complicated as that."

He laughed as he said the last sentence, and I understood that he was trying to make light of the heavy things he had just said. I made myself laugh as well, to show him that I wasn't insulted or anything by what he said.

The airport wasn't anything like what I had imagined. I had seen photographs of paved runways with giant hangars, shiny, metal, multi-engine planes and a "control tower" with a striped "windsock." This one had none of those, except for the windsock. The windsock flew from a metal pole on the side of a large, green field. At one end there stood a small, wooden hangar with the familiar curved roof and wide doors. There were a few open-cockpit airplanes to one side of the hangar, and then some that were similar to the one in the picture the senhor had given me, standing on the other. One plane was just starting to taxi away, and a man was doing something to the side of one of the others.

Sr. Segiera parked the Chevrolet near some other cars and we started walking towards the airplanes. I was pretty sure I recognized the one in the picture by the shape of its tail. It was a blue airplane. As we passed the man who was doing something to one of the planes, Sr. Segiera stopped to exchange a few words.

I saw what the man was doing. He had a large needle and thread, and he was sewing up the material that covered the side of the airplane. I was surprised—I had thought the airplane would have been all-metal, or, at least, solid wood. Looking more closely at the airplane, I could see its ribs showing as humps through the skin and realized that it must have been covered with fabric all over. I had had no idea that airplanes weren't built as solidly as cars. It sent a slight shiver up my spine. Suddenly, I wasn't at all happy about going flying.

When we walked on and approached the blue plane that I had thought was the senhor's, I had a feeling of dread. The senhor opened the door for me to look inside. It wasn't at all like the interior of a car. The seats were one in front of the other, and, instead of being upholstered, they were plain metal with cushions that didn't even look attached. The side windows were of some kind of transparent material that wasn't glass, because it was flexible and all scratched. And there wasn't even any steering wheel, only a stick in front of each seat.

The senhor told me to get in the front seat, but not to touch any of the controls. I wished I hadn't come. As I waited in the cockpit, the senhor walked all around the airplane, checking things. There were oil and gasoline smells in the airplane. Then Sr. Segiera made me pull myself up, while he slipped an extra cushion under me and one behind me, and then began strapping me in. I didn't like the feeling of being strapped in. In a moment he was sitting behind me, and he pulled the door closed. It didn't make a solid sound like a car door, but more of a slap, as though it could open again, if you leaned against it. I saw the stick in front of me moving in all four directions, and realized that it must be attached to the one in front of the senhor, and that he must be checking out the controls.

Two men had appeared at the sides of our airplane, holding lines that attached to wood blocks under the wheels. Then the engine started with a terrible noise, and the plane began to shake. "Here we go," the senhor yelled above the noise of the engine. I saw the men pull the blocks out from under the wheels. We began to roll forward. I was about to grab a little black handle on my left, but I saw it move, and realized that it was one of the controls. I knew enough not to touch the stick in front of me. I didn't know what I could hold on to.

We were bumping along on the grass now, and I wasn't feeling well at all. I had a feeling in my stomach like the one I had had on the ship one windy day. I had almost thrown up that day, but managed to keep it down. Then we were turning, and I saw a long stretch of well-worn grass ahead of us. We stopped and the engine began to roar much louder, and the airplane shook.

With a lurch, we began rolling forward again, but faster than before. We were bouncing along the grass, going faster and faster. And, suddenly, I was vomiting all over my lap and the floor.

The silly thing was that, after Sr. Segiera had slowed the plane down again, and, instead of taking off, we taxied back to the hangar, I didn't feel sick anymore. Of course, I did feel very embarrassed and angry at myself.

"Don't worry," the senhor had assured me, as he sponged me off in the bathroom. "I got sick the first time I flew too. And I was a lot older than you."

But, we had never even gotten into the air. The senhor had told Mother, earlier that day, that Paolo had actually flown with him and loved it. I doubted that the senhor considered me an adequate companion for his son now, even though he probably didn't even know that I was Jewish.

# CHAPTER XII

WHEN SR. SEGIERA BROUGHT ME HOME, I could tell by Mother's tense face and the state of the ashtrays in the room, that things had not been going well in my absence. "I don't like this," she said to the senhor. "Don't ever do this to me again!"

"He is a boy, Basia," the senhor said. "Boys need to experience these things."

"He doesn't need to experience going up in an airplane."

I noticed that Irenka was not in the room and the door to the bedroom was closed.

"Basia, please be reasonable. I wouldn't do it if it was dangerous. I've brought Paolo up."

"Because Paolo's mother is dead."

"Basia."

"I don't want to see you right now."

"I'll go home and change and pick you up."

"I don't want to see you."

"Basia, we are expected at the Salazars."

"I'm not going. Go by yourself. Say that I have a headache."

"It's you they want to meet."

"Me? He's your supervisor."

"I told him something of your story, and they want to hear it from you and to meet you."

Mother sighed. "I have to take a bath. Look at how I look. And I have no idea what to wear."

"You'll find something."

"You think it's easy?"

"Basia, I know that you're an artist about your clothes, and you work hard at making the exactly right impression. And when I get back, you will look terrific again."

"Well, don't hurry. You know it takes me a lot longer than it does you."

"I know, Basia. I'll see you in a while."

Mother got up on her tiptoes and gave the senhor a quick kiss on his closed lips. Then the senhor left, and I heard Mother say, as she passed through the bedroom, "Irenka dear, would you please iron my blue skirt and the green blouse. You know, the one with the little cuffs?" I could hear that Irenka was already filling Mother's tub. Then, later, I heard Mother say from the bathtub, "He keeps dragging me to meet these dreary, people, but, I suppose, it's important for his career, so I go."

Sr. Segiera had said nothing about my throwing up, or even about the fact that we never got off the ground. In fact, there had been nothing for Mother to be worried about. In fact, also, Mother had sounded very enthusiastic about my going up in the plane, when she mentioned it yesterday.

The senhor and I had stopped for lunch at a funny little restaurant that was open to the street, with no front wall. The senhor ordered for me, and I had a sandwich of some sort and a delicious, chocolate drink called a *milchek*. Some months later, I would learn to pronounce it *milk shake*. The senhor didn't seem the least bit angry with me. But he didn't say anything more about me and Paolo doing things together.

When Mother and Sr. Segiera came back to our suite that night, I wasn't asleep, though I pretended to be. They didn't turn the light on, but they whispered together for a minute or two, and I heard Mother giggle twice. There was a long silence, and then the senhor left.

It was two or three weeks later that I came home from school, when it was raining, and suggested to Irenka that we put on our raincoats and walk to the movies. From the bus, I had seen some new posters that showed soldiers in frilly, three-cornered hats confronting men in round, fur hats, with the animal's tail hanging from them. I recognized the outfits from a book I had had in Warsaw, and knew that the story took place in America, before they had streets and skyscrapers.

But Irenka said that we couldn't go because Mother was coming home early to take me to that café where Polish people met. She had a surprise for me.

A surprise for me at the café, meant meeting some person or persons. It could have been my aunts, Edna and Paula with Miss Bronia and my cousins, Fredek and Sonia, all of whom we had left in Durnoval before our escape. The only one of them that it would have been a pleasant surprise to see, would have been Miss Bronia. Or, maybe, Mademoiselle, who had taught me French in Lvoof. Or it could even have been my governess, Kiki!

Suddenly, I was frightened. I had changed so much since Kiki and I had parted. What would I say to her? How was I supposed to act toward her now, now that I could walk in the street by myself, buy things in stores, and had those strange, embarrassing desires regarding Irenka.

I didn't miss Kiki anymore, and I certainly didn't want to go back to our old relationship. I grew quite anxious, waiting for

Mother. I could handle the others, but I didn't want to face Kiki. But then I realized that the probability of its being any one of these people was very slight. Mother and I were the only people we knew, who had escaped from Poland after the war. And none of the people whom I was afraid of meeting was the type to go climbing the Carpathian Mountains. The only exception was my cousin, Fredek, but he was six months younger than me.

"I have a surprise for you, Yulian," Mother said, when she came home, and I could tell that she was very pleased with that fact.

"Is it Kiki?" I asked. While the odds were very small, as long as the possibility existed, I wanted to be prepared.

Mother's tone softened immediately, "No darling, it's not Kiki," she said. In an uncharacteristic gesture, she stroked my head. Evidently, she had mistaken my concern for a longing. "I have no news about Kiki. But I'm sure you'll be very excited."

All the way to the café I was trying to figure out who the surprise could possibly be. The number of people that I knew and cared about was very limited. My concentration on the question was so great that when we arrived at the café, I realized that I had, actually, been holding Mother's hand.

There were people sitting at three tables, but I didn't recognize any of them. I was relieved to see that none of them was a child. Of course, my "surprise" may not have arrived yet. We would sit at an empty table and wait for them.

But Mother did not hesitate to select a table. She led me directly toward a man and woman whom I could not imagine having ever seen before. How this could be my surprise, I could not imagine. The man stood up, as we approached. He had gray hair and a long, triangular face that ended in a narrow chin and a long, sharp nose. On one cheek, there was a large, brown spot.

"Hello Basia," the man said, and he kissed Mother's cheek.

"How are you, Yulian?" she responded.

So the man's name was Yulian. Well, that *was* a surprise, since I had never met another one, but hardly worth all that excitement. Now she was leaning down to kiss the woman.

Then she turned to introduce me. "Yulian," she said to me, "this is Yulian Tuwim."

It took absolutely no time for the name to register. Yulian Tuwim was the poet who had written the *Locomotive* poem that Kiki and I loved so much. He was a famous poet.

Mr. Tuwim had his hand out. "I'm glad to finally meet you, Yulian. You're a poet too."

Something, about what he said, struck me as odd. He had not, I realized, said anything like, *I hear,* or, *Your mother tells me.*

"Your poems are very *good*," he said, as I put my hand into his.

*He had read my poems? How did he get them?*

"I hope you'll keep on writing," he said.

"Say something to Mr. Tuwim, Yulian," Mother said.

"He does his speaking with his pen," Mr. Tuwim said, with a little laugh.

Mother laughed too, a little. "He used to have such beautiful manners, in Poland."

"He should keep writing, you know," he said to Mother.

"Oh, I'll have some of that," Mother said, pointing to the tea-pot on the table, as she sat down. The waiter went to get her a cup. "Do you think he has enough talent to become famous?" she asked Mr. Tuwim.

"Well, Basia, fame is so much a matter of chance."

"I know that. But does he have the talent?"

"He's very young still. Who knows what he'll be interested in when he gets older. He may want to build bridges."

That was all silly talk. Mother talked as though we weren't Jewish. She pretended that we weren't, which was all fine for her.

But people would find out and they wouldn't want to read my poems. Jews didn't become famous people.

The waiter brought me a *milchek*, which I must have ordered without even realizing it. The grownups were in conversation, now, about something that didn't have anything to do with me or my poems. Mother must have found my poems under my shirts, in the bureau drawer, where I had been hiding them, and given them to Mr. Tuwim some time ago. I had a hard time keeping my eyes from the big brown spot on Mr. Tuwim's cheek. I remembered the fact that I had been introduced to the man who had written the *Locomotive* poem, in our Warsaw apartment, some years ago, though I could not remember the actual event. I certainly didn't remember the brown spot on his cheek.

There was something different about Mr. Tuwim—different from other men I knew. There was a gentleness about the way he spoke, even the way he moved, that was different. He moved his hands a lot, when he spoke, but not quickly. Those hands, with their long fingers, had written *The Locomotive* and the one about the farm family trying to pull a turnip out of the ground. I would have loved to become a poet like Mr. Tuwim. I didn't need to fly airplanes or be a soldier or a cowboy, or even build bridges. I wanted to write poems that people read and loved, the way Kiki and I loved *The Locomotive,* and talk gently like Mr. Tuwim.

But I knew that would not be possible for me.


I wrote two more poems, over the next couple of weeks, and Mother promised that she would show them to Mr. Tuwim as well.

One evening, when she came home from work, Mother said to Irenka, "I think we need to go and buy you a tennis dress."

I could tell that Irenka was as surprised by this statement as I was. "I don't know how to play tennis," she said.

By the smile on Mother's face, I could tell that she was enjoying the confusion she had just created.

Then Irenka seemed to grasp something that I didn't. "Oh yes?" she said. "Your friend?"

"He wants me," Mother said, walking on into the bathroom and speaking as she went, "to go with him to the home of some friends of his for the weekend, where, he says, there will be tennis and swimming and dancing. You should like that."

Irenka followed her into the bedroom and spoke through the closed bathroom door. "It sounds like you would have a good time," she said. "Don't you want to go? And I don't know how to play tennis."

"I'm sure he'll be happy to teach you. I don't need tennis or swimming or dancing. And I just don't want to go overnight with him. I don't know what's on his mind. It would be different with you—you'll have just met. It's not exactly the meeting I had in mind, but I think it will work out fine. And I really *don't* want to go."

I guessed that they must be talking about Andre, since Irenka knew Sr. Segiera, and that there must have been a whole lot more to the conversation prior to all this, that I had missed out on.

"Would he want to bring a total stranger to his friends?" Irenka asked the same question that was on my mind.

I heard Mother come out of the bathroom. "Once he meets you," she said, "that's exactly what he'll want to do."

"No, really."

"Yes, really."

"Are you sure?"

"I'm sure."

Mother did not come out into the living room, and I guessed that she was changing her clothes. "He's a perfect gentleman, you know," I heard her say. "It's just that I've been out enough times with him now, that he's likely to be having ideas. That's how men are. The worst thing that can happen to you, is that you'll have to slap his face once. You'll have a good time. Now go fix your face."

Then somebody closed the door, and there was more talk going on, that I couldn't quite hear.

Then we were in the store and Irenka was trying on tennis dresses. She came out of the dressing room in a knee-length white dress with blue trim, shook her head, and said, "I can't do this."

"What do you mean, you can't?" Mother said. "Don't you like the dress? I don't like it either. Try another one."

Irenka shook her head again. "It's not the dress. I can't pretend."

"Pretend what?"

"You know. It was all right when Tadek and I were pretending together. He did all the talking."

"And now, Andre will do all the talking. Believe me. All you'll need to do is smile and say, *yes* and *no*."

"But I'd be lying to your friend."

"What do you mean *lying?*"

"Who I am."

"Who are you? This isn't Poland. Nobody knows who your parents are. You were brought up in a good house. You speak well—you have good manners. You're not going to pick up your soup bowl and drink from it. Don't be stupid. Try a different dress—I don't like the way this one fits around your bust."

When Irenka had gone back into the changing room, Mother said, "She can't pretend. What does she want to do, go back to being somebody's maid?" This was one of those times when she was talking partly to me and partly to herself. Then she turned to me and said, "Yulian, do you remember how you pretended to be sick, when we were staying on the farm, last fall?" That was when we were afraid of the Ukrainian peasants, right after the Russians had come. But the Ukrainians didn't show up that day, and I waited, all day, in bed and never, actually, got a chance to pretend. Now I nodded my head.

"Well, tomorrow, I want you to pretend you're sick again. Would you do that for me?"

I nodded again.

"When Andre comes, you'll pretend to be sick, and I'll tell him how sorry I am, but we can't go with him."

"A... nd th... en I... renka w... ill go w... ith h... im?" I asked excited to, finally, be included in the subterfuge.

Mother nodded her head, a conspiratory look on her face.

I loved it when Mother was like that. It was like the time we were walking back from the American embassy and making fun of things in shop windows.

"I think I w... ill h... ave as....thma," I said, as though I were selecting from a menu and remembering my cousin Fredek having an asthma attack in those damp rooms in Durnoval, before Mother and I escaped.

"We don't need anything quite that dramatic," Mother said, a little laugh in her voice. "How about a nice, quiet sore throat?"

"A s... ore th... roat it w... ill be," I agreed, glad to be on the team.


The following morning, when Andre came to pick us up, I was in bed, on my sofa, Mother's scarf around my throat. I had suggested a wet cloth on my forehead, but Mother had rejected it.

The look of disappointment on Andre's face, when Mother told him that we couldn't go, could have been mistaken for nothing else. He had on his blue jacket, with its brass buttons, and white pants and white shoes. "Why doesn't your friend stay with him?" he suggested.

Seeing an opportunity to ad lib here, I put a look of terror on my face. "He really needs to be with me," Mother said. "I'm sorry, but he's terrified to be separated from me at night. He's been through so much, you know."

"You're supposed to be my tennis partner, this afternoon," Andre said, with almost a wail in his voice.

"And I've found you a new partner. You'll have to teach her to play, of course, but she's a wonderful dancer."

I wanted to add that he would have to teach her to swim, too, but realized that I would be stepping out of character.

Andre tilted his head to one side. "Is she good looking?" he asked.

"That you'll have to judge for yourself. She is from a very old Polish family. And you'll be able to speak Portuguese to her. She doesn't speak French."

Mother's exaggerations no longer surprised me, though, technically speaking, Irenka's family went back to Adam and Eve, just like anyone else's.

Now Mother walked to the bedroom door, opened it only enough to pass through, and closed it behind her.

Andre looked at me, a worried look on his face. "Is she good looking?" he whispered.

I nodded, reassuringly. The look remained. He lit a cigarette, then paced back and forth across the room, glancing at the closed door. "It's the woman who lives with you?" he whispered.

I nodded again. Andre did not seem reassured. I could not imagine what was taking so long in the bedroom. Irenka had been ready and waiting before he arrived, and only ducked into the bedroom when Mother told her to, after the desk clerk called. Andre looked nervously at his watch, then at the door again.

Finally the door opened. Andre spun around to face it, but it was only Mother. "Irena will be right out," she said. She had her little brown suitcase in her hand, and she set it down by the front door.

"Irena?" Andre repeated.

"Don't you think it's a beautiful name?"

"Yes, yes, very beautiful," Andre agreed. Then I saw his mouth drop open.

Facing Andre, I had not seen Irenka step through the door. She was wearing her beige, silk blouse and a very full blue skirt that I had not seen before, with her sunglasses on top of her lush, wavy, brown hair. I had never seen anyone so beautiful. She was looking down at the floor. "She's very shy," Mother half whispered in French.

Then, turning to Irenka and straining the limits of her Portuguese, Mother said, "Irena, let me present Sr. Andre O'Brien," her tone suddenly formal, a smile fixed on her face. "Andre, this is Senhorita Irena Troboska." Then she whispered in Polish, the one word, "Hand," the smile still on her face. In French, she said, "Brought up by the good sisters."

Irenka extended her hand, and Andre flew across the room to shake it. They exchanged formal greetings.


Mother and I went to the beach that afternoon and to the movies on Sunday. Irenka was sitting in the living room, when we got back. "It was awful," she said. I could tell that she had been crying.

"Awful?" Mother said. "What happened?"

"Nothing happened. I just didn't know what to say—I couldn't hit a tennis ball, and I made Andre lose terribly. Then I didn't know any funny stories. I didn't know any of the people or the places they talked about. I know I embarrassed him."

"Nonsense. Andre doesn't know how to be embarrassed."

"He was very nice to me all the time. And I was so stupid."

"Of course he was very nice to you. You're a very beautiful woman."

"I'm stupid."

"You're not stupid. You're being stupid now. You don't know any people in Rio because you just got here. You don't know funny stories or how to play tennis. So what? You were brought up by the Sisters. Go fix your makeup, and we'll go somewhere for supper."

"You told him I was brought up by the Sisters? That's blasphemy."

"It's not blasphemy. Go fix your face."

"I don't want supper."

"Yes, you do. We'll sit down someplace nice, you'll have a cocktail and tell me all about the weekend."


"You watch," Mother said to me a few days later. "Andre is coming to take us all out to dinner tonight. But what he really wants is to take Irena out and thinks he's going to hurt my feelings, if he doesn't ask me too."

"H... ow do y... ou k... now th... at he w... ants to t... ake I... renka out, and n... ot y... ou? Sh... e s... aid that sh... e em....bar....rased h... im."

"She just *thinks* she embarrassed him. He's a sweet boy. I'll be very surprised if he isn't in love with her."

"L... ike y.. ou're in l... ove w... ith S... enhor S... egie... ra?"

Mother blushed suddenly. "Who told you I was in love with Sr. Segiera?" She said it with one of those smiles that isn't really a smile.

"Who t... old y... ou An... dre was in l... ove w... ith I... renka?"

Suddenly, Mother grew very serious, and I was afraid I had spoiled our fun by saying something I shouldn't have. Mother was sitting at the desk with her solitaire, and she said, "Come here, Yulian."

She didn't sound angry, and I walked over from my sofa. Mother took my two hands. "Sr. Segiera," she said, in a very serious voice, "has asked me to marry him."

I wondered if that had been before or after my aborted airplane ride. "Are y... ou g... oing to?"

"What do you think I should do?"

I wasn't surprised by this, and I had my own opinion, but I shrugged my shoulders.

"You like Ernesto, don't you?"

I nodded.

"He likes you too. And you like Paolo, don't you?"

I nodded again.

"Well, I have to think about it."

This was cold water. "Wh... at do y... ou h... ave to th... ink a... bout?"

"Well, we're on our way to America, you know."

"We're an o... cean aw... ay fr... om Eu....rope n... ow," I said, using a phrase I had heard Mother use.

Mother sighed. "Yes, we are. And Ernesto is very sweet. But I want you to grow up to be an American."

An American Jew, I thought.

"Being American means you can do and be anything you want."

"I d... on't w... ant to be a c... owboy."

"Oh, be serious."

"I want to live with Paolo and his grandmother."

Then Mother said, "We'll talk about that some more later."


It was only a few minutes before Andre was supposed to arrive, that Irenka came home.

"Where is she?" Mother had asked, several times, which I knew was a question that wasn't really directed at me. Mother was dressed and ready to go, though I knew that, at the last moment, she would go back into the bathroom and fix her makeup. "Oh, that woman!" she said as well, crushing out her cigarette. "The only thing she's learned since she came is the Brazilian custom of being late."

That wasn't at all fair. For one, Irenka had learned a lot more Portuguese than Mother had. And Andre would, of course, be late himself. Then we heard someone at the door, and, on the chance that it might be Andre coming early, Mother made her exit into the other room.

But it was Irenka, and she wasn't alone. She was accompanied by a man who looked very nervous and slightly familiar. She introduced him to me as Diego, and, as we shook hands, he looked at the floor and his hand was completely limp in mine.

Mother came charging out of the bedroom. "Get out!" she shouted in Portuguese, and I suddenly recognized the man as one of the hotel waiters.

"Get out!" Mother repeated, advancing toward Diego, who quickly made his exit.

"What are you doing?" Mother demanded of Irenka.

"I don't want to go," Irenka said. "I... I don't think I should go."

"What are you babbling about? Of course you're coming. Do you want to go back to being a chambermaid?"

"Diego says that I could... "

"Oh my God, you're talking like an idiot!"

I could see how scared Irenka was, and I felt sorry for her. Mother was being mean to her.

"I mean... "

"Look, you are from an old Polish family. Remember that," Mother said, not as though she were informing Irenka of it, but as though Irenka should be ashamed of acting the way she did. "Your father was a colonel, and was killed defending Warsaw against the

Nazis. He was a hero. You were brought up by the Good Sisters. Now go get dressed."

"I really…"

Mother had taken Irenka by the hand and she led her into the bedroom. "Talk to Andre," she said to me, over her shoulder, as the door closed behind them.

Andre was, of course, twenty-seven minutes late. I let him in and invited him to sit down, since Mother and Irenka would still need a few minutes. He asked me how school was, and I told him that I was now reading aloud, like the others, except, of course, not as quickly. He told me that he had been a very bad reader, himself. But he was good at numbers. He was working at the bank that his father had owned or run or something. He had, also, been the fastest runner in his class, which made him popular with the girls. I told him that I was the fastest runner in my class, too, but I didn't know any of the girls. Andre said that he would introduce me to some. We men had to stick together.

I really liked Andre, but I was glad that it was Sr. Segiera that Mother loved. Andre would have made a great older brother.

Then he asked me if I knew how to dance. Irenka, he told me, was a wonderful dancer….as was my mother, though I was sure that was an afterthought. Then he said that he would have to teach me to dance, and got up. "Come on," he said from the middle of the room, holding his arms out.

Suddenly, I was embarrassed.

"Come on," he repeated, but nicely.

I got up and let him hold me like they do in dancing. He started humming the tune to a waltz that I knew, and pushed me backwards. "Come on, follow me," he urged. I took a step backwards, but he was already stepping to the side. I would have fallen, if he hadn't been holding me. Andre laughed, and I laughed with him. "Just pay attention to which way I press you, and step in that direction," he said and began humming again. After a bit, I think I was actually dancing. "That's good," Andre said. "That's good."

I realized that, with Sr. Segiera, I would have been very embarrassed to dance, but with Andre, it was all like make-believe. Then Mother was standing in the bedroom doorway. "What are you teaching my son?" she asked, laughing.

"A little waltz step," Andre said. "I'm going to introduce him to some girls."

Now I was embarrassed again, so I laughed to show that he was joking. I had no interest in meeting any girls, but I enjoyed being friends with Andre.

Andre had brought a car bigger than his white sports car. It was a black Buick, and he made a big show of being particularly attentive to Mother, who sat in front with him, while I sat in back with Irenka.

At the restaurant, he asked Mother to dance, but she said that she had a headache, and didn't feel like dancing, but he should dance with Irenka.

Andre and Irenka danced a number of times through the evening, and when we got home, Irenka was still smiling.

"So, was it terrible?" Mother asked.

Irenka smiled with clamped lips and shook her head.

"He's sweet, isn't he?" Mother said.

Irenka nodded her head.

"You like him, don't you?"

Irenka's tight-lipped smile grew bigger, and her head nodded again.

"Next time," Mother said, "if he asks me, I'm going to have a very bad headache."

Irenka bent over and kissed Mother on the cheek. Then she ran into the bedroom. Mother had a cigarette in the living room, before following Irenka.

Apparently, Andre and Irenka spoke on the phone, when I was in school, because he surprised Mother and me, when he arrived a few days later. He came to take Irenka to dinner and brought a bouquet of flowers, which he presented to Mother.

Irenka wasn't around much on weekends, anymore, and she was out with Andre many weekday evenings, as well. She still managed, though, to wash, iron, and mend my clothes, have a snack waiting for me after school, and have supper with me, when Mother wasn't there.

As for Mother and me, we spent time with Sr. Segiera, going to that deserted beach, driving in the mountains, and he even persuaded me to fly my wind-up airplane again, in a field with long grass, where it wouldn't get hurt when it crashed. Sometimes, he would have to fly away to different places for the government. Once he tried to get Mother to go with him, but she wouldn't go up in the airplane. "What will happen to Yulian if I'm killed?" she asked.

One weekend, both the senhor and Andre were away, and the three of us went to the beach. I was sure it was the first time that the three of us had been to the beach together, and Irenka even got Mother to go in the water with us. I was concerned about Mother's ring, but she was very careful and didn't get wet much above her ankles.

Then we went home, and, while Irenka was in the shower, Mother suddenly said, "Where's my ring?"

We searched the suite. When Irenka came out of the bathroom, we searched the bathroom, but there was no ring.

"I know I had it, when I came out of the water," Mother said. "I had my fist clenched all the time."

The only place it could be was on the beach, and if it was there, Mother said, it had either worked its way into the sand, by now, or someone had picked it up. Mother explained that she had broken the nail on her ring finger, the day before, and it was sore, and she would not have felt the ring slipping off.

I volunteered to go to the beach and search, even though Mother said I would never find it. But I figured that this was a matter so important, that it was worth pursuing even the most infinitesimal chance. And it did not escape me, what important a mission I had volunteered for, and what a coup it would be, if I did happen to find it. I didn't ask permission, but just told her I would go, and Mother, sitting in the armchair and looking stunned, nodded her head.

I went down and found the spot where I was sure we had spread our blanket and began to dig around. There was no ring. I walked around to see if anyone near our spot was wearing it. There wasn't much chance that anyone who might have found the ring would be wearing it now, but I felt I had to take that chance too.

When I came back, Mother was still sitting in the armchair, looking very, very sad. She looked as though she was trying very hard not to cry. Irenka was kneeling beside her and patting Mother's hand. She, I could see, *had* been crying. They both looked up at me, as I came in, but I shook my head, feeling incredibly important.

"All right," Mother said, sitting up suddenly. "We are not going to sit here and cry anymore. That won't accomplish anything. Let's go downstairs and have some tea and nice cake to make us feel better."

Irenka and I both looked at her in surprise.

Mother had forced a smile onto her face. She clapped her hands. "Come on, no sad faces," she said.

"Yes, yes, that would be good," Irenka said, finally.

I did not feel much like drinking tea, under the circumstances. Of course, with the ring gone, we probably would not be able to go to America, and Mother would have to marry Sr. Segiera. But I could not shake our group sadness.

As it had happened more than once before, our noisy little elevator was out of order, and we had to walk. The late afternoon sun came in in rectangular bars, through the windows at each landing, between floors. They were directly below our bathroom window, looking out over the open space above the hotel lobby. As we reached the landing on a level with the lobby roof, I saw a man with a big push broom, sweeping the blacktopped roof.

"Oh my God!" Mother cried. "Look, look!"

I thought the man had fallen off the edge of the roof, but he was still there, still sweeping.

"What?" Irenka said.

"Look there, there!" Mother cried. "It's my ring!"

And, looking where she was pointing, I did, indeed, see the ring lying there, in the still-unswept portion of the roof.

Irenka and I rushed to the window. I reached it first, and climbed out onto the lobby roof. When I climbed back in, the ring in my hand, Mother was crying, and Irenka was holding her.

"Oh thank you, thank you, Yulian," Mother said, as though it was I who had found it. "I... I shook out my beach jacket outside the window, like I always do." She was laughing through her tears. "I didn't feel it come off!"

Over tea, Mother told us stories about her childhood. She told about her brother, Paul, who was afraid to climb trees and had said that she was too dumb to know that she could fall. She told about how, in her teens, she was fat, and how Grandmother would take her to fashionable places all over Europe and get young men to dance with Mother by bribing them with socks from Grandfather's factory. And she told about what a great gentleman my late father had been and how many *mistresses* he had, before they got married, though, from the context of the story, I was sure that *mistress* meant something different than just *lady friend*, as Mother explained it. Irenka and I sat listening, and I had never heard Mother tell so much about herself before. It seemed as though she couldn't stop talking. Eventually, she began to cry, and Irenka said that Mother was just very, very tired, even though she had done nothing but just sat there and worried all afternoon, while I was the one who was doing all the digging at the beach.

One evening, Mother was sitting, cross-legged, on her bed, in her sheer, blue nightgown, her face covered with cream, and she was doing her solitaire on top of the pillow. I was teaching Irenka to play gin rummy in the living room, when there was a knock on the front door. I went to see who it was, and was surprised to see Mr. K. standing there.

"Good evening, Yulian," he said, in a very friendly tone.

"G... g... od e... vening," I said, catching myself in mid stutter, as Mr. K. stepped past me.

"Hello, Irenka dear," he said, crossing the room toward her.

But, suddenly, Mother, in her bare feet and nightgown that you could see through, was standing between him and Irenka. "Get out!" she shouted. "Get out of here! She doesn't want to see you!"

"She is my wife, Basia," Mr. K. said.

"She is not your wife, you son-of-a-bitch, and don't you *Basia* me!"

Now Mother had her hands against Mr. K's chest, and she was pushing him backwards toward the door.

I opened the door again, and then Mother and Mr. K. were both out on the landing. "But Basia," I heard him say.

"You come here again, and I will have you arrested!" Then Mother was back inside. "Close the door, Yulian," she said.

I closed the door.

"Oh, Barbara," Irenka said. "He's going to be so mad at me now."

"Don't worry about him. I will tell Ernesto to have some of his friends tell him that it would be a good idea to leave Rio."

I wondered what Sr. Segiera's friends might tell Mr. K. to convince him that it would be a good idea to leave Rio.

# CHAPTER XIII

CHRISTMAS WAS IN THE HOTTEST PART of the Brazilian year. Mother had taken me aside to explain that I shouldn't expect much in the way of presents, because of our precarious finances, which wasn't, at all, necessary to tell me. I suggested we forego a tree, and Mother agreed, saying we would make up for it next year, when we were in America.

But Irenka brought us a little, tabletop tree, which she decorated with stars, angels, and balls that she had cut out of colored paper. She even bought me a box of watercolor paints, that she said were from her and Andre. And, so that I could buy something for my mother, she gave me some money, with which I bought two pieces of bath soap, shaped like an angel, for Mother and Irenka. Mother gave me a cowboy gun belt with two cap pistols.

Because Mother had gotten word that our entry permit to America would be coming soon, she decided that I did not need to go back to school, which was a big relief to me, particularly since it would save us money.

Three weeks after Christmas, January 13th, was my ninth birthday, and I got a cowboy hat from Mother, to go with my gun belt. Irenka gave me a leather-bound notebook, to write my poems in, and I immediately set to transcribing my existing poems into it, so that Irenka would know how much I appreciated it.

Then, Mother said that Mr. and Mrs. Tuwim had a present for me as well. We had met Mr. and Mrs. Tuwim a number of times at that café, and we set out for the café that afternoon.

I wore my gun-belt and hat, so as not to hurt Mother's feelings, though it was not the image I wanted to project to Mr. Tuwim. As usual, the Tuwims were there before us, Mrs. Tuwim immediately happy to see us, with a kiss for Mother and a birthday hug for me, Mr. Tuwim sitting back in his chair, his legs thrust out in front of him, and deep in thought. Mother immediately ordered a dish of ice cream for me, chocolate and vanilla. "I can't get him to eat anything," she said to Mrs. Tuwim, and I felt instantly guilty over my lack of appetite. "Look how thin he is."

"He looks fine to me, Basia," Mr. Tuwim said. "He's busy growing." What he was saying was that the process of growing somehow took effort and concentration on my part, and I appreciated fully the humor and the creativity of the remark.

"Give the boy his present," Mrs. Tuwim said to her husband, when we had been sitting there a while.

"I don't have it," Mr. Tuwim said. "You have it."

"I gave it to you before we left," Mrs. Tuwim said. "You put it into your left trousers pocket."

Mr. Tuwim felt both his pockets and said he didn't have it.

If Mr. Tuwim had lost it, I was embarrassed for him, but I didn't much care about the present itself. All of us refugees, facing uncertain futures, had little money to spend on things like birthday presents.

Then Mr. Tuwim found a flat box with a gold bottom and a blue top, about six inches long, and tied with a little bow, in the pocket of his jacket. "You must have transferred it to your jacket," his wife explained.

Mr. Tuwim tried to hand it to his wife.

"No, you should give it to him," she said.

"It's from both of us."

"Yes, but it's better coming from you."

Mr. Tuwim handed me the box, and I thanked him.

"Kiss him," Mother whispered.

I pretended not to hear. There was no way that I was going to kiss Mr. Tuwim.

A box of those dimensions could contain a fountain pen, a mechanical pencil, both, or a wristwatch. But wristwatches were expensive items, and I guessed it to be a pen or pencil, with which to write my poems. I ruled out a pen-and-pencil set, because the same gift gesture could be achieved with just a single item.

I untied the bow slowly and opened the box. Lying inside was a wristwatch.

I had received a wristwatch from my parents for my seventh birthday, in Warsaw. I was told that it was a "pilot's" watch because it was shockproof, waterproof, antimagnetic, and glowed in the dark, and I took it as a mark of my maturity. I was immediately told to wind it carefully every night and lay it on the table beside my bed, where I could see it, and to take it off and lay it aside before washing my hands, all of which I promised to do faithfully.

From my uncle Jacob I had received another symbol of maturity, a sheath knife, about eight inches overall. This, I was allowed to wear, hooked to the button that connected my short pants to my shirt, as long as I never took it out of its sheath.

Then, when my stepfather, Lolek, went into the army at the beginning of the war, he had taken my pilot's watch, because his own watch was gold and expensive, and because he said he had the right to take it, since he had given it to me. He also took my sheath knife, with which, I supposed, he would be able to kill some thin German soldier.

But the generosity of the Tuwims' gift surprised me. This one wasn't a "pilot's" watch—it wasn't waterproof, shock resistant, or antimagnetic, and it didn't have the green numbers that glowed in the dark—but it was from Yulian Tuwim, the great poet, which made it doubly or triply precious. But I didn't feel any of the thrill that I had felt on that day, two years ago. I wound my new watch, set the time from Mr. Tuwim's watch, and had my mother buckle it onto my wrist. Then I sat and watched the little second hand, at the bottom of the dial, go round and round, while I tried to appreciate how generously I had been treated.

It was at that same café, with the Tuwims, a few weeks later, when I was studying the metal pipes that held up the awning, as I had that day months earlier, that I suddenly heard Mother say, "Oh Yulian, tell me what I should do."

She was, of course, talking to Mr. Tuwim, but it was the note of pleading in her voice that pulled my attention from the overhead rigging.

"Basia, dear, it's a decision you have to make for yourself," Mr. Tuwim said.

"But I don't know what to do."

I had never, before, heard Mother make that particular statement in any form.

"I think I am in love with him," Mother continued, and I knew immediately that she was grappling with the decision that I had seen coming for some time.

"Oh, I have no doubt that you are," Mr. Tuwim said.

"So tell me what I should do."

"I can't tell you what to do."

Now I saw Mother turn to Mrs. Tuwim. "What do you think I should do?" she asked in that little girl voice I had heard her use on occasion.

Mrs. Tuwim shook her head. "I can't tell you, Barbara."

I knew very well that it was the question of whether to go to America or marry Sr. Segiera that was on Mother's mind. She was wringing her hands and biting her lips now, and, suddenly, I was feeling very sorry for Mother. I had seen her angry and sad, but I had never seen her seem so helpless.

"He's so sweet and so understanding and good to me," Mother was saying now. "I've been a real bitch to him sometimes, but he just worships me. And he has that lovely, crippled boy, who would be a good friend for Yulian. He's the only boy Yulian has ever gotten along with. But then, on the other side, there is Yulian becoming an American and my book and… "

I found that I was hurting for Mother. I was feeling her pain. I remembered the agony of my separation from Kiki, more than a year ago now, and not wanting Mother to have to endure the same thing.

"You can write your book in Portuguese as well as in English," Mr. Tuwim interrupted her. "As far as I know, you can't write in either language."

I couldn't agree more with him. In either case, she would have to have help writing her book, so why not stay here and write it in Portuguese.

"But I want Americans to read my book. Americans can do something about this war."

That was true. I knew that America had many more people than Brazil, and that it was America that had influenced the outcome of the last war.

"So go to America," Mrs. Tuwim said.

"But I love Ernesto."

I knew exactly how that felt, and I hated Mother having to endure the pain of separating from him.

"So stay," Mr. Tuwim said.

"But I want Yulian to become an American."

I didn't need to be an American. I could be very happy being Brazilian.

Now I could see a tear on Mother's face, and Mr. Tuwim changed the subject suddenly. "Yulian, what plans do you have for Carnival?" he asked.

I shrugged my shoulders. I had heard mention of the Carnival, but assumed it to be a place you went to and paid admission, which put it beyond our budget.

"It isn't for him," Mother said.

"Why not? It's a time when people dress up and become somebody else. They step outside of themselves for a few days, and everyone has a good time."

"It's for the common people," Mother said.

"Oh come on, Basia. Everyone in Rio gets involved."

"And what are you dressing up as, a circus clown?"

Mr. Tuwim laughed. But I knew that he wasn't going to dress up as anyone.

But the idea of becoming someone else had an immediate appeal for me. I would get a wheelchair and become Paolo. I would wheel around in it, talking to all sorts of strangers, and everybody would have to talk to me and be nice to me because I was crippled and because I was coping so well with my disability.

Irenka told me that she and Andre were going to do something with some other people for Carnival, and Mother was going to go on working at Sra. O'Brien's as usual. For weeks, my mind was filled with vignettes and entire scenes of me wheeling my way around the street in front of our hotel, zipping up to groups of people, who would turn to let me join them and then return my greetings, marveling at how unaffected I was by my handicap. Way in the back of my mind was the question of where in the world I was going to get a wheelchair. But the knowledge that there was, really, no way for me to obtain one, kept the thought in its back corner.

Then, two days before Carnival was about to start, I finally realized that, even if I did find my wheelchair and learned to operate it the way Paolo did, I did not have the capacity to wheel, uninvited, up to strangers and start a conversation. In a word, my plans for becoming Paolo were not going to happen.

So the start of Carnival found me leaning out of our window, looking at the activities on the street below. In the morning, there were people, individually or by twos and threes, in brightly colored and strange clothing hurrying up or down the street, as though late for an appointment. There were women in skirts that were cut very short in front and dragged on the ground in back, men in trousers with one leg of one color and the other different. Shirts had collars that were large and pointed or very round with large bows or just with long strips hanging down. There were hats of all sorts, usually very large. Some hats were made of fruits or vegetables; some fruits were worked right into hairdos. Some people wore masks that covered their entire faces, some had their masks on top of their heads, as they hurried to their destination. They weren't, mostly, masks that made people look better, but uglier, with long noses, weird beards, huge, hairy ears, or, even, horns. I thought of Irenka's impression of Jews.

Then, as the day progressed, a sort of parade developed, moving from right to left along the street. But it wasn't a parade like any I had seen before. There were no soldiers marching in step and no brass bands with brass-buttoned uniforms. The people walked or rode on the back of trucks or open cars, the walkers making no particular effort to keep in step. Every once in a while a group of musicians passed, sometimes playing a marching beat and sometimes music to dance to. Some of the people in the parade danced to the music, others seemed to ignore it completely.

People, along the sidewalk, stood watching the parade, or ignored it, going about their business. Every once in a while, someone, or two or three, from the sidewalk would join the parade and be acknowledged by the people they had joined, as though they had been expected.

I wondered whether you really had to be expected or whether anyone could join. I wondered whether I could put on my cowboy hat and gun belt and march along with the parade for a few blocks.

I didn't have a mask, but if I tied a handkerchief around my nose and mouth, the way the crooks did in cowboy movies, people wouldn't know who I was and might think that, maybe, I was someone who was supposed to march with them.

In my mind, I now saw myself marching in the parade with grownups in their weird costumes all around me and accepting me as one of them and all of us marching in the same direction. It would be a wonderful feeling, I was sure, and I stepped away from the window to sit in the armchair, close my eyes, and concentrate on the image.

When Mother came back from Sra. O'Brien's she asked me whether I had watched the parade, and I said that I had. Then she asked whether I had gone downstairs in my cowboy outfit, and I assured her that I hadn't, though I had the feeling that she no longer felt as negative about the parade and its participants as she had talking with Mr. Tuwim. In the evening, we both leaned out of the window, as the street lights cast a whole new character on the activities below.

"The music is going to be playing all night," Mother said. "Why don't you sleep with me. We'll close the bedroom door, and it won't be as loud. Irena won't be back tonight."

I said that the music wouldn't bother me, and Mother said that, of course, it would, but, in the end, she agreed to let me sleep in my own bed, certain that I would regret it.

As Mother had said, and I had known it would, it took a long time for me to fall asleep, as I lay, tense with anticipation of my proposed plunge the next day. But I would have had a difficult time entertaining these thoughts with Mother's presence beside me, even though I was sure she couldn't read minds.

In an effort to be realistic and knowing my own self, I realized that I might, very well, not have that courage to do what I was planning. I knew that I would probably just stand there or walk along the sidewalk, without finding the nerve to make that step. But, maybe, I would find a way to, as Mr. Tuwim had said, "step out of myself."

The next day, Mother asked whether I wanted to come to Sra. O'Brien's with her and swim in the pool, while she worked with the senhora, but I said that I would rather watch the parade some more.

The moment I saw Mother pull away in Sra. O'Brien's black car, I stepped away from the window to strap on my guns. I did that deliberately, lest I lose my nerve for the whole adventure. The parade hadn't formed yet, and I expected that it would take some time before it did, but I was also aware of a need for precautions against my loss of nerve. The more prepared I was, I figured, the harder it would be to back out, if my nerve disintegrated.

Then, when there was a parade again, I forced myself out of our suite and onto the landing. I hoped that I would not encounter anyone in the elevator, and I didn't. Then I was out on the sidewalk within a few steps of the moving stream, wondering what I should look for as an appropriate place to make my move.

A number of the revelers did wave to me, as they walked or rode by, but none seemed to be extending a definite invitation to join their ranks. And then I saw seven boys, about my own age, walking by with their arms around each other's shoulders and singing. They weren't in any sort of costume, except that one of them had some sort of cap on his head.

Before I realized it, I was walking along the sidewalk, keeping abreast of them. Then, one of them raised his arm and waved for me to join them. I was positive he was inviting me to join them. And then the others waved for me to join as well.

Not permitting myself to think about it, I made the few sideways steps necessary, and soon I had my arm around the shoulders of the nearest boy, and his arm was around me. I didn't know the song they were singing, but I marched in step to their rhythm.

Then, at one corner, as though by previous plan, my companions veered out of the parade and down a side street, I, of course, right with them. We stopped in front of a store, and one of the boys went inside. He came out a few minutes later with a paper bag of candy that he proceeded to distribute among us. I got a cylindrical, chewy, chocolate something that I had never tasted before, but was delicious.

In a moment we had rejoined the parade. Our mouths full of candy, we were not singing, but marching to the beat of some nearby musicians.

Conscious of being the only one in any sort of costume, I had pushed my hat back to hang from my neck by its strap and pulled the kerchief down to hang on my neck as well. We were now some five or six blocks from the hotel, at the limit that I had set for myself, and I knew that I would have to leave the group. But that was all right. The exhilaration that I felt from the few minutes of this experience would last me for some time. My only problem was how to make my exit, particularly since I was now in pretty much the center of the line.

Then our entire group veered away from the parade again and turned down another side street. In the middle of the street we stopped. Then the boy, who had gone into the store last time, addressed me with words I didn't understand at first. Seeing the confusion on my face, he repeated them louder.

Now I understood that he wanted me to give him my guns.

My exhilaration turned, suddenly, into fear. I shook my head.

The other boys took up his cause, repeating his command in my ear.

I shook my head again.

I felt hands grab my arms and the boy in front of me reach for my belt buckle.

Instinctively, I raised my arms, breaking the grips on them. Then I began to run.

I heard their shouts for me to stop and the footsteps behind me. I did not dare look back, but ran as fast as I could back to the parade street.

They were still calling, and I felt a hand graze my back. But I was still running. One boy, bigger than me, was on my left now, so I angled to the right and increased the distance between us.

I was running in the opposite direction of the parade, heading back to the hotel. The bigger boy on my left seemed to have dropped back, and I, suddenly, had the certainty that I could outrun my pursuers.

Their shouts were beginning to turn into hard breathing and their footsteps grew fainter. I was now filled with a new exhilaration, far greater than what I had felt while marching. I had outrun them all.

I could no longer hear them behind me, and I knew that I could turn my head to make sure, then slow down to a walk. But it felt too good to be running. I felt as though I could run forever, maybe even rise off the sidewalk and soar through the sky.

# CHAPTER XIV

I NOTICED THAT MOTHER had stopped smoking altogether, or, at least, when I was around. Instead, she would drum her long, red nails on the table a lot. She also seemed to hold herself extra straight, and I often saw her biting her lip now. I knew very well that she was either trying to decide whether to continue on to America or that she had already made a decision and that it was hurting her. I imagined what it would have been like if I had known, weeks in advance, that Kiki would be leaving me, and I would, probably, never see her again.

And Mother hadn't been able to sell her diamond, which, as far as I knew, she still needed to sell for our trip to America... if we were going. But, in view of what she was going through, I did not mention my earlier suggestion of selling it to a jewelry store.

With Sr. Segiera very busy with his work, right now, we seemed to see more and more of the Tuwims. Sometimes, at the café, Mother would ask me to take a walk around the block, so that she could talk privately to them. I thought that those talks must comfort her, and I was happy to do my part.

One afternoon, when I was completing just such a walk and attuned my ear to hear if it was safe to return to the table, I heard Mr. Tuwim utter words I could not believe. What I heard was, "... for me, as a Jewish poet... "

*For me as a Jewish poet*—that meant that, if I had heard right, Mr. Tuwim, the famous poet, was a Jew, just like me. Of course I had heard right. He *had* said that—I was certain. He was a Jew, and he was a poet—a poet whose poems were published and sold and read by many, many people. I was amazed. That meant that, when I grew up, the things I wrote could be published and read, as well. It meant that I didn't have to hide the fact that I was a Jew or be ashamed of it. It meant a million things. I sat down.

"Are you all right, Yulian?" I heard Mother ask, alarm in her voice. I didn't know what I was doing, but evidently there was something in my manner that was communicating my excitement.

"I'... m f... ine," I said.

"Did somebody do something when you were walking?"

I shook my head.

Mother put her hand on my forehead. Then she asked Mrs. Tuwim to feel my forehead as well. Mrs. Tuwim stood up and reached across Mother to feel my forehead. She found nothing amiss.

"Yulian," Mother said to Mr. Tuwim, "you're sitting next to him. Feel his forehead."

"I'm not going to feel his forehead. He says he's all right, you both felt nothing, what do you want me to feel?"

"He's not right." Mother's face looked definitely worried, and she felt my forehead a second time.

"Leave him alone," Mr. Tuwim said. "He's probably just thinking about girls."

I hadn't been thinking about girls, but now it occurred to me that Mr. Tuwim, being a poet, might very well be able to read minds. I had better not think my beach thoughts about Irenka.

Suddenly I had a tremendous desire to get back to our suite, where I could tell Meesh about Mr. Tuwim being Jewish. He was the only one who would understand the significance of that. I had not spoken to Meesh for a while, and I felt guilty about it. But I felt too good for the guilt to dampen my spirits. Meesh and I would have a very long talk that evening.

"More ice cream for the boy," Mr. Tuwim said to the waiter, and I realized that I had eaten all my ice cream.

"He ate all his ice cream," Mother said, great surprise in her voice.

"A sure sign of sickness," Mr. Tuwim said. I was proud of my understanding of sarcasm, though that word was not in my vocabulary either, and very pleased to hear the poet apply it.


I could not remember any previous time in my life when I had been eager to get to bed. But I kept visualizing Meesh sitting on the chair beside my bed, while I pulled the sheet over my head and spilled out my heart.

I had tried to be careful not to give Mother any more cause to worry about my health, but forgot what ideas my eating my supper quickly might put into Mother's head. But I was in a hurry, and, for the first time in a long while, I had an appetite. I saw Mother fret and then realized that any visible desire to go to bed, on my part, would only confirm her suspicions. After supper I suggested that I take a walk along the street, because, walking by myself, I would be free to think about whatever I wanted. But Mother said that I couldn't do it in the evening. She did, however, suggest that we play some Gin Rummy, which was how I, finally, spent the evening.

When I was at last in bed, with Mother behind the closed bedroom door, doing her solitaire on her pillow, and Meesh was on the chair beside my bed, I pulled the sheet over my head and proceeded to tell Meesh about Mr. Tuwim, his *Locomotive* poem, which every child I knew in Poland was familiar with, his other poems in the book, which Kiki and I didn't think were as good as *The Locomotive,* but still very good, and the fact that he also wrote poems for grownups. And then I explained that Mr. Tuwim was a Jew, like I was and like Meesh was.

After thinking about this for a while, Meesh asked why Mr. Tuwim's being Jewish was important, to which I responded by telling him that I hadn't thought that Jews could be poets. Of course, Jews could write poetry, as anyone could, but nobody, except maybe other Jews, would ever read their poems. But, if a Jew like Mr. Tuwim, could write poems that everyone read and admired, that meant that, if the poems that I wrote when I grew up were good enough, everyone would read and admire them as well.

This explanation seemed to satisfy Meesh, but then, suddenly, the image of Gustavo sitting on the ground and looking up at me with his bleeding face, appeared in my mind again, and I immediately tried to wipe it out by thinking of the pleasing image of lying on the beach with Irenka. But Gustavo would not go away. Except that now I felt even more guilty for trying to ignore him, in his pain.

There was a new persistence in Gustavo's bloody image forcing itself into my mind, that I had not known before, and I did not fall asleep for a long time. Gustavo's face kept changing. At times it was his normal face, wet only with tears, but, at other times, it was covered with blood, though he had not fallen on his face. And then, strangest of all, I could see the black and gray bristles of a beard covering the lower part of his face.

It was then that I remembered Kiki's old warning about going crazy from touching my genitalia, my *birdie,* as she had called it, while warning me that repeated, extracurricular contact with it would make me crazy. And I had taken the warning as a challenge and had, foolishly, darted secret, instantaneous touches with the tip of my finger under my nightshirt, tempting fate to strike me.

But, over the past year, I had lost faith in a number of Kiki's declarations, this one among them, and lost all interest in that activity. But now it occurred to me that perhaps what Kiki had told me had not been an old wives' tale, after all, and that I was, indeed, suffering the consequences of my recklessness. While I still could see no logical way that unauthorized contact between my finger and that organ, which I had to handle, routinely, several times a day in front of the toilet, could, possibly, lead to mental consequences, that may well have been the reasoning of an, already compromised, mind.

If my brain could manufacture blood and even whiskers on little Gustavo's face, then what credence could I give to any of my conclusions? Had I really heard Mr. Tuwim refer to himself as a Jew, or was that a fabrication as well? Had he really said that my poems were good and that I should continue writing them? Was that really Yulian Tuwim, writer of *The Locomotive*, with whom Mother and I met at the café and who had given me the wrist-watch? Was there really such a poem? Were Kiki and Warsaw really gone from my life, and was I really living in Brazil with Mother? Was there really a war going on? Was a crazy man in Germany really gobbling up Europe?

With my world crumbling around me, I had finally fallen into an exhausted sleep. Waking up the next morning, I tried hard not to think about any of the things that had plagued my night. Since the end of school, Irenka and I had resumed occasional trips to the beach, the pool, or the movies. While I was allowed to go to the beach by myself, I could not go into the water without Irenka to watch me, which left looking at scantily-clad women as the only reason for going, and I had not been aware of any great desire to do that, for some time. Before she had left for Sra. O'Brien's, I had told Mother that I would go to the beach and dig in the sand, but I had no intention of following through.

I sat in our living room, staring out of the window at people and cars going by in the street. I thought about the few hours of utter ecstasy that I had experienced the previous afternoon, and how the image of Gustavo had obliterated it. As with the witches and goblins that had visited me on earlier nights, the prospect of my "insanity" had faded with the coming of daylight, but I felt myself swathed in a gloom far thicker than the one that Mr. Tuwim's revelation had, temporarily, lifted.

When Irenka came home, with her little suitcase, that afternoon, she found me still sitting by the window and, evidently, looking quite distressed, because her greeting words were, "What is the matter, Yulian?"

I found myself wincing, as though I had been caught in some shameful act. I loved Irenka, but how could I possibly share my issues with her?

Not waiting for the answer, which I was still formulating, she walked right across the room to, first, feel my forehead and then wrap her arms around me.

The moment I felt her arms around me, I knew that I could stop looking for words to answer her question. I pressed my head against her and remembered the way Miss Bronia had held me when German planes had strafed the road along which we were escaping from Warsaw and people around us were crying in pain. Now, I found that I, too, was crying.

It felt very good to cry in Irenka's arms. But it felt particularly good to be able to cry without having to explain what I was crying about. It wasn't just that I would not be able to explain my problems in any way that Irenka could understand, but that the freedom to cry without explanation suddenly seemed a great luxury, a luxury I could not imagine being granted by Mother.

I don't know how much time I spent in the security of Irenka's embrace. But, eventually, I found that I was feeling better.

"Do you want to tell me about it?" Irenka asked gently, when my sobbing had stopped. I shook my head and, again, experienced the satisfaction of having my refusal accepted at face value.

Suddenly, it occurred to me that, in the freedom that she granted me, to cry without explanation, there was a bond between us, even stronger than when we used to share our embarrassing secrets.

By the time Mother returned, I was using Irenka's birthday gift to color in the photographs in a newspaper, and Irenka was washing out blouses in the bathroom sink. That does not mean that my gloom was, in any way, lifted. What it was, maybe, was pushed a little to one side, giving me room to enjoy Irenka's proximity in the other room, while still looming as large as before. While I could not say with any certainty whether or not I was crazy, Gustavo's bloody and bearded face was never far from my mind. When I wasn't actually seeing it, I was thinking about seeing it.

"That's nice," Mother said, observing my coloring activity, though the watercolors made a terrible mess on the porous newsprint. "Now why don't you take a fresh piece of paper and write a thank-you poem to Mr. and Mrs. Tuwim, for the beautiful watch they gave you for your birthday, and illustrate it with your new paints."

I did not feel like writing a poem, and I hated it when Mother told me to write one. But the last thing I wanted right now was an argument with Mother. I took a fresh piece of paper out of the drawer and poised my pencil over it to look as though I was thinking. But nothing came, of course, since my mind kept turning to a multitude of things, not in any way related to my birthday gift.

"Why don't you begin by finding a word that rhymes with *wristwatch*," Mother suggested, when she saw my lack of progress. If there were words that rhymed with *wristwatch*, in Polish, my mind was, clearly, unable to produce them. Yes, there was one, the word for *canary*.

"What *is* wrong with you?" Mother said, a little later.

I shrugged my shoulders.

Mother checked my forehead again. I saw her roll her eyes. "I don't know what to do with him," she said to Irenka, in the other room. "He doesn't have a fever."

"My brother went through something like this," Irenka said. "Boys have moods."

"He had such a wonderful governess in Poland."

I knew what Mother was really saying. She was saying that if Kiki were here, she would have known what to do about this, but I knew that she wouldn't have.


At supper, I forced my food down so as not to provoke any more distress or questions on Mother's part. Then, somehow, I got through the evening, till my bedtime.

Irenka gave me a hug before closing the door to the bedroom, and Mother came in, when I was in bed, felt my forehead again, and then kissed it. I realized that Mother was hoping that I did have a fever, and she could give me aspirin. I pulled the sheet over my head, closed my eyes, and tucked my knees up against my chest. Trying not to think about Gustavo, of course, only made him appear more often.

Then I heard Meesh ask, "Why did you trip him?" It was, I was sure, the first time I had heard Meesh initiate a conversation.

"I didn't," I said. "I pushed him, when we were playing tag."

"Not Gustavo."

"Not Gustavo? Whom?"

"The Jew."

"What Jew?"

"The Jew shopkeeper in Hungary."

Now I remembered about the man that Mother had told me that I had tripped, when I was with Carlos, the count's chauffeur.

"Was he a Jew?" I asked.

And then I remembered the man's bearded face, with its hooked blade of a nose and long ear locks. Of course he had been a Jew—I had forgotten that. I remembered his frightened face, as Carlos pushed him up against the wall of his shop. There had been old pots, dusty clocks, musical instruments, stuffed animals, and articles of used clothing scattered all around the weird shop.

Then Carlos had released the man and I watched him scurry past me, to the other end of the shop.

"That's the way to do business with Jews," the Russian chauffeur with the Spanish name, whom I had admired so much, said to me as we watched the frightened man take a box out of a drawer and scurry back towards where Carlos was waiting. Most of that, up until that point, I had remembered before—I guess all except Carlos calling him a Jew. And it was at this point that my memory had ended.

But now, for the first time, I was remembering more. As the man is about to pass me, I stick my foot out, tripping him. He falls face down, and I watch his glasses bounce and roll over the floor towards where Carlos is standing. Carlos looks frightened, scaring me as well. The man on the floor gets to his knees. He looks up at me from the floor, his bearded face covered with blood.

Carlos leans down to pick up the glasses. A fat woman in a long, peasant skirt has come out from some back room. The man on the floor is holding a towel to his bleeding nose. The woman has found some blood splattered on my camel's hair coat, and she is kneeling in front of me, blotting it with a wet sponge. The man is still looking up at me from the floor, except that he's not down on the floor anymore, but standing, and I feel terrible, horrible over what I've done. And then I black out.

"I didn't mean to hurt the man," I said to Meesh. "I didn't. It was an accident."

"God hates lying," he said.

"I wasn't lying."

"He knows everything."

"There may not even be a God. Kiki was wrong about a lot of things." I could still see the man with the beard and the blood looking up at me, his eyes squinting to see without his glasses, and I felt horrible. Meesh was right. I had tripped the man on purpose. I hadn't intended to do that to his nose, but I probably broke it. And the man was looking up at me wanting to know why I had done such a terrible thing. "I don't know why I did it. I never meant to hurt anybody."

"You did it because you wanted Carlos to like you."

Meesh was right. "I did want Carlos to like me."

"And you wanted him to think that you weren't Jewish."

I didn't have an answer to that. Meesh was right again—I wanted Carlos to think that I was Catholic, like him. Being Jewish was something ugly and detestable.

I could see the question on the man's face. Because when he looked at me, he could see in my face that I was just like him.

I reached my arm out from under the sheet and pulled Meesh into bed with me. With the crook of my arm, I held him tight to my chest, feeling, again, the familiar sensation of the scratchy plush, through my nightshirt.

Then I began to cry. I cried for the Jewish shopkeeper whom I had deliberately tripped. I cried for his damaged nose, that I hadn't broken on purpose. I cried for the old woman who had gotten on her knees to sponge the blood splatters off my camel hair coat. I cried for Carlos, who had looked so frightened. And I cried for me.

# CHAPTER XV

I WOKE UP THE, the following morning, with Mother's hand, again, on my forehead.

"How are you feeling?" she asked. She was dressed to go to Sr. O'Brien's, and I realized I had slept late. My eyes and throat had that dryness that was the result of insufficient sleep.

"I....m all r... ight," I said. From the tone of Mother's question I sensed that she would have much preferred it if I had a sore throat or stomach ache to report.

"Did you have a bad dream?"

That was a relief. One of my bad dreams would give Mother the explanation she was looking for. From past experience, I knew that I must have had a bad dream—which I wouldn't be able to remember—and thrashed around enough, during the night, to attract Mother's attention. That had been going on fairly frequently, since we left Warsaw. "Y... es," I said, quite certain that I must be telling her the truth.

Mother sat down beside me, on the bed. "What did you dream?"

I shrugged my shoulders. I had never been able to answer that question for Mother, but, this morning, I had the feeling that something more than a dream had taken place during the night.

Then I remembered the Jewish shopkeeper that I had tripped, and telling Meesh that I hadn't meant to do it. I, again, had that taste in my mouth and the feeling in my stomach of having done something awful. That had not been a dream. It was a true memory that I had had before falling asleep… wasn't it? Had it been a dream? I was wishing that it could all have been a dream, but I knew that the memory was true; the question was whether I had recalled it when I was awake or asleep. I felt Meesh's presence against my thigh, under the sheet, and was assured that it had not been a dream.

"Try to remember."

I made a split second decision. "I d… reamt about the m… an who fell d… own in H… ungary," I said.

"Man who fell down?"

"W… hen I was with C… arlos."

"You mean the shopkeeper?" I saw something begin to register on Mother's face.

"The o… ne I t… t… t… tripped. He w… as J… ewish."

At my last word, Mother's hopeful expression disappeared. "Your memory is coming back?" she said, not totally pleased.

I nodded.

"I have to go. The car is probably waiting downstairs. I'll wake Irena up— she'll stay with you until I get back. You like talking to her. Tell her the story—just don't say the man was Jewish. Just say he was an ugly looking, crooked shopkeeper with a beard. And the beard scared you—tell her that."

Then Mother went back into the bedroom, and I heard voices. In a moment they were both beside me, Irenka wrapped in her bathrobe, smelling of toothpaste.

"You had a bad dream?" Irenka said. She sat down and put her arms around me.

"Call me if you need to," Mother said to Irenka. Irenka nodded and waved for Mother to leave.

"You have the phone number," Mother said.

Irenka waved at her again, and Mother left.

Now I heard Irenka humming some tune I didn't recognize. She continued holding me, and we rocked back and forth a little. I wondered what I might want to tell Irenka of last night's experience.

And then I felt a strange calm come over me. It was like the time Kiki and I had been at that summer resort on a dull day, and watched a bank of fog sweep over us, with its moisture cooling not just our skin, but our very bones. There was nothing to see, this time, but I could actually feel the peacefulness sweep over me and settle around me.

Now, I realized, I didn't feel the need to tell Irenka anything of what had taken place last night. And I also realized something else. Now that I had remembered what I had done to the man in Hungary, did that mean that I would no longer stutter? I had remembered it on my own, not from someone telling me about it, as Mother had done in Lisbon, so it was different. And I *was* feeling different, so maybe something had happened to take my stutter away.

I could have continued clinging to Irenka, but I had to test out my speech. "L… et's go h… ave breakfast," I said. I hadn't stuttered, but I realized that I had forgotten how to speak without dragging out the words.

"All right," Irenka said. "I'll put some clothes on."


It was difficult, trying to speak, again, the way I did before I learned to drag the sounds out. "I….think… my… stuttering is… better," I said to Irenka over breakfast. What I was doing now, I realized, was dragging out the silences between the words. Whether this was an actual improvement or just an improved technique, I couldn't tell.

Irenka agreed that my speech was better, and suggested that we just spend a quiet day at the beach and, maybe, a walk with a stop for ice cream in the afternoon. I advocated for a movie, but she said it was best just to be very quiet today. When Mother came home, Irenka convinced her that my speech was, indeed, improved.

Then Mother said that the three of us were going to have dinner at a restaurant outside the hotel, because this was a special evening. I felt a little bit guilty, in the event that my speech "improvement" wasn't really an improvement, but, over soup, Mother clapped her hands and said, "Yulian, we're sailing to America next month."

I was well aware of the pain inherent in Mother's decision and didn't want to voice my disappointment. Not only would my dreams of Paolo and Sr. Segiera not be coming true, but I would also be leaving Irenka.

"That's wonderful," Irenka said, but I could tell that she had already known about it.

"America is the strongest and the safest country in the world," Mother went on. But we had discussed this issue already.

"You will grow up to be an American," Irenka said to me.

"You can be a great poet, like Mr. Tuwim says," Mother said. I didn't believe that Mr. Tuwim had committed himself to that degree regarding my ability.

"You can become an American millionaire," Irenka said. "Andre says that the American dollar is the strongest money in the world." There, I had no idea what she was talking about, but I well understood that this had all been planned to assuage my disappointment, and now I didn't want to disappoint them by beating what I knew to be a dead horse.

Nor did I want to raise the tender issue of finances. But I knew that Mother must, certainly, be aware of the predicament every time she looked at the twin diamonds on her finger, and that she must certainly be making some kind of plans.

There was a palpable sense of things winding down, now. Sr. Segiera seemed to be very busy with his work, and we did not see much of him. Each time Irenka and I went to the beach, I had the strong feeling that this might be our last time. We spoke little and of nothing of importance. On the other hand, I found that the contours of Irenka's tanned body, as she sunned herself on the hotel blanket, now held a renewed fascination for me. I had to fight the urge to lay my hand on one of the soft convexities that she presented so generously to the world.

One evening, Sr. Segiera did come to take Mother out to dinner. There was not, on either of their faces, the smile that I was used to seeing on such occasions. They kissed only lightly on the cheek, as though they were angry with each other. The senhor had brought a bouquet for Mother and a little, square box, tied with a piece of yarn for me.

My present was from Paolo, he said, and I proceeded to open it with great surprise and curiosity.

"Oh, what is it?" Mother said, looking over my shoulder, and then, "Oh my God!" as I lifted the lid.

Sitting inside the box, nestled in a wad of cotton, was the glass eye from Paolo's collection.

"Who gives a thing like that?" Mother said.

"Boys collect those things, Basia," the senhor said.

"But that's an eye."

"It's a glass eye."

"Yes, I know that. Who collects glass eyes and gives them as presents?"

"Boys do, Basia. Boys do."

Then Mother laughed. She kissed the senhor's cheek again, but for real. "Let's go," she said, taking his hand.

I was racking my brain for what to give Paolo. If I gave him my airplane, Sr. Segiera might think I didn't want it, and Paolo

might have difficulty flying it. Then I thought of my cowboy outfit, and that was perfect.

"Just… a… second, Monsieur," I said, "I have… something
for Paolo, too." I dashed for the bedroom door, but stopped and
opened it quietly, because I knew Irenka was trying to sleep off a
headache.

I came back, a few moments later, on tiptoes, my gun belt and
hat in my hands. I noticed Sr. Segiera and Mother both looking
intently at me, as though they had been discussing me.

"Thank you, Julien," the senhor said. "Paolo will really like it."
But he was looking at me as though there was something funny
about the way I looked. There was a silence, which I realized was
an expectation for me to say something. It was my speech they
wanted to hear.

"I hope so, Monsieur," I said, making a great effort to not
stutter.

"Don't you think so?" Mother said.

"Yes, you're right, Basia," the senhor said.

I, of course, knew very well what they were talking about. I
had learned that if I made a great effort, I, *usually*, or maybe just,
*often*, could refrain from stuttering.

Then I realized that Mother had begun to cry. "Oh, my God,"
she was saying under her breath, in Polish. She had her hands
clasped against her mouth.

Sr. Segiera put his arm around Mother's shoulders.

"He… he doesn't stutter anymore," Mother said, in the little-
girl voice she used sometimes, "does he, Ernesto?"

"Why don't you tell *him* that," the senhor suggested.

Mother reached her arms out to me, in a way that I could see
was uncomfortable for her. I found it awkward for me, too.

"Give your mother a hug," the senhor said.

We hugged awkwardly.

"We should go now," Mother said suddenly. "You won't wake Irena up, will you Julien?"

I shook my head. But Irenka was standing in the doorway. "I am awaking. Julien and I will go look at a movie," she said, in slightly awkward French.

"Oh, that's good," Mother said. "Now let's go."

As Mother took his arm, I saw that her ring, that had had two diamonds on it, now only had one. I hoped she had gotten a good price for the other one.

Sr. Segiera was at the dock to say goodbye. "Paolo says that when you learn to write in English, you'll write to him," he said. "He is learning English in school."

I said that I would.

"And when you begin writing poems in English, you will send some to me? I read a little English, too."

Mr. and Mrs. Tuwim were there as well. "Make him promise to keep writing poetry, Yulian," Mother said to Mr. Tuwim.

"If he wants to write poetry, he'll write poetry," Mr. Tuwim said.

Irenka gave me a very big hug, then pulled the handkerchief out of Andre's breast pocket to wipe her tears. On her left hand, I saw Mother's missing diamond.

# EPILOG

"WAKE UP, YULIAN, WAKE UP," Mother was saying, shaking me out of a deep sleep.

I thought we had been torpedoed or something, and reached for the life preserver under my berth, as we had done in the lifeboat drill.

"Just put on your bathrobe and come up on deck. I want you to see something."

I could see, through the porthole, that it was the middle of the night. "What?"

"Come up on deck."

I was rubbing my eyes, as Mother's hand, on my back, urged me down the hall.

There was a crowd of people on deck, many, like me, in bathrobe and slippers, crowding against the rail. Beyond, there was a dark gray fog. It must have been just before dawn. The air was clammy. The people were pointing something out to each other in a multitude of languages.

"Look out there," Mother said, pushing me through the crowd, to the railing. "See that?"

I saw nothing but dark gray fog.

"See, right there, right there?"

Where Mother was pointing, there was fog of a darker gray than the rest. "That's the Statue of Liberty," she said.

"What?"

"The Statue of Liberty. Oh my God, Yulian, **the Statue of Liberty**. Do you see it?"

I didn't want to argue, but I had little interest in seeing someone's idea of what liberty was supposed to look like, so I said that I did. "N… ow can I go back to bed?"

My stuttering did not go away completely. When I was nervous, it would come back, and I still have vestiges of it. I continued to write poetry, switching to English, but what I really wanted to do, as I grew up, was to write prose.

It wasn't easy to find decently paying work as a writer, when I came out of college in 1954, but I found a niche in documentary film writing and production. The poetry that I write now is, mostly, humorous and not directed to publication. Framed copies of my poems make great gifts to friends.

Mother stormed into the publishing offices of Duell, Sloan and Pearce in New York and got them to give her an advance and a collaborator to write her book. *Flight to Freedom* by Barbara Padowicz, was published in 1942 and, as the first of the WW II escape stories, enjoyed a brisk circulation. Soon after, having divorced my stepfather, she met a handsome French war hero, named Georges Pierre Gabard, who had lost a leg defending access to the Suez Canal against Erwin Rommel. After the war they married, and Pierre entered the French diplomatic service, his career culminating with the post of Consul General to Philadelphia in the 1960's.

In Philadelphia, Beautiful Basia quickly became one of that city's leading hostesses, entertaining luminaries of Society, the arts, government, and industry in their beautifully decorated, Spruce Street townhouse. Pearle Buck, Edith Piaf, Eugene Ormandy,

John F. Kennedy, Grace Kelly, Marcel Marceau, and Spyros Skouras were only a few of the names to glitter on their guest lists.

Pierre passed away in 1967 and Mother in 1973. Because they had made numerous trips between Europe and America, not always together, there is a considerable quantity of letters, some typed, some handwritten, and all in French and tied up with a ribbon, among Mother's papers. Because I read French with great difficulty and because they deal, mostly, with housekeeping issues, I have only passed a casual eye over the typed letters, and had not even tried to decipher the handwritten ones.

That was until my wife, Donna, alerted me to the fact that some of the latter were dated after Pierre's death. That warranted a closer examination, which revealed the signature at the bottom of the letters to be "Ernesto."